Between Fires

21 Feb. 2002

Between Fires
Fifteen Perspectives on the Estrada Crisis

Edited by AMANDO DORONILA

Featuring essays by

Jose V. Abueva

Fermin D. Adriano

Arsenio M. Balisacan

Maria Cynthia Rose Banzon Bautista

John J. Carroll, S.J.

Teodoro Casiño

Karina Constantino-David

Randolf S. David

Emmanuel S. de Dios

Carolina G. Hernandez

Joseph Y. Lim

Guillermo M. Luz

Cayetano W. Paderanga Jr.

Raul J. Palabrica

Michael Vatikiotis

Anvil Publishing, Inc.
and
Philippine Daily Inquirer, Inc.

Between Fires: Fifteen Perspectives on the Estrada Crisis
Edited by Amando Doronila

An Inquirer Books publication

Co-published by

Anvil Publishing, Inc.
2/F Team Pacific Building 14 P. Antonio Street, Barangay Ugong, Pasig City 1604 Philippines
Telephones: 671-1899 (sales & marketing)
Fax: 671-1308
Email: pubdept@anvil.comph

and

Philippine Daily Inquirer, Inc.
Chino Roces Ave. corner Yague and Mascardo Streets, Makati City, Philippines
P.O. Box 2353 Makati Central Post Office, 1263 Makati City, Philippines
Telephone: 897-8808 (connecting all departments)
Fax: 897-4793/94
Website: www.inq7.net

This book is published with the assistance of the Konrad Adenauer Foundation.

Copy editor: Vergel O. Santos
Book designers: Ibarra Crisostomo and Ani V. Habúlan
Cover photo: Dennis Sabangan

The National Library of the Philippines Cataloguing-in-Publication Data

Recommended entry:

Between fires : fifteen perspectives on the Estrada
    crisis / edited by Amando Doronila ; featuring
    essays by Jose V. Abueva... [et al.] - Pasig City :
    Anvil Pub., c2002
    1 v

    1. Estrada, Joseph E., 1937- 2. Philippines.
President (1998-2001 : Estrada). 3. Philippines - Politics
and government. I. Doronila, Amando. II. Abueva,
Jose V. III. Title.

DS686.8.E8 959.9059 2001 P013000035
ISBN 971-27-1155-2 (bp)
ISBN 971-27-1170-6 (np)

Printed in the Philippines

Contents

Introduction

The Specter of the Politics of Mass Mobilization

AMANDO DORONILA

THIS VOLUME IS AN INDISPENSABLE SEQUEL to the gripping account of the events that led to the fall of President Joseph Estrada, the accession of Vice President Gloria Macapagal-Arroyo to the presidency, and the rapid counter-revolution exploding in a mob attack on the presidential palace on May 1, 2001.

The rebellion took place just 101 days after Macapagal-Arroyo had been installed. Paradoxically, the attack, and the peaceful upheaval that preceded it, erupted within the framework of representative democracy. Few democracies have gone through such a swift turnover of power, raising issues about the stability of Philippine democracy and about its direction. The two People Power upheavals—in February 1986 and in January 2001—capped by the "rebellion of the poor" on May 1, 2001 have provoked questions, among Filipinos and foreign observers alike, over whether the Filipinos have unlocked and harnessed the powers of mass political mobilization to redefine the conventional formats of election-driven representative democracy.

If the first volume, *The Fall of Joseph Estrada*, presented a narrative of swiftly moving events as they unfolded from day to day, this second volume allows us to pause, catch our breath, and understand the flow of the tide of political change.

The title of this volume, *Between Fires*, highlights the turbulent transition from the Estrada administration to the successor government of President Macapagal-Arroyo.

Historic Opportunity

FOR THE PURPOSE OF PUTTING THE EVENTS leading to the ouster of Estrada under the more rigorous spotlight of scholarship, we have asked leading Filipino academics and key players in People Power 2 to provide perspectives and insights. None of those we invited to write turned us down despite the short notice. That was very gratifying if we consider that in this country it is hard to engage academics in a project to mount a collection of studies. I like to believe that our contributors were acutely aware of the historical importance of the events which they have analyzed. They applied their analytical discipline to interpret events while they were relatively fresh. The result is a comprehensive study in perspective of one of the most turbulent episodes of political change in this country's history since World War II.

This volume does not pretend, however, to be the final word in explaining the upheavals of January to May 2001. Rather, it should be regarded as the beginning of a thorough study into the issues of democratic development in developing societies and, in particular, the role of military intervention in political change in relatively new democracies, such as the Philippines. If this study serves as a catalyst for further debates on the issues of democratic consolidation or transformation, in relation to political stability and economic development, we should be more than happy.

15 Perspectives

THIS STUDY OFFERS 15 PERSPECTIVES covering the sociological, political, and economic aspects of the events narrated in the first volume. Essentially, it is a study of democracy as it underwent wrenching changes in the context of Philippine social problems, chief of which are widespread poverty, the vast gulf between the rich and the poor, and the lopsided distribution of economic and political power in Philippine society. This social environment provides the setting for mass-mobilization politics on which the foundations of regular democratic elections and other democratic institutions have rested for nearly a hundred years. The last rising, on May 1, in particular, saw the mobilization of the Filipino poor—constituting the masses—for political action manipulated by a faction of the Filipino elite, albeit wearing the tag and trumpeting the slogans of populism.

The first essay, by sociologist Cynthia Rose Banzon Bautista, examines the class issues that propelled the second People Power, which led to the toppling of President Estrada. She counsels against reducing the People Power phenomenon into the "facile interpretations of political developments as the 'revenge of the elite on the masses' or of the 'poor on the rich'". Her study confronts the issue of class conflict as the mobilizing theme of the Estrada presidency. Estrada has fostered the myth that People Power 2 was a conspiracy of the rich and the middle class to depose a pro-poor president elected with a large plurality in the 1998 elections.

The strength of Bautista's essay lies in her marshalling of fresh empirical data to define the composition of Filipino social classes. As far as we know, this is the first time that new data have been deployed to determine the base of the social constituency of Estrada, and of the Estrada-resign movement, in a presidency that raised for the first time in Philippine democracy the theme of class politics as an element to mobilize mass support to win power and retain it. Noteworthy is the examination of the polarization of Filipinos along "lines that coincide with the class divide" provoked by the arrest of Estrada after he was charged with plunder in the anti-graft court. Her study defines the multi-class character of People Power 2 by fleshing out the class composition of the street mass movement. Her study is most helpful in amplifying the middle class, the class credited for the mass mobilization for People Power 2, bringing forward our knowledge of what the middle class is.

Emmanuel S. de Dios's essay inquires into the central role corruption played in the downfall of the Estrada administration. He argues that perception of widespread corruption was an important reason for the steep decline in investor confidence, affecting the rate of economic recovery since the beginning of the 1997 Asian financial crisis. More directly, he argues, "corruption was at the heart of the entire impeachment process", with the events leading to the end of the process as the immediate reason for People Power 2 and the erosion of Estrada's loss of capacity to govern.

Market-Mediated Corruption

DE DIOS ARGUES that public demonstrations and rioting that followed Estrada's arrest show "that a large segment of the population still has not understood the reason for his downfall". His essay proceeds to explain how and why Estrada provoked a popular reaction against his administration so powerful that it led to its downfall and what this may portend for the future of Philippine politics.

While conceding that corruption—defined as "the misuse of public resources for personal gain"—is endemic in Philippine politics, De Dios points out that Estrada "contributed his own innovations to grand corruption".

A new element was "the leveraging of government assets and authority to undertake deals that were ultimately mediated by markets", according to De Dios. "This went beyond simple kickbacks or public contracts, since the rents…did not directly originate from the usual exercise of bureaucratic functions (e.g., government procurement, auctions, etc.) but arose or were realized through the workings of markets or what would appear to be autonomous private-sector decisions". One example of market-mediated corruption "involved the use of government-controlled financial institutions, particularly pension funds…to implement private strategies for take over".

This typology gives a nuanced picture of presidential corruption. Equally insightful is De Dios's observation that a more fundamental consequence of the impeachment trial was "how it exposed the extent of the rot in many of the nation's institutions". De Dios observes that Estrada was a creature of a culture of corruption. "He was also the product and logical culmination of political and social institutions that had been long permeated by corruption and betrayal of the public [trust]," he writes.

The pivotal role played by the military in the collapse of the Estrada government by withdrawing its support comes under scrutiny from a leading Filipino specialist on military intervention in politics, Carol G. Hernandez. Her essay describes the similarities and differences between People Power 1 and People Power 2. In both events, the military played a crucial role in bringing down the sitting government.

One similarity, she points out, is that in both cases people had been at first prepared to take the constitutional route. In 1986 the people participated in the snap election, but they took to the streets when President Marcos stole the election. In December 2000 they acquiesced in the impeachment process but again took to the streets after the impeachment trial had collapsed with the suppression of the prosecution's evidence.

She disagrees with the interpretation that People Power 2 was a form of "mob rule" undermining democracy. She argues that both instances of People Power were peaceful, that protest groups were orderly in expression of opposition to the Estrada administration, and that theirs was a "demonstration of democracy in action". She warns, however, that the specter of coups "continues to haunt the nation". She argues that "a more empowered citizenry can be harnessed to protect democracy from military intervention if the government delivers" good governance.

Exercise in Direct Democracy

JOSE V. ABUEVA ASSESSES THE IMPACT of the Estrada presidency on Philippine democracy. He examines the implications for democracy of the impeachment trial. And he explores the crisis of political leadership transiting from "electoral democracy" to "substantive democracy", during and after the crisis of the Estrada government.

In his view, People Power 2 was a "massive exercise in direct democracy after the institution of impeachment had failed because of the inability of the senator-judges, and the senate as an institution, to act with integrity, impartiality, and wisdom as the people had expected".

Abueva rejects the "lynch mob" description of People Power 2. Abueva argues that People Power 2 "was an extraordinary assertion of popular sovereignty that resulted in the incapacity of President Estrada to govern, his peaceful removal from office, and the succession by Vice President Macapagal-Arroyo".

Abueva recognizes the need to reorient the politicized military to its professional role in a democracy. But he also highlights the flaws of "electoral democracy", characterized by regular elections. He contrasts it with "substantive democracy", which "enables most of the people to realize and enjoy not only their political rights but also their social and economic rights".

Poor Record on the Poor

DID THE ESTRADA ADMINISTRATION benefit the poor?

Arsenio M. Balisacan, a specialist in poverty studies, puts Estrada's record in this regard in the context of his pro-poor rhetoric. His study uncovers a big gap between rhetoric and delivery. One indicator is that, despite the Estrada administration's "resounding rhetoric for the war against poverty", it failed to lower poverty incidence. Access by the poor to education, electricity, and health services was in fact reduced during Estrada's administration, according to Balisacan.

While sustained growth is necessary, he argues, it is not enough. He describes Estrada's war on poverty as unfocused and diffused. Although the Estrada administration reduced the proportion of the population deemed poor, "the rate of reduction was so slow that there are more poor people now than in 1997", says the study. "On an annual basis, the rate of reduction was slower than that achieved in 1985-1997. Among the major Asian countries, the Estrada administration's track record in terms of poverty reduction was quite pathetic."

Economist Joseph Y. Lim puts the thesis that the political and economic crisis during the twilight days of the Estrada administration "showed the clear link between weak institutions and governance structures and the poor economic performance of the country". His study seeks to demonstrate how biased policies, meant to benefit narrow vested interests at the expense of national interest, made a negative impact on the economy. Within this framework, Lim then argues that, if corruption charges against Estrada and his friends are true, his election "should be seen as a takeover of a faction of the old elite that viewed election victory as a feudal conquest that would put the state apparatus at the helm of the winning clique and friends". He substantiates this view by citing specific transactions in which the president tried to "influence various agencies to give special consideration to his friends, many of whom allegedly turned out to be acting as his proxies".

Among the cases is the air war between the Philippines and Taiwan over the liberalization of civil-aviation policy. In that conflict, the Estrada government took the side of the Philippine Airlines, controlled by his friend and campaign-fund contributor Lucio Tan, in curtailing Taiwanese airline flights with stopovers in Manila. The restrictions and policy reversals levied a heavy economic toll on the Philippine economy.

The focus on details of the transactions is helpful. The paper showed how weak institutions and governance structures failed to withstand the pressures "of a particularly vicious type of patronage politics that have gained authority and power".

Diary of Disenchantment

SOCIOLOGIST RANDY DAVID is a disenchanted academic. He had cast his lot with Estrada, together with several University of the Philippines academics who believed they could provide an intellectual content to Estrada's agenda or that they could "make a difference". While some of his UP colleagues stayed with Estrada up to the end, hoping they still could save him and reform him, David withdrew his support when he began to see Estrada "in a different light".

His essay, "A Diary of Disenchantment", confesses he was one of those wide-eyed academics from the University of the Philippines who, like the rest of the Filipinos, were fooled by this "clever politico". Although David did not take up any position in the Estrada government, he has more intimate knowledge than most about the emptiness of the president's populist façade. He calls his disenchantment, in Weberian terms, "an awakening from the spell of custom and charisma; in short, the beginning of rationality". It's best to let him tell his story.

The economy during the Estrada administration comes under review from economists Cayetano W. Paderanga Jr., Christine Atienza, Ferdinand Co, and Flora Belle Villarante. Their paper highlights the political and economic importance of employment generation. After a survey of the economic and financial developments in the country, in the wake of the 1997 Asian financial crisis, the paper concludes that, more than any other economic undercurrent, the "unemployment situation appears to be the main explanation" for the Estrada administration's collapse.

Mindanao War Toll

THE "ALL-OUT WAR" unleashed by Estrada on the separatist Moro Islamic Liberation Front and on the Abu Sayyaf, the latter for taking hostage foreign holiday-makers in Sipadan, Malaysia, contributed to the fall of the Estrada government, according to Fermin Adriano.

While the *jueteng* scandal and the impeachment trial triggered the eventual collapse of the government, Adriano argues, it was the heightened-armed conflict in Mindanao that highlighted the incompetence of the administration. Adriano's paper counts the high social and economic costs of the war and describes as mere Pyrrhic victory the military's proclaimed success after over-running the MILF camps.

Inside the PR

KARINA CONSTANTINO-DAVID was head of President Estrada's housing program until October 1999, when she resigned after Estrada reorganized the housing agency to make way for the appointment of his friend Jose 'Sel' Yulo as co-chairperson (with Estrada) of the newly formed Presidential Commission for Mass Housing. The housing scheme was one of the legs of the president's pro-poor program. In fact, it was a showcase of his socially oriented projects.

Within two years of involvement with the program, Constantino-David not only discovered it was a sham and was in fact in disarray. She also came to know intimately the president's lavish life style and erratic, if not desultory, work habits. Her essay, "Surviving Erap", is an insider's account of what went on behind the housing program and propaganda and in the presidential residence, where bacchanal took place in the feasting and drinking among the president and his cronies.

The Dam Breaks

RAUL J. PALABRICA, a lawyer, was the *Inquirer*'s legal expert who wrote articles analyzing the day-to-day developments on the Estrada impeachment trial. His articles translated to layman's language the legalistic jargon that often shrouds lawyer's debates. In his essay, Palabrica describes the highlights or turning points of the trial leading to its breakdown when the senate majority suppressed the second envelope.

"What 35 witnesses and 24 trial days failed to accomplish, one envelope did in five days," Palabrica writes. "The refusal of 11 senators to open the envelope that purportedly contained information about Estrada's P3.3-billion bank deposits raised serious doubts about the ability of the impeachment process to impartially pass upon Estrada's culpability for the impeachment charges."

The "dam of resentment and frustration that had built up since Day

One of the impeachment trial finally broke," his essay concludes. "The constitutional process could no longer be trusted. Neither can the senators be relief upon to protect the people's interests against an abusive president. So the people took to the streets and gave sovereignty a new dimension."

Civil Society

FATHER JOHN CARROLL, a Jesuit scholar, provides us with a detailed account of the role of the Roman Catholic church and civil-society forces in the removal of Estrada from power. While Jaime Cardinal Sin, the archbishop of Manila, was a key figure in the 1986 People Power revolution, the church under him also played a crucial role in People Power 2.

The composition of civil-society forces was, however, different in People Power 2 from the one in People Power 1. Father Carroll's essay takes us into the behind-the-scenes squabbling within the protest movement and reveals the tensions within the Estrada-resign coalition of the streets.

He reveals that the entire church hierarchy was not monolithically involved in the protest campaign to remove Estrada. According to Father Carroll, not more 30 out of 100 bishops were actively involved in the movement. Many bishops not only stayed on the sidelines. His account reveals that "many noted with some distress" the refusal of Ricardo Cardinal Vidal of Cebu to speak out firmly on the Estrada resignation issue. His paper defines the groups that compose "civil society". The paper is uncertain over whether the civil-society groups that backed Vice President Gloria Macapagal-Arroyo could "hang in there" and remain coalesced with the president, given their different outlooks.

The Left Reverses

IN PEOPLE POWER 2, the Left was a key participant. Its involvement is a departure from its boycott of the political movement that led to the toppling of Ferdinand Marcos in 1986. In its involvement in political action, the Left organizations were thrown in the company of moderates and even conservatives in the business community. Teodoro Casiño, one of the militants of the Left, provides the "view from the streets". He also writes about the tensions between Left-wing contingents and the Makati Business Club (MBC), and the difference between the Left's strategy to march to the presidential palace and church-backed conservative forces who were issued confusing marching orders by Cardinal Sin.

Business Perspective

GUILLERMO LUZ WAS THE ARTICULATE SPOKESPERSON for the Makati Business Club during the campaign to step up the demand for Estrada's resignation. But all was not sweetness and light among the big businesses and between them and the other activist groups in the coalition of the streets. In his article, Luz reveals the MBC's friction with the activists over funding of rallies. He also describes the acceleration of the MBC's involvement with, and participation in, the anti-Estrada movement. He writes about what the business community expects of the administration of President Macapagal-Arroyo.

A Regional View

MANY IN THE PHILIPPINES were offended by comments of the foreign press, describing People Power 2 as a "soft coup" or something close to "mob rule". Those reactions were shaped by the experience of Western journalists accustomed to the resolution of conflict through stable political and social institutions. The clash of political cultures between Filipinos and foreign observers over the events in the Philippines, where conflict has increasingly been resolved by mass political action, is at the root of the Filipino reactions.

We have asked Michael Vatikiotis, editor of the *Far Eastern Economic Review*, to present his point of view on the Estrada ouster. Being an old Asia hand, Vatikiotis has intimate knowledge of the cultural and political contexts of the West and Asian societies. He writes that Estrada's "ignominious exit from power... solved a thorny problem of bad leadership in the Philippines, but underscored the frail foundations of democracy in the region".

With the Macapagal-Arroyo government sitting on the fragile foundations of an unstable democracy, still shaking from the aftershocks of the new round of criminal trial of Estrada for plunder charges, and a weak economy, the essays in this volume could help illuminate our reflections on the prospects of the future of democracy in the Philippines.

Between Fires

Fifteen Perspectives on the Estrada Crisis

People Power 2
'The Revenge of the Elite on the Masses'?[i]

MARIA CYNTHIA ROSE BANZON BAUTISTA

Estrada's Class-Based Electoral Victory

POVERTY HAS BEEN A CONSTANT THORN in the nation's flesh. When Joseph Estrada launched his bid for the 1998 presidential elections, about 37% of the country's population lived below the official poverty threshold. For government economic planners then, this figure represented a marked de-cline from much higher levels of poverty incidence in previous years. But for many grassroots organizers, it underestimated the magnitude of poor Filipinos at the time. A more realistic assessment of the minimum require-ments for a decent life would, accordingly, reveal that at least half of Fili-pino families lived in poverty in 1997.

Even more striking than persistent poverty, gross inequality character-ized the late 1990s, as it did earlier decades. The Philippine social struc-ture during the 1998 presidential elections reflected class cleavages that had undergone very little transformation since the country's independence from colonial rule. Although the class structure had become far more com-plex than the two-tiered model of rich patrons and poor clients, its shape, nevertheless, remained pyramidal. A small proportion of rich citizens formed the apex, while a huge mass who are poor or on the brink of poverty con-stituted the broad base. Although the middle class has expanded in size and political significance since World War II, it still made up a relatively narrow segment between the apex and the base.

Filipino social scientists generally construct an image of the class struc-ture from measures of indirect income and status. For instance, the Social Weather Stations, Inc. (SWS) and Pulse Asia, Inc., two of the biggest opin-ion polling institutions in the country, use housing characteristics to clas-sify respondents into four categories: AB, C, D and E. Although more complex and theory-based classification systems exist, the ABCDE system based on type of dwelling is widely adopted in the Philippines because it is simpler and more reliable than direct income estimates or employment-based classifications.[ii] It rests on the validated assumption that Filipinos spend their incomes on the appearance of their homes, unless they are too poor to adequately meet survival needs. Thus, their socio-economic standing may be inferred from specific features of their houses.

In the ABCDE system, AB constitutes the upper class while C corresponds to the middle class. The D and E groups make up the lower classes. D is further subdivided into D1 and D2, with the former owning the lots on which their houses are built.

AB houses are made of heavy and high quality materials and are located in exclusive villages or stand out in mixed neighborhoods (Arroyo, 1990). They are usually well maintained and have sprawling lawns, gardens and expensive furnishings. On the other hand, C houses combine light and heavy materials. They are also well maintained and have adequate furnishings. Located in middle class subdivisions or mixed neighborhoods, some C houses have lawns or gardens.

Compared to C houses, D homes are made of light and cheap materials. Found in crowded neighborhoods, they are generally shabby in appearance and have scanty furnishings. But the most unkempt houses are reserved for the E class. E respondents live in dilapidated, makeshift structures often found in cramped spaces or slum districts.

Using this classification system, SWS estimated that during the 1998 presidential elections, the voting population nationwide could be categorized as follows: 10% belonged to ABC; 18% were from the poorest E class; while 72% came from D. Of those categorized as D, 43% were from the upper lower class (D1) and 29% belonged to the lower-income D (D2).

Among all the candidates in the 1998 presidential elections, former President Joseph Estrada was most aware of the potentials of class-based politics. He exploited the class divide in his campaign to the full. Having risen in the political hierarchy, first as a town mayor, then as a senator and vice-president, on the strength of the mass vote, Estrada, not surprisingly, cast his net throughout the presidential campaign on the D and E bulk of the voting population.

Aprodicio Laquian, chronicler of Estrada's rise to the presidency, relates that strategists in the Laban ng Makabayang Masang Pilipino

(LAMMP), Estrada's political party, initially focused on the ABC-oriented Metro Manila media. But they soon found this strategy off the mark. Opinion polls at the time emphasized clear differences between the concerns of Metro Manila's voters and those from the provinces. They also revealed a solid constituency for Estrada among the D and E classes. Heeding the surveys, Estrada's subsequent campaigns directly addressed these groups. He engaged in face-to-face encounters with the masses in places where they congregated—markets, bus depots and factories. His sorties penetrated the squatter and slum settlements in urban areas.

The surveys also revealed why his constituency in these classes preferred him to other candidates. They saw in him a caring, approachable and compassionate man who sympathized with the plight of the poor. Capitalizing on these perceptions, the LAMMP strategists reinforced the image. They published photographs of Estrada sharing meals with squatter families and putting food into the mouths of their children. They also launched a radio program—*Jeep ni Erap*—that allowed lower class listeners to air their problems directly to Estrada.

The masterstroke communication line *Erap Para Sa Mahirap* (Erap for the Poor) captured the essence of Estrada's message. But the campaign imagery went beyond that of a charismatic politician serving the poor. Despite his upper middle class origins and flashy lifestyle, Estrada succeeded in making the masses feel that he was not just for the poor. He was one of them in spirit and circumstances. Like the masses, he did not possess the conventional credentials of the educated class. Like them, he felt alienated from an elite that questioned his capacity to govern and openly rejected his bid for the presidency.

Illusion and reality meshed in the campaign as the masses equated Estrada with the poor but always golden-hearted characters he portrayed throughout his movie career—as a jeepney driver, stevedore, tricycle driver and ice cream vendor, among others. More importantly, his cinematic roles as a local Robin Hood in the movie, *"Asiong Salonga"*, and as heroes of poor people's uprisings (e.g. *"Kumander Alibasbas"*) made him a larger-than-life savior in the eyes of the poor. Estrada's psychological identification with the masses in real life, which accounts for his immense credibility with them, further reinforced such images.

The bond between Estrada and his mass constituency was most evident in LAMMP campaign rallies. Marginalized in a society indifferent to their needs, his mass audience empathized with him each time he declared that the rich were against his election to the presidency. He aroused their sympathy as the underdog whenever he proclaimed that the personal attacks on him by the wealthy were also attacks on the masses (Laquian, 1998). His "us versus them," "the poor versus the rich" line roused wild cheers and drove people to agitated frenzy.

Reciprocating Estrada's affinity to them, the masses gave him an overwhelming victory at the polls. The SWS exit polls in May 1998 revealed that almost half of the poorest E population and 40% of the D class across different regions nationwide elected him to office. Their votes, in turn, made up 25% and 63% of the total, respectively. The sundry intellectuals who supported Estrada hailed his rise to power through a popular vote. For compared with his predecessors, he won the presidency as a relative outsider to the traditional system of national patronage politics. Since he was less beholden to elite power brokers, Estrada could, accordingly, transcend entrenched interests and more vigorously pursue democratizing reforms.[iii]

The Road to People Power 2

THE MISSION TO LEAD THE LIBERATION of the masses from poverty and inequality was not lost on Joseph Estrada, who, upon being proclaimed as the 13th Philippine president by Congress, promptly described himself as a "modern Bonifacio". (Almario, 1998; Locsin, 1998). In Estrada's view, he too, like Bonifacio, was condemned by the Catholic church hierarchy and the country's bourgeoisie. His ascent to the presidency was therefore the equivalent of the plebeian-led "revolt of the masses" in 1896. Thus, as the "Centennial president"—elected 100 years after the nation's independence from Spain—he would complete Bonifacio's unfinished revolution by breaking the chains of poverty.

Unfortunately, Estrada as president failed to live up to this promise. Analysts who reviewed his administration's efforts to improve the lot of the poor found an incoherent and fragmented anti-poverty program (De Dios, 1997; Karaos, 1997; Bautista, Angeles and Dionisio, 2000). In response to rising criticism, government launched a national poverty action agenda in August 2000. By then, however, the prospect of equity reform and poverty alleviation under Estrada was growing dim. For one thing, Estrada would be embroiled in another scandal, this time, over his alleged unexplained wealth which investigative journalists exposed in a series of meticulously documented articles. Several political fiascoes—including the ill-fated attempt to launch a new anti-corruption superbody—would likewise bring criticism on government. Eventually, two months after it was launched, Estrada's national anti-poverty agenda would be swept aside by the brewing political crisis.

The emergence of a new set of cronies under Estrada's watch undermined the president's script of social action and devotion to the masses. With Ilocos Sur Gov. Luis 'Chavit' Singson's disclosure that Estrada had received regular payoffs as the virtual head of a nationwide syndicate running an illegal numbers game (*jueteng*), his pro-poor rhetoric began to lose its ring even among some of his supporters. For if Singson's allegations were true, massive funds must have flowed from the poor, who put their small monies in *jueteng*, to Estrada and his cabal of wealthy friends including Singson (Doronila, 2000).

The televised morality play that unfolded in the wake of Singson's October 2000 expose turned an initial business confidence problem into a political crisis. Months earlier, the business community had become increasingly restive over the rising incidence of corruption, cronyism and arbitrary decision-making in government. But Singson's revelations as to how the spoils of *jueteng* were being allocated introduced a criminal element to the administration's character. The existence of a "sub-rosa bureaucracy" extending all the way from the president to the smallest *jueteng* collector, "paralleling and intertwining at key points with the formal government hierarchy", further eroded the business sector's confidence (Bello, 2001). In the end, business severely judged Estrada's administration for "morally wounding" the rule of law itself (Fabella, 2000).

Outrage against Estrada's shady business deals and the spate of revelations in the impeachment trial was not confined to the business community. Within days of Singson's expose, various civil society forces formed the Kongreso ng Mamamayang Pilipino II (Kompil II), a pluralist coalition composed of NGO networks (e.g. Code-NGO), issue-based and sectoral coalitions (e.g. Freedom from Debt Coalition and the National Peace Conference), church based organizations (e.g. Gomburza), Left political blocs (Bisig, Social Democratic Caucus, Sanlakas), party list groups (e.g. Akbayan) and individuals. Similarly, organizations and movements of the national democratic Left, anti-Estrada politicians and known progressive individuals formed the Erap Resign Movement (Reyes, 2001). Both multisectoral networks succeeded in mobilizing huge support for the major anti-Estrada rallies in the last quarter of 2000. Other organized players that emerged included the United Opposition led by then Vice President Gloria Macapagal-Arroyo, Council on Philippine Affairs (Copa), Kangkong Brigade, the People's Consultative Assembly, Couples for Christ, Bigkis Pinoy, Barangay RJ and the Jesus is Lord Movement (Casino, 2001).

The call for Estrada to step down from office began months before October. In March 2000, the so-called "Silent Protest Movement", an initiative led mostly by middle class personalities, launched a series of actions to demand the president's resignation. But these protests eventually fizzled out because of lack of public support. Singson's expose, however, served as catalyst for the widespread rallies and demonstrations that culminated in the People Power 2 uprising in mid-January 2001. The eventual ouster of Estrada as president of the Republic, on the other hand, was sparked by the fateful vote of the 11 senators in the impeachment trial against the opening of the second envelope said to contain evidence of Estrada's unexplained wealth.

While drawing parallelisms between him and Bonifacio in May 1998, Estrada highlighted a crucial difference. Unlike the Great Plebeian, he claimed he would not allow his *ilustrado* enemies to execute him. Not surprisingly, in the months preceding People Power 2, Estrada vigorously fought back.

He decried the charges against him as part of a mere destabilization campaign being launched by his elitist detractors. He made the rounds of poor urban communities, where he branded the anti-Estrada protests as attacks by the elite against the poor he had vowed to defend. In a Kongreso ng Masa (Congress of the Masses) organized by the People's Movement Against Poverty (PMAP) in December 2000, Estrada accused the business elite of trying to undermine him because of his success in uplifting the conditions of the poor. By opposing his efforts to improve the quality of life of the masses, the rich, according to him, were preventing their empowerment. Estrada brought his gripes to the *masa* where he was most comfortable, and it was among them that he sought refuge for his drained spirits.

Composition and Character of People Power 2

HARPING ONCE AGAIN on the class divide, Estrada virtually labeled People Power 2 the revenge of the elite, specifically the "Makati-based *insulares* and *peninsulares* who never accepted his election", on the poor majority who voted him into office. But was People Power 2 indeed an elitist uprising?

Instead of referring to those who participated in the four-day demonstrations that ousted Estrada as members of the ruling elite, the local and international press projected People Power 2 as an essentially middle class protest with strong support from the business community. It is easy to imagine why this impression stuck. The images on television were those of clean-cut participants in black mourning attire, many of whom carried cellular phones. Furthermore, middle class activists, intellectuals and professionals led the multi-sectoral coalitions against Estrada (Rivera, 2000). In addition, the vanguardless, decentralized and spontaneous uprising was coordinated through messages transmitted by numerous but interlocking texting networks and electronic discussion groups, technology available mainly to the upper and middle classes.

Personal observations of the crowd at the EDSA shrine and interviews with resource persons, however, suggest a more heterogeneous class composition. Comparing People Power 1 and People Power 2, political analyst Ricardo Reyes noted the deeper grassroots imprint of the latter. Mass-based organizations formed a significant core of the mobilization in People Power 2. All shades of the Left were represented. A strong Moro contingent and a small section of the peasantry, including organizations such as Pakisama and Kilusang Magbubukid ng Pilipinas (KMP), were present at the shrine. In an unprecedented move, all major labor groups spanning the ideological spectrum—i.e., the conservative Trade Union Congress of the Philippines (TUCP), the Center-leaning Federation of Free Workers (FFW), and the three socialist labor federations and centers, namely, Bukluran ng Mangagawang Pilipino (BMP), Kilusang Mayo Uno (KMP) and the Alliance of Progressive Labor (APL)—made their presence felt organizationally although they did not come in full force. Interestingly, the TUCP had endorsed the presidential tandem of Estrada and Edgardo Angara in the 1998 presidential elections.

Among the sectors, young students were the most visible group in EDSA. The high energy and exuberance at the shrine may be attributed to their presence especially at night. Contrary to the impression that most of the youth who participated in the rallies were from exclusive Catholic schools, participant observers noted sizable delegations from the university belt and other educational institutions attended by the D and E classes.

Estimates of the actual distribution of the People Power 2 participants by social class are unavailable. However, data from Pulse Asia's February 3-5 nationwide survey, conducted two weeks after Estrada's ouster, provide a snapshot of the class composition at the EDSA shrine in mid-January. In a sample of voting-age respondents in Metro Manila, 18% claim to have participated in the uprising. Of these, almost half (47%) came from the ranks of the middle C class while close to one out five participants (18%) were from the upper class. Although the majority belonged to the ABC classes, the lower income groups were represented as well. Slightly more than a third of the participants (35%) were from the D and E classes (Figure 1). It is worth noting, however, that less than 5% of those who participated in the uprising represented urban poor slum communities where E households proliferate.

The estimated proportion of Metro Manila-based middle class participants in People Power 2 could be higher if the D rallyists with at least some college education and those in middle class occupations were added to the C group.[iv] Doing this would result in slightly more than half of the EDSA rallyists (56%) falling under the middle class category. As a result of the reclassification, three out of four People Power 2 participants in Metro Manila would belong to the ABC classes.

The low incomes of D respondents engaged in otherwise middle class jobs (e.g. professionals, managers, routine white-collar workers, proprietors) reflect the wage differentials within the same occupations in the Philippines. Studies have shown that the wages of people belonging to the same occupational cluster vary considerably depending upon a host of factors including the sector of the economy (private versus public), years of experience, the geographic location of the firm and the female density of the industry (Alba, 1997). Belonging to the D group, however, does not preclude these respondents from sharing the work orientation and values of their educated counterparts in the upper and middle class.

Figure 1

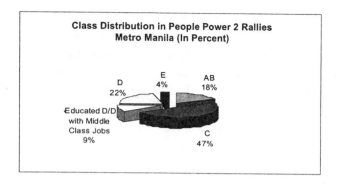

Class Distribution in People Power 2 Rallies
Metro Manila (In Percent)

E 4%
D 22%
AB 18%
Educated D/D with Middle Class Jobs 9%
C 47%

Source: Pulse Asia, Inc. Thames Nationwide Survey, 3-5 February 2001, N=54 of 300.

Outside of Metro Manila, the composition of those who joined the anti-Estrada rallies that erupted in major urban centers nationwide also reflected the visibility of the upper and middle classes. However, half of the participants (53%) were from D and E households (Figure 2). Even if the educated D and those with middle class occupations were included in the middle class, the proportion of D and E respondents who joined these rallies nationwide (44%) would still be higher than in Metro Manila (26%).

Survey findings and observers' assessments suggest that the People Power 2 participants consisted of the educated segment of the voting population in the ABCD classes and the organized D and E groups. Representing grassroots civil society, most of the D and E participants may not have reached college. However, compared to their unorganized counterparts, their involvement in various movements implies a higher level of informal education along the issues and principles of their respective organizations.

One would expect the laborers who joined the uprising, for instance, to have previously undergone some form of political education. Labor unions, regardless of ideological persuasion, use training modules, reading materials and focused discussions in pickets and demonstrations to raise their members' social and political consciousness. Similarly, one would expect D and E members of religious organizations, like the Couples for Christ, to have participated in regular area-based prayer meetings and bible readings involving couples from other social classes. Like the conscientization (i.e., action, reflection, revised action) tools of the labor movement, such activities serve to enhance the functional and political literacy of these groups' D and E members.

The class composition at the EDSA shrine and other sites of urban protest[v] accounts for the distinct character of People Power 2. Attended predominantly by the middle class with significant representatives from the organized segments of the lower classes, the four-day uprising vented a righteous indignation. A broad spectrum of institutions, organizations and individuals vehemently protested the suppression of truth when a majority of the members of the impeachment court voted to keep the controversial second envelope—containing potentially damning evidence against Estrada—sealed. But they also congregated to demand the end of a regime marked by brazen corruption, cronyism, and abuse of power.

Figure 2

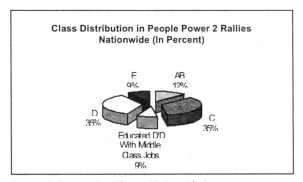

Source: Pulse Asia, Inc. Thames Nationwide Survey,
3-5 February 2001, N=80 of 1200

In the context of a highly personalistic political culture, People Power 2 was a significant accomplishment. It galvanized participants around abstract principles such as truth, justice, and good governance.[vi] Earlier, political observers had expressed serious doubts about the possibility of an EDSA 2. When the *jueteng* scandal escalated, they argued that while similar principles animated the protests in 1986, the moral outrage at EDSA 1 had a rallying point in Corazon Aquino, bereaved widow of slain oppositionist Benigno Aquino, whose victory in the snap elections was snatched by Ferdinand Marcos. As the underdog of Philippine politics then, Corazon Aquino easily aroused the sympathy of an enraged citizenry.

In contrast, the rallying issues of the anti-Estrada struggle were not embodied in any single person. The series of protest actions that culminated in the uprising had no aggrieved personality for Filipinos to rally behind.

Nor did it have an unequivocal leader. In fact, Macapagal-Arroyo, the constitutional successor, was not popular among those demanding Estrada's resignation. Her net trust rating at the opinion polls even dropped significantly at the time. Thus, it was remarkable that People Power 2 rallied behind a set of ideals instead of a person. Sovereign citizens trooped to the streets to mourn the suppression of truth and justice. And when they succeeded in ousting President Estrada extra-constitutionally, People Power 2 "went back to its constitutional shell". It accepted Gloria Macapagal-Arroyo as the new head of state even if she was not the participants' choice for the post (Reyes, 2001).[vii]

What the skeptics failed to consider in assessing the likelihood of mass mobilization for EDSA 2 was the impact of the impeachment trial. Commencing on December 7, it gripped the nation as no other show had. About half of 1189 respondents in the SWS ABS-CBN nationwide survey on January 6-9, 2001 closely followed the impeachment trial while 40% followed it occasionally. Only one out of ten respondents ignored the trial (Figure 3). As expected, the proportion of Metro Manila respondents who keenly monitored the impeachment proceedings was much higher than the rest of the nation. Seven out of ten respondents from the metropolis followed it closely; 28% followed it occasionally while an insignificant 2% did not bother to monitor the trial (Figure 4).

Figure 3

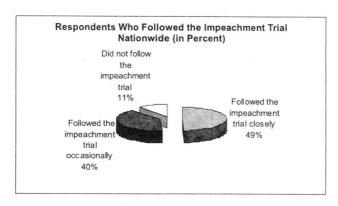

Source: Social Weather Stations, Inc.
ABS-CBN Nationwide Survey 6-9 January, 2001, N=1189

Figure 5 reveals that, nationwide, nine of ten respondents from the AB class; eight of ten from C; five of ten from D; and four of ten respondents from E kept up with the trial. An overwhelming majority of them watched the proceedings on television. Figure 5 also shows that in Metro Manila, 93% of the AB respondents; 81% of the C respondents, 66% of the D respondents and 53% of the E respondents closely followed the televised impeachment proceedings.

In a nation addicted to *telenovelas*, the full media coverage of the six-hour daily impeachment proceedings offered the Filipino audience a thrilling melodrama, complete with real-life characters, an unfolding plot, suspense and unexpected twists. Beating the television ratings of the most popular prime-time shows, the trial provided faces and images to an otherwise abstract and issue-oriented struggle. Without it, the public would not have fully understood how Estrada violated its trust. Without it, moral outrage would not have erupted when 11 senators voted to dismiss the controversial envelope. Without it, People Power 2 would have been difficult, if not impossible, to stage.

Figure 4

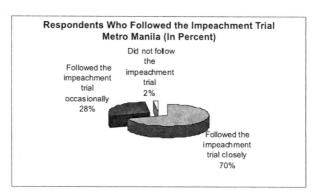

Source: Social Weather Stations, Inc. ABS-CBN Nationwide Survey 6-9 January, 2001, N=295

Figure 5

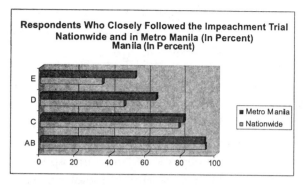

Source: Social Weather Stations, Inc. ABS-CBN Nationwide Survey
January 6-9, 2001, N=1189; 295

The impeachment trial profoundly affected the viewing public. Phrases like "yes, your honor" or "objection, your honor" infused the everyday speech of ordinary Filipinos. They were exposed to the meaning of legal constructs like relevance, materiality and *subpoena duces tecum*. They not only learned how trials were carried out in court but also got a glimpse of the workings of institutions such as the stock market. More importantly, however, the viewers saw themselves as members of the jury and acted accordingly when the trial was aborted (Pertierra, 2001).

The resulting indignation at the EDSA shrine articulated a consensus among disparate groups and individuals that Estrada had lost the moral ascendancy to govern. Despite marked ideological and class differences among them, their assessments of the Estrada government converged. A broad acceptance of common intellectual and ethical reference points made this convergence possible (Magno 2001). Moral reference points constitute, after all, a much broader ethical frame whose normative standards are shared by contemporary religions, social movements and professions in the modern world.

This modern sensibility is universal, transcending culture, religions and politics. It is imbibed through humanist education, attained formally through schools and universities or achieved in the practice of ideologically motivated social movements and religious organizations. It is notable, for instance, that the First Quarter Storm in 1970 heralded the most significant educational reorientation since the coming of the Thomasites during the American colonial period (Doronila, 1989).[viii] Accomplished outside the formal educational system, it skirted the bureaucratic problem of access. Thus, it succeeded in awakening the consciousness of huge segments of the marginalized to the possibilities of a transformative project within the framework of modernity.

Given their formal and informal education, a critical mass of People Power 2 participants from the upper-, middle- and the organized lower classes would have imbibed a modern sensibility. This explains the spirit of People Power 2. For four days, a sense of community prevailed at the EDSA shrine, the symbolic center of protest and change. Social hierarchies were suspended and the distinct groups merged in an atmosphere of overwhelming unity (Pertierra, 2001). A deep sense of moral renewal characterized the mood of the participants. They were upbeat, confident in the efficacy of their actions to change a corrupt government and hold its successor accountable to the principles of a morally grounded politics (Bautista, 2001).

The sense of hope and future-oriented ethos of People Power 2 is rooted in the composition of its participants. The middle classes, in particular, have the means to imagine and create the possibilities of a better future for themselves and their progeny. Many of them would have concretely experienced social mobility, even as past political and economic crises may have threatened the sustainability of their lifestyles and the fulfilment of their dreams. On the other hand, members of the organized lower classes, while themselves embroiled in the daily struggles for economic survival, would be less desperate and cynical of the future than the unorganized among their ranks. In the course of their participation in political, sectoral or religious organizations, they would have experienced small but significant improvements in their lives. They would have also borne witness to the efficacy of collective action, thereby allowing them to imagine the possibility of social change and future reform.

Class and the Numbers Game

THE SENSE OF MORAL RIGHTEOUSNESS at the EDSA shrine made the size of the rebellious crowd less salient to the People Power 2 participants. This was not the case, however, for the pro-Estrada forces. At the height of the four-day uprising, Malacañang spokespersons questioned the legitimacy of the demand for Estrada to resign. As they put it, a few hundred thousand wealthy citizens could not claim to represent 70 million Filipinos.

They argued that 10 million Filipinos voted Estrada to office and most of them were not at the EDSA shrine to recall his mandate.

It was not the first time that Estrada's publicists played the numbers game. On August 20, 1999, or more than a year before Singson's expose, Estrada defended his proposal to amend the Constitution before a mammoth crowd that had gathered at the Luneta for El Shaddai head Mike Velarde's birthday. Estrada's publicists lost no time claiming that the beleaguered president commanded a much bigger support. The Luneta crowd after all dwarfed the multisectoral but much smaller anti-Charter change rally in Ayala.

The issue of numbers would be raised once again in the major mobilizations at the height of the political crisis. The prayer rally led by El Shaddai and Iglesia ni Cristo on November 11, 2000, for instance, was projected to have brought more than a million Filipinos to Luneta in support of Estrada. This rally was organized a week after Jaime Cardinal Sin and Corazon Aquino spearheaded the first anti-Estrada demonstration in EDSA that mobilized a much broader spectrum of participants. Noteworthy for the mix of upper, middle and lower class protestors, the EDSA rally was, nevertheless, smaller than the religious festivities at Luneta.

The pro-Estrada forces downplayed the multisectoral composition of the anti-Estrada rallies. Instead, they harped on the size and class differences between the EDSA or Ayala rallies and the Luneta congregations. The presence of the lower classes who constituted a significant section of El Shaddai's membership was said to reflect the masses' continuing faith in the charismatic idol and leader they catapulted to the presidency.

But the charges of corruption and cronyism against Estrada in the first two years of his term did affect his level of mass support. In the three-part series *The Movie in Erap's Mind*, Pulse Asia director Romeo Manlapaz analyzed Pulse Asia's data from May 1999 to October 2000. He found out that from May to September 1999, approval for Estrada's performance plummeted drastically.[ix] It continued to drop, though at a slower rate until March 2000, but recovered somewhat between March and August 2000 because of the perceived success of the Mindanao war. Another round of falling ratings began once again from August to October. In this light, Manlapaz argued that the *jueteng* scandal merely accelerated Estrada's fall in the ratings.

Manlapaz also revealed that public approval of Estrada's performance fell at a rate of 0.79 for all classes nationwide from May 1999 to October

2000. But it was among the lower income D (D2) that his approval ratings fell at the highest rate (0.97) in the same period. This was quite notable since the same class gave him higher ratings than the general population in May 1999. As for the E respondents, their approval ratings of Estrada were consistently higher than the rest of the population during the same 17-month period. But it had also fallen by as much as the general population by October 2000. The approval ratings of the middle class (C), on the other hand, were consistently lower than the general population from May 1999 to October 2000.

In a March 2000 sample, Manlapaz further studied the predispositions of those who voted for Estrada in 1998. Of the 47% who claimed to have voted for him, 20% said they would not vote for him anymore, 14% said they were ambivalent and only 13% would choose him again. Since 96% of the sample came from D and E, the much lower share of Estrada's supporters in the D and E classes who would elect him again suggests some disenchantment with his performance long before Singson's expose.

Further analysis of Pulse Asia Inc.'s nationwide surveys from July 2000 to February 2001 qualifies this apparent erosion of Estrada's support among the masses. Since Filipinos are not accustomed to assessing the performance of their leaders, the analysis focuses instead on the respondents' trust in the former president. In the context of the Filipinos' personalistic culture, exploring the *tiwala* or trust they have in a leader may be more meaningful (David, 2000).

Figure 6 shows the net trust rating of Estrada—i.e., the proportion of respondents who trust him minus those who distrust him. As expected, his net ratings for the AB and C classes were negative in October. It remained almost at the same level in December and plunged to as low as –74% and –55%, respectively, two weeks after People Power 2. Classifying those who were undecided as trusting Estrada did not affect the trend for the upper and middle classes. While the levels of those who trust him would be higher, the net ratings would still be negative.

Among D respondents, Figure 6 also shows ratings dropping significantly from 22% in July to 7% in October. Their net trust rating of Estrada remained a positive but low 5% in December. Two weeks after People Power 2, this plunged to –28%. If the high share of undecided D respondents were classified as trusting him, the declining pattern of the ratings would remain but the levels would be much higher (50% in July, 32% in October, 35% in December, –7%). Interestingly, the net trust in Estrada would still be negative in February 2001.

The E class deviated from the general pattern of decreasing net trust in the former president. His ratings hardly changed from July to December (36% in July, 31% in October and December)[x] although it dropped to –10% in February. But if the undecided E respondents were classified as trusting Estrada, the ratings would have been +10% after his ouster.

Figure 6[xi]

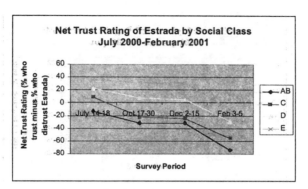

Sources: Pulse Asia July 14-28 Ulat ng Bayan (nationwide); Pulse Asia October 17-30 Ulat ng Bayan (nationwide); Pulse Asia December 2-15 Ulat ng Bayan Survey (nationwide); Pulse Asia February 3-5 Thames Survey (nationwide)

Reclassifying respondents by employment class rather than type of dwelling reveals negative net trust ratings since July for capitalists, professionals, managers and routine nonmanual workers (Figure 7). This trend was not as apparent among small proprietors and artisans whose net trust fluctuated from –33% in October to 8% in December and –53% in February.[xii] Among the working class and the economically inactive or unemployed that made up close to half of the voting population, the pattern was similar to that of the D class (Figure 6).

Focusing on the masses, young E respondents, that is, those less than 30 years old, had low and consistently declining positive net ratings until December (Figure 8). By February, the ratings of the young and older E (30 years old and above) had become negative although the former had a –20% rating compared to the latter's –4%. The ratings of D respondents younger than 30 years old, on the other hand, did not differ significantly from their older counterparts.

In terms of education, D respondents with at least some years in college consistently registered negative and lower net trust ratings than those with less years in school. Similarly, the educated E respondents had declining ratings which became negative in December 2000 (Figure 9).

Figure 7[xiii]

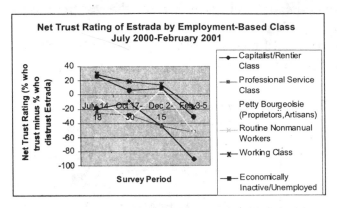

Sources: Pulse Asia July 14-28 Ulat ng Bayan (nationwide); Pulse Asia October 17-30 Ulat ng Bayan (nationwide); Pulse Asia December 2-15 Ulat ng Bayan Survey (nationwide); Pulse Asia February 3-5 Thames Survey (nationwide)

Figure 8[xiv]

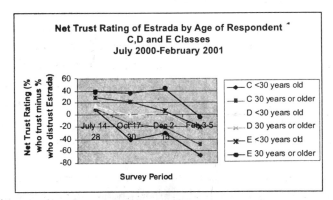

Sources: Pulse Asia July 14-28 Ulat ng Bayan (nationwide); Pulse Asia October 17-30 Ulat ng Bayan (nationwide); Pulse Asia December 2-15 Ulat ng Bayan Survey (nationwide); Pulse Asia February 3-5 Thames Survey (nationwide)

Figure 9[xv]

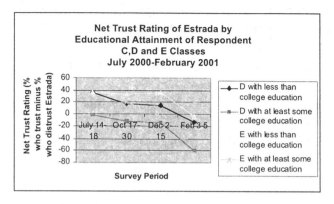

Sources: Pulse Asia July 14-28 Ulat ng Bayan (nationwide); Pulse Asia October 17-30 Ulat ng Bayan (nationwide); Pulse Asia December 2-15 Ulat ng Bayan Survey (nationwide); Pulse Asia February 3-5 Thames Survey (nationwide)

Estrada's net trust ratings among the E respondents in major cities (including Metro Manila) also reveal an interesting pattern (Figure 10). They were consistently decreasing and much lower than the net ratings obtained for the same class nationwide. But among the urban sample, Metro Manila's E respondents gave Estrada net trust ratings that were higher than those he obtained in major cities. Interestingly, the E ratings for the metropolis hardly changed between December (18%) and after People Power 2 (17%). This was in stark contrast to the nationwide E ratings, which plunged from 31% in December to −10% in February. In the wake of the uprising, therefore, the E voting population with a positive net trust rating for Estrada was found only in Metro Manila. If the undecided among Metro Manila's E class were classified as trusting Estrada, his rating in February among them would have even been higher at 37%.

Estrada's net trust ratings among the E class in the metropolis deviated considerably from those found among D respondents. In July and October, while the ratings for the Metro Manila D group were higher than those of the D class found nationwide and in major cities, they declined more sharply (Figure 11). By December, the D respondents in Metro Manila had a negative trust rating (-4%) that was only slightly higher than the general urban rating (-10%). By February, however, more respondents from the metropolis distrusted Estrada (-44%) than in urban areas in general (-32%) and the country as a whole (-28%).

The divergence between the poorest E class in Metro Manila and other E and D respondents is reflected as well in their opinions regarding Estrada and the charges against him. Figures 12 to 14 present the share of respondents who believe in the charges against Estrada by social class. As expected, majority of the ABC classes believed that he used Jose Velarde's name, received *jueteng* money, obtained a share of tobacco funds, amassed wealth in office and granted special favors to family and friends. On the other hand, from 41% to 51% of the D and E classes did not believe the charges against him. There are significant differences, however, in their levels of disbelief.

Figure 10[xvi]

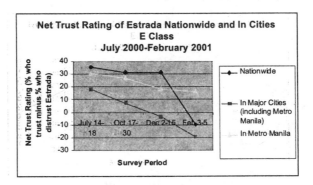

Sources: Pulse Asia July 14-28 Ulat ng Bayan (nationwide); Pulse Asia October 17-30 Ulat ng Bayan (nationwide); Pulse Asia December 2-15 Ulat ng Bayan Survey (nationwide); Pulse Asia February 3-5 Thames Survey (nationwide)

Figure 11[xvii]

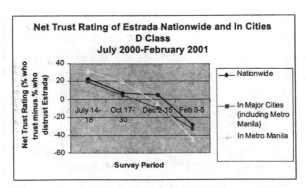

Sources: Pulse Asia July 14-28 Ulat ng Bayan (nationwide); Pulse Asia October 17-30 Ulat ng Bayan (nationwide); Pulse Asia December 2-15 Ulat ng Bayan Survey (nationwide); Pulse Asia February 3-5 Thames Survey (nationwide)

Figure 12[xviii]

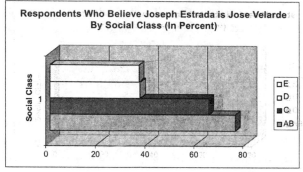

Source: Social Weather Stations, Inc. ABS-CBN Nationwide Survey,
January 6-9, 2001

Figure 13

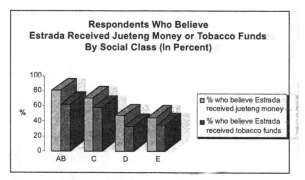

Source: Social Weather Stations, Inc. ABS-CBN Nationwide
Survey, January 6-9, 2001

Figure 14

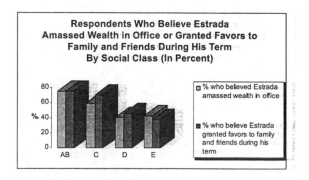

Source: Social Weather Stations, Inc. ABS-CBN Nationwide
Survey, January 6-9, 2001

While 51% of D and 52% of E respondents nationwide did not believe that Jose Velarde is Estrada, almost 7 out of 10 E respondents in Metro Manila dismissed this charge compared to only 4 out of 10 D respondents in the metropolis (Figure 15). This pattern prevailed even among those who followed the televized impeachment trial closely. Although the sample of educated E respondents was too small to generate valid conclusions, Figure 16 further suggests that Metro Manila's more educated urban poor respondents (70%) could have even disbelieved Clarissa Ocampo's watershed testimony that Estrada and Velarde are the same person. This is in stark contrast to the situation of the college-educated D respondents in Metro Manila who, like the middle C class, tended to believe rather than disbelieve Estrada's use of the Velarde alias (Figure 17).

The pattern of disbelief of the D and E classes in the allegation that Estrada used an alias in his banking transactions, held for the other charges as well. Less D respondents in Metro Manila than nationwide tended to disbelieve that he received *jueteng* money (Table 1). The proportion who disbelieved the other charges against Estrada did not differ much between the D voting population nationwide and those in Metro Manila, except for the allegation that he granted special favors to friends and family. Less D respondents from Metro Manila did not believe this charge.

On the other hand, much higher proportions of E respondents in Metro Manila did not believe the charges against Estrada than their counterparts nationwide. This was also the case among the educated E in the metropolis. More of the latter did not believe the charges compared to the educated E nationwide. Interestingly, educated E respondents in Metro Manila had lower levels of disbelief than their counterparts nationwide only on the allegation that Estrada amassed wealth in office. Note, however, that the trends found among the E class in Metro Manila and are inconclusive because of the small size of this group.

*Figure 15*xix

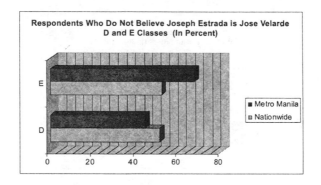

Source: Social Weather Stations Inc. ABS-CBN Nationwide
Survey, January 6-9, 2001

*Figure 16*xx

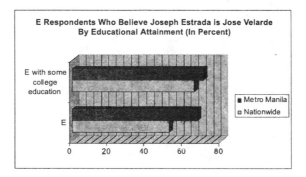

Source: Social Weather Stations Inc. ABS-CBN Nationwide
Survey, January 6-9, 2001

Figure 17[xxi]

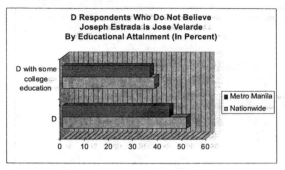

Source: Social Weather Stations Inc. ABS-CBN Nationwide
Survey, January 6-9, 2001

Table 1. Respondents Who Do Not Believe Specific Charges Against Estrada, D and E Classes (In Percent)*

Charges	D nation-wide	D Metro Manila	D with some college education nation-wide	D with some college education Metro Manila	E nation-wide	E Metro Manila	E with some college education nation-wide	E with some college education Metro Manila
Estrada received jueteng money	42	34	28	31	41	60	35	50
Estrada received tobacco funds	47	44	35	33	44	69	59	70
Estrada amassed wealth in office	46	44	39	33	46	58	47	40
Estrada granted special favors to family and friends during his term	39	35	30	19	44	60	35	50
N	806	139	215	58	232	45	34	10

* The entries in the Table are not too different from the figures obtained for those who followed the impeachment trial closely.

If the trends observed among Metro Manila's E class are not statistical flukes, then the urban poor in the capital region are Estrada's staunchest constituency. Not even some college education could persuade those who followed the impeachment trial closely to doubt that Estrada was innocent of the charges against him. They were only too willing to defend him and be counted in the pro-Erap demonstrations held in Mendiola during the political crisis. It did not matter that some of them were paid to attend the rallies. In Metro Manila's slums, accepting such money was not incompatible with their genuine support and affection for the former president.

Whence springs the metropolitan urban poor's unwavering loyalty to Estrada? His televized departure from the presidential palace showed elderly urban poor women crying inconsolably in his arms, reflecting their deep and personal identification with him. This scene is best understood in its context. In the squalor and wretchedness of life in the slums, they pinned their hopes on someone bigger than themselves. Estrada's cinematic career molded him to be that person. Most of his films revolved around poor, insulted and belittled men who fought for the masses and triumphed in the end (Lacquian, 1998). Movie fans in the metropolis, especially among the poor, no longer distinguished him from the roles he played.

Estrada unwittingly encouraged this meshing of reality and fantasy in the minds of his loyal constituency. Even before he officially launched his campaign for the presidency, Estrada's mobile cinema—featuring a 45-minute documentary on his life, followed by a movie—had traveled all over the country. It was quite remarkable that his movies penetrated the interiors of depressed communities (Laquian, 1998). This meant that younger slum dwellers were exposed to the same movies their parents had watched in an earlier time, portraying Estrada as champion of the underdog and marginalized. No wonder, the young E in Metro Manila deviated from their age group in terms of positive net trust in Estrada especially after his ouster.

Estrada sustained the myths and images projected in the cinema. On his occasional visits to Metro Manila's squatter communities as president, he spoke to the poor in the language and metaphors of his movies. At the height of the protests in November, for instance, he cavalierly announced before Tondo's teeming poor that he was letting the villains in the impeachment story beat him up. Amid their cheers, he proudly proclaimed that he would knock out all his enemies.[xxii] He appropriated the *"kanto boy"* lingo when he threatened prior to the impeachment trial that his detractors would find themselves in the *"kangkungan"*, the lowliest patch to end up in after a brawl.

A closer look at Estrada's movies reveals that some of the more popular ones had urban poor settings. By capturing the precarious conditions in communities much like their own, the movies facilitated the urban poor's psychological identification with him. He embodied in his cinematic roles some of the values permeating life in slum communities. Under conditions of uncertainty and occasional violence, for instance, the group serves as paramount source of support and protection. As a result, *barkadahan* (group life) and loyalty to the group are extremely valued.

The urban poor have translated Estrada's cinematic loyalty to the marginalized as real devotion to them. In return, they pledged to give him as much loyalty, vowing never to leave him right or wrong. *"Walang iwanan!"* (we will stick together until the end), which became the buzzwords of Estrada in the last few weeks before his ouster, merely captured the urban poor's deep sense of allegiance to leaders and relevant groups that defend them from exploiters.

People Power 2 and Class Polarization

THE COMPELLING IMAGES OF PEOPLE POWER 2 included a clash between the pro-Estrada rallyists and the white-collar workers of the Makati Stock Exchange on January 19, 2001. Writing for the Pearl of the Orient Seas, Clarence Henderson vividly described a scene he personally witnessed:

> A group of 300 or so pro-Erap rallyists, mostly headbanded teenagers in raggedy shorts, tank tops and the ubiquitous flip flop slippers of the Filipino working class, had assembled on Ayala Ave. to have a little demonstration. Many looked pretty drunk and quite a few were carrying pointed sticks, but initially, they pretty much minded their own business...However, when the white-collars (mostly from the Philippine Stock Exchange) started coming out for lunch, things quickly turned nasty. Most were dressed in black, and several carried "Erap Resign" streamers. Perhaps predictably, the white collars couldn't resist taunting the tank tops. Equally predictably, the tank tops reacted with angry obscene gestures. The white collars responded with more taunting and chants of "Erap resign". Back and

forth it went. Chaos soon ensued—flying rocks, screaming curses and more obscene gestures, scurrying white collars. Once safely back inside, a fair number of the white-collars ascended to the roofs of their buildings, from whence they showered the tank tops with plastic water, bottles, rocks and miscellaneous building materials.

The Ayala incident was ugly. It illustrated the wide gap between Makati's urban poor and its middle classes. The latter consisted of a mixed bag of People Power 2 participants spanning a wide range of social classes. Some of them were economically well off professionals and managers in the AB and C categories. Others were routine non-manual workers (administrative and sales workers) belonging to the C and D classes.

The chasm between the urban poor and the middle classes was more than a difference in lifestyle or socio-economic status. The gulf was between two different worldviews. Regardless of economic position, the middle classes were unified by a common moral sensibility. They espoused clear-cut ethical standards of right or wrong based on universal principles. Applying these principles to governance problems, they judged Estrada accordingly and found him sordidly lacking.

On the other hand, the urban poor who supported Estrada, many of whom lived subhuman lives, continued to pin their hopes on him. In their eyes he would remain their champion. Arguing that the Estrada administration had terribly failed them, by not seriously addressing poverty, for instance, would not change their minds. This steadfastness was not solely borne out of personal conviction that Estrada was innocent of the charges against him. After all, 37% of the E and 45% of the D classes in Pulse Asia's February 3-5, 2001 survey thought he was probably or definitely guilty. His mass supporters were resolute because of their cynicism toward these charges.

Die-hard pro-Estrada squatters in Commonwealth, Quezon City, interviewed for this paper argued that past presidents and local politicians could just be as guilty of the same public offences. They were certain that Macapagal-Arroyo would commit similar acts, if she had not done so before. A few even considered receiving funds from illegal gambling or amassing wealth an integral part of Filipino politics. Some of those who believed that Estrada enriched himself in office did not find anything wrong in the act per se because they were convinced he would redistribute such wealth to the poor. When asked if their lives had changed during Estrada's incumbency, they were quick to cite word-of-mouth accounts of his generosity to other underprivileged families. In the end, they put their faith in him because he walked with their kind and touched their hearts.

Estrada's ouster in mid-January did not undermine the loyalty of his die-hard supporters among the urban poor. Interestingly, however, the impeachment trial and Estrada's silence in the last few days of the crisis downplayed the usual rhetoric that fomented class rifts. Perhaps not surprisingly, when Estrada left Malacañang on January 20, 2001, his ardent supporters did not come out in droves to publicly assail his "upper class tormentors". Instead, his San Juan constituency massed in front of the municipal hall and along the streets leading to his home to express their continuing support for and personal loyalty to their fallen leader. Their deep-seated class grievances would be conveyed more dramatically several months later in May when the lines of polarization would harden.

Pulse Asia's nationwide February 3-5, 2001 survey provides material to construct a plausible interpretation of the events that unfolded in the months following People Power 2. Two weeks after Estrada's ouster, his mass supporters, particularly the urban poor in Metro Manila, commiserated with him in silence. As his supporters in Commonwealth put it, they empathized with his humiliation. Despite his fall from power, they did not waver in their loyalty to him as ally, friend and protector.

But while unstinting in their support and affection for Estrada, the thought of restoring him to the presidency did not cross the masses' minds in February. At that point, they seemed to have conceded his loss of political authority to govern. Pulse Asia's survey reveals that 59% of D and 60% of E considered Macapagal-Arroyo's assumption to power, legal and constitutional (Figure 18). Almost the same proportion of AB (61%) and a slightly higher proportion of C respondents (67%) shared the same opinion. Interestingly, 64% of the D respondents in Metro Manila saw Macapagal-Arroyo as the current head of state. The E class in Metro Manila, which usually deviated from the opinion patterns of the rest of the E nationwide, did not differ significantly this time in their acceptance of the government turnover.

Figure 18[xxiii]

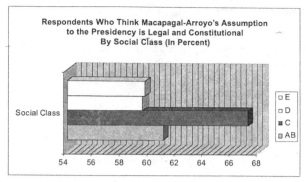

Source: Pulse Asia, Inc. Thames Nationwide Survey February 3-5,
2001-05-17

The legitimacy of the Macapagal-Arroyo government in the eyes of the poor as of February 3-5, 2001, could be gleaned as well from their opinion of her support from the people. About 66% of D and 67% of E respondents nationwide thought the majority of Filipinos backed her up, an opinion shared by Metro Manila's D and E classes (Figure 19).

The SWS survey findings at about the same time (February 2-7, 2001) arrived at similar conclusions. Sixty-one percent of Filipinos nationwide accepted Macapagal-Arroyo as Estrada's replacement. Majorities in all social classes accepted her: 58% of ABC, 64% of D and 54% of E (Mangahas, 2001).

While subsequent SWS and Pulse Asia surveys underscored the legitimacy of Macapagal-Arroyo across classes, the next chapter in the Estrada saga would radically shift the position of a segment of the poor on the rightful constitutional leader. Prior to his arrest, the cues emanating from Estrada and his advisers were unclear. They were relatively quiet, hoping to achieve immunity from suit for the fallen president, by raising the question of constitutional leadership to the Supreme Court.

The High Court's unanimous ruling that Macapagal-Arroyo's assumption of the presidency was legitimate and that Estrada no longer enjoyed immunity from suit, allowed the new administration to file charges against the former president for plunder and other offenses. Well-publicized plans for his inevitable arrest—as plunder was a non-bailable offense—drove ardent urban poor followers to camp out in front of his residence and provide a human shield. By then emotions were running high. Following his legal advisers, Estrada's mass supporters initially demanded that Estrada be placed under house arrest. But even before he was actually taken into custody, they began to articulate the constitutional ambiguity of Macapagal-Arroyo's rise to power—a discourse that had trickled down from earlier pronouncements of Estrada's inner circle

Figure 19

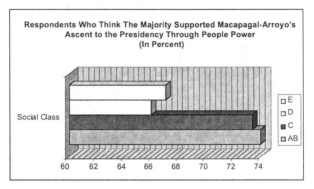

Source: Pulse Asia, Inc. Thames Nationwide Survey February 3-5, 2001-05-17

The turning point in this continuing melodrama was Estrada's arrest on April 25, 2001. Like the earlier clampdown on the controversial envelope, Estrada's arrest proved to be a catalyst. It drove the masses to congregate at the EDSA shrine and stage a mirror image version of People Power 2. Dubbed as "Poor People Power", the crowd that swelled each evening from April 25 to April 30 eloquently expressed their grievances. Sensing the opportunity to score political points, pro-Estrada politicians who were then running for the May 11 elections, gave fiery speeches to this crowd and quickly turned the April 29 demonstration into a massive *miting de avance.*

Estrada's arrest clearly upped the political ante. The mammoth crowd who had gathered at EDSA no longer insisted on house arrest for their fallen leader. Instead, they demanded the reinstatement of Estrada as the constitutionally elected president. (La Liga Policy Institute, 2001) By the evening of April 29 and 30, reclaiming Malacañang for Estrada became their battle cry.

Angered by the humiliating arrest of the man they voted into power, thousands of urban poor rallyists stormed Mendiola in the early morning of May 1. A combined contingent of police and military personnel forcibly dispersed them but the marchers fought back. By the end of the day, at least four rallyists and policemen were killed and more than a hundred injured in an exchange of rocks, sticks, tear gas and bullets. Infuriated by their dispersal and the injury suffered by fellow marchers, the retreating rallyists burned down media and Red Cross vehicles, looted stores and broke streetlights as they disappeared into the maze of congested slum communities.

Even before his fateful arrest, Filipinos were already divided over the most judicious way of dealing with Estrada. In the Pulse Asia nationwide February 3-5, 2001 survey, about a third of the respondents thought he should be charged with corruption and punished accordingly. As expected, the share of respondents who held this opinion was highest for the middle (C) class (42%) and lowest for E (21%). About 39% of the upper class (AB) and 33% of D thought this move appropriate.

Some 7% of the respondents took a related but more extreme position on the same issue. They said the proper step to take was to lock up Estrada in jail, without bail, while his case was pending in court. In contrast, 11% asserted that the former president must be reinstated because he was innocent. Among those who took the latter view, 11% belonged to the D class while 17% were from E. Other opinions on how to treat Estrada were as follows: (a) exile him and ban his return (5%); (b) leave him in his current state without any power (11%); and (c) let him spend time forming a legal defense to clear his name (34%).

In time, however, public opinion gravitated around two positions on Estrada's arrest. The first asserts that no one, not even a former president, is above the law. Justice from this viewpoint requires subjecting Estrada to the same legal and judicial processes that apply to less powerful suspects of plunder and corruption. Thus, since Estrada is charged with a non-bailable offense, his arrest and detention is but a consequence of the need to implement the spirit and substance of the law.[xxiv]

Frustrated over the failure of succeeding governments to punish the Marcoses and recover their ill-gotten wealth, proponents of this position also contend that if Estrada is able to get away with plunder, future leaders will not be deterred from committing similar crimes. They draw inspiration from the arrests of former high government officials charged with corruption in maturing democracies, the latest of which were two of South Korea's former presidents, General Chun Doo-hwan and Roh Tae-woo. By successfully prosecuting Estrada, they believe Philippine democracy will evolve and mature faster.

The other position in the controversy claims that subjecting Estrada to the regular procedures of the criminal justice system does not befit a former head of state, who still enjoys popular support and whose guilt has not yet been established by the courts. The La Liga Institute's April 29, 2001, "Conjunctural Analysis" succinctly articulates this view and attempts to explain why Estrada's arrest sparked EDSA 3. In light of the Macapagal-Arroyo government's "pro-Erap vs anti-Erap campaign that has only worked to further divide society", the institute claims:

> The overkill in the arrest of Estrada was an event waiting to happen. The campaign to demonize the past administration provided incentives to government officials and civil society actors to treat the former president like nothing more than a common criminal. The more indignities they heaped on his person, the more media mileage or political capital they seemed to gain. Unwittingly, however, this mean-spirited campaign *(in a context where Macapagal-Arroyo's Arroyo's rise to power is laden with constitutional ambiguities)* * grated on the Filipino psyche that tends to sympathize with the underdog.

But Estrada was a phenomenal underdog. The masses, especially among Metro Manila's urban poor, embraced him as their stalwart defender. If the February surveys are correct, they silently accepted his ouster as legitimate. If indeed Estrada was guilty, his shameful fall from grace was enough punishment in their eyes. However, they could not bear to see their leader, who already lay wounded on the ground, suffer further humiliation with his arrest. Thus, they streamed to EDSA to vent their anger and frustration.

As politicians further riled them up with condescending comments heard from some People Power 2 groups about their shabby appearance, crass demeanor and lack of integrity, the anger they felt with the way government treated their symbolic leader merged explosively with their long-standing grievances against society's gross inequities. In their minds, the government—who has continued to crucify their hero—and the elite—who has benefited from such inequities—became one. Emboldened by their numbers and the fiery speeches of Estrada's allies, this "poor People Power" marched to Malacañang to take their revenge and turn the tables against the elite.

People Power 2, EDSA 3 and Poverty

ESTRADA'S ARREST AND EDSA 3 polarized Filipinos along lines that coincide with the class divide. In the politically charged atmosphere that prevailed after EDSA 3, the former president's loss of moral authority to govern, his prosecution and the deep-rooted grievances of the poor were muddled in the public mind. The schedule of national and local elections barely two weeks after the march to Malacañang aggravated the confusion. Without adequate time to unpack the issues, intense pro- and anti-Estrada sentiments dominated the 2001 polls.

From the perspective of his poor supporters, Estrada's rise and fall from the presidency are conflated with their own long-standing struggle to lift themselves from poverty. Traditional politicians and Estrada himself used this view and the very real class divide to obfuscate the issues. They peddled his prosecution as an attack on the poor rather than on the very system of "old politics" that Estrada represents and which has, in large part, prevented the liberation of the poor.

The conflation of issues is holding back the nation's democratization and social development. They ought to be disentangled for Filipinos to move out of a debilitating period of uncertainty and address the urgent demands of poverty alleviation, economic growth and people empowerment.

Democratization and development require a transformation of the country's system of political governance. In this regard, the exercise of People Power in 1986 and 2001 ushered profound changes in the nation's highly personalistic political culture. Proof of this is the preoccupation of politicians with reinventing their image to avoid the *"trapo"* (traditional politician) label. The remarkable development of grassroots institutions linked to mechanisms of local governance in certain parts of the country also attests to the erosion of patronage systems. But the bigger proof is the impeachment trial and its historic outcome. Estrada's arrest, despite its politically inconvenient timing two weeks before a decisive national and local elections, brought the nation to an unprecedented point of holding its highest government official publicly accountable. For once, those in the top echelons of power are no longer as free to get away with plunder and blatant corruption.

By toppling a brazenly corrupt administration, People Power 2 upheld high ethical standards of public service and inspired a constituency for new politics. Unfortunately, the uprising superceded existing institutional processes in particular the impeachment trial in the senate. Thus resulting in constitutional ambiguities that sustain the call for Estrada's reinstatement. Nevertheless, the strength of the moral arguments against Estrada's presidency impelled state institutions like the judiciary, the military, and Congress to define the legal framework more broadly and reinforce the constitutional shell around the new government.

From an institutional perspective, Estrada's ouster through the impeachment process would have been preferable. It could have avoided the constitutional dilemmas that continue to hound Macapagal-Arroyo. But the way events unfolded in January, moral sensibilities and the question of national integrity overrode procedural considerations. In the process, People Power 2 ironically circumvented an institution it had hoped to eventually strengthen. Not surprisingly, this generated problems.

Many Filipinos equate the form of People Power 1 and 2 with their essence. The idea conveyed is that massing up legitimizes political demands regardless of goals, principles and circumstances. Thus, since the ouster of Ferdinand Marcos in 1986, many losing candidates for political office— including those genuinely rejected by a majority of their constituents— have mobilized People Power to protest electoral outcomes. Office subordinates have also utilized it to subvert unpopular decisions by bureau heads or disliked superiors. In EDSA 3 Sen. Miriam Santiago, in one of her fiery speeches, agitated the crowd by declaring they had sufficient numbers to force Macapagal-Arroyo to resign.

But while People Power often takes the form of a massive gathering, it is more than a numbers game. It is future oriented, moved by the hope that Filipinos can reinvent their destinies and proudly march forward in the community of nations (David, 2001). Higher principles transcending vested individual or group interests motivate it. In the context of democratization, People Power aspires to imbed itself institutionally. By channeling its energies to the onerous task of building democratic and accountable political institutions, it expects to eventually become a relic of the past, never to be called upon again to resolve divisive political issues.

EDSA 3 denounced People Power 2 for various reasons. For one, it accordingly violated the constitutional provisions on the legitimate transfer of power. After all, EDSA 3 participants contend that Estrada had not formally resigned when the Supreme Court administered Macapagal-Arroyo's oath on January 20. EDSA 3 also countered the moral foundation of the ouster. Noting the prevalence of corruption in high government circles, Estrada's supporters asked why he was singled out when other officials have also committed acts of corruption in the past.

Although their sentiments may be founded, nevertheless, Estrada's brazen and reckless disregard of high ethical standards of public service made him vulnerable to public scrutiny. The timing of his actions added to his misfortune. Congress had previously passed a more stringent legislation on plunder, motivated in part by the failed prosecution of the Marcoses for their ill-gotten wealth. Unfortunately for Estrada who also was among the senators who passed the new law, he was the first high government official prosecuted for violating such law.

The resolve to pursue Estrada's cases in court emanate from civil society's righteous demand for justice as a requisite for reconciliation. The recent life imprisonment sentence imposed on a middle-level Bureau of Internal Revenue employee caught stealing from the public coffers further dramatizes the need to publicly prosecute higher and more powerful officials in the interest of justice.

More significant than the question of singling Estrada out is the cynical view held by many that corruption is integral to Filipino patronage politics. This view considerably diminishes the seriousness of the crime in the eyes of his supporters. As a result, they decried the punishment that befell their fallen leader, which they considered too grave for his offence.

As far as Estrada was concerned, he had done nothing wrong. Experienced in the ways of small town politics, he saw himself as the patron generating resources legally or illegally and distributing privileges to loyal constituents, while appropriating his share. As president, he merely applied the values and practices of traditional local politics on a grander scale. Thus, in the face of the charges against him, Estrada constantly defended his integrity and argued that he had not stolen a single centavo from the people. For instance, while he claimed to have received Singson's P200 million "gift" without inquiring into its sources, he justified it as a contribution to a scholarship fund for deserving Muslim scholars.

Many of Estrada's supporters share his worldview. Even those in the D and E class who thought his government was brought down by too much corruption, would have probably viewed his corrupt practices as character flaws that pale in comparison to his service to the masses.[xxv] His poor supporters' psychological identification of their struggles and interests with Estrada's saga makes it extremely difficult to disentangle poverty from governance issues in their minds.

But these issues ought to be unpacked for development and democratization to proceed. The experiences of the developing world reveal that the struggle against poverty cannot be effectively waged within the framework and institutions of patronage politics. Under such a regime, deeply entrenched vested interests could successfully undermine the equity reforms required for effective poverty alleviation. The prevalence of cronyism, arbitrary decision-making and the uneven implementation of rules' guiding economic activity would also hamper the growth required to generate wealth and employment. Thus, pushing for Estrada's reinstatement after repudiating his government for failing to address corruption and poverty would constitute a leap backward.

Disentangling the question of addressing poverty, from the need to make Estrada accountable for his actions, will advance the democratization process. However, it would entail more than conceptual clarification. In the current context of political and class polarization, the potential backlash of making hard political decisions poses real risks of waylaying efforts to institutionalize development and democratic processes in the immediate period. The challenges of containing the backlash and minimizing the risks, therefore, are daunting.

The political realities confronting the nation are such that the most recent episode in its unfolding saga threatens to be repeated unless poverty is addressed. For as long as the poor do not share the fruits of development, their marginalization and lack of opportunities will make them vulnerable to the machinations of traditional politicians. For as long as they live sub-human lives, desperation will force them to pin their hopes on ineligible candidates created by television and cinema. For as long as they do not experience mobility, an undeveloped sense of efficacy will prevent them from critically holding their leaders accountable for their actions. For as long as they remain poor, therefore, the democratization process will be severely constrained (Bautista, 2001).

While alleviating poverty is necessary to erode systems of patronage politics, it is not sufficient. Conscientization through formal and informal education and the development of strong social institutions on the ground are equally important. When citizens are empowered through their own grassroots organizations, they will cease equating the personal interests of charismatic politicians with their legitimate grievances. When citizens experience working institutions that transcend class and political lines, they will put their faith in democratic processes. When the wide gap between the rich and the poor is narrowed, they will ignore manipulative politicians who foment class war for their own vested interests. Only then will facile interpretations of political developments as the "revenge of the elite on the masses" or of the "poor on the rich" cease to take hold.

* Itals by the author. The phrase was taken from another section of the La Liga analysis.

ENDNOTES

[i] The author is grateful to Pulse Asia Inc. and SWS Inc. for sharing their SPSS data files. She derived the statistical figures and graphs presented in the text from two sets of data sources: Pulse Asia, Inc.'s nationwide surveys conducted on July 14-28, 2000 (Ulat ng Bayan), October 17-30, 2000 (Ulat ng Bayan), December 2-15 2000 (Ulat ng Bayan) and February 3-5, 2000 (Thames Survey) as well as the SWS, Inc.'s January 6-9, 2001 SWS ABS-CBN Survey. Specific data sources are cited in the text or graphs. The surveys utilized a multistage cluster sampling design. For details on the sampling design, refer to the Pulse Asia and SWS documents.

The author also acknowledges the invaluable contributions of Teresa Melgar, Manuel Sapitula, Pia Bennagen and Mia Mangalindan to this paper. Teresa's incisive and critical comments on an earlier draft helped sharpen its analysis and flow. Manuel reviewed newspaper, magazine and tabloid accounts of all relevant events and rallies from the presidential campaign period in 1998 to January 20, 2001. He also gathered background information on the movies former President Joseph Estrada produced or starred in. Pia graciously clarified questions regarding four of Pulse Asia's data sets while Mia patiently guided the author through the SWS CD containing the January 6-9, 2001 survey.

[ii] Apart from housing characteristics, it is important to note that market researchers also utilize other variables such as types of appliances owned and the educational attainment and occupation of the household head. For a review of various systems of operationalizing social classes in the Philippines and other methodological issues, see Bautista, Rivera Tabunda and Arguillas (2000), Chapter 1.

[iii] Those who were more conscious of Estrada's political and financial support from the Marcoses, Eduardo Cojuangco and some influential Chinese businessmen genuinely thought they could influence his political agenda.

[iv] In an employment-bases class system, the middle class would consist of the following clusters of occupations: *Service Class or New Middle Class* (higher grade professionals, administrators and officials; managers in large industrial establishments; lower grade professionals, administrators and officials, higher grade technicians, managers in small industrial industrial establishments and supervisors of nonmanual employees) *Petty Bourgeoisie or Old Middle Class* (small proprietors, artisans without employees or with 10 or less employees) *Routine Nonmanual Workers or Marginal Middle Class* (higher grade employees in administration and commerce; lower grade employees in sales and services).

[v] The other sites include Davao, Iloilo, Cagayan de Oro, General Santos, Naga and Baguio (Reyes, 2001).

[vi] Good governance constituted the minimum platform around which groups with opposing interests converged after the Singson expose.

[vii] The divergent position among the People Power 2 groups came from Sanlakas, which called for the resignation of Vice President Macapagal-Arroyo to give way to a caretaker government to be headed by Supreme Court Justice Hilario Davide.

[viii] Citing David Wurfel's insight in the book *Filipino Politics. Development and Decay.* Ithaca, New York: Cornell University Press, 1988, Doronila listed three major periods of reorientation in Philippine education, the introduction of Spanish mass education in 1863; the coming of the Thomasites and the institution of the American mass educational system in the early 1900s, and the First Quarter Storm in 1970.

[ix] The SWS October 1999 survey found 68% of the voting-age Filipinos nationwide considering the problem of cronyism serious. Manlapaz used polynomial regression models.

[x] If the undecided among the E respondents were classified as trusting him, the net trust ratings would have been 57% in July, 51% in October, 55% in December and 10% in February.

[xi] The average class distribution of respondents in the four surveys is as follows: AB (3%); C (11%); D (66%) and E (20%).

[xii] Interestingly, about 56% of the professionals and managers and 65% of routine white-collar workers belonged to the D class although on the average they made up only 9% of this class.

[xiii] About 3% constitute new middle class professionals; 2% are old middle class merchants and small commodity producers; 5% are white-collar marginal middle class

workers; 37% are in the working class and 53% are economically inactive (e.g. house-wives) or unemployed. Note that because of the small proportions of respondents in capitalist middle class occupations, observed trends for this group are indicative but inconclusive.

[xiv] The average size of the D and E classes by age in the four surveys is as follows: D <30 (240); D 30+ (551); E <30 (81); E 30+ (161).

[xv] The average size of the D and E classes by educational attainment in the four surveys is as follows: D with some college education (268); D with less than college education (523); E with some college education (36)); E with less than college education (36).

[xvi] The average size of the E class by geographic location in the four surveys is as follows: E in Metro Manila (42); E in major cities nationwide (98); E nationwide (243).

[xvii] The average size of the D class by geographic location in the four surveys is as follows: D in Metro Manila (139); D in major cities nationwide (380) D nationwide (792).

[xviii] The distribution of respondents in the SWS ABS-CBN 6-9 Nationwide January 2001Survey by class is as follows: AB (16); C(145); D (806) E (203).

[xix] The relevant sample sizes for the classes in the Figure are as follows: D nationwide (806); D Metro Manila (139); E nationwide (232); E Metro Manila (45).

[xx] The relevant sample sizes for the classes in the Figure are as follows: E nationwide (232); E Metro Manila (45); E with some college education nationwide (34); E with some college education in Metro Manila (10).

[xxi] The relevant sample sizes for the classes in the Figure are as follows: D nationwide (806); D Metro Manila (139); D with some college education nationwide (215); D with some college education Metro Manila (58).

[xxii] See Philippine Star, December 22, 2000., November 5, 2000 Phippine Daily In-quirer.

[xxiii] The distribution of respondents by class in Pulse Asia Inc.'s 3-5 February 2001 Nationwide Survey is as follows: AB (23) C (161) D (1813) E (203).

[xxiv] Those who hold this view, however, differ on whether or not Estrada is to be given any special consideration as befits his stature as a former president, even as he goes through the same judicial process. One area of debate along this line is the question

of where to keep him while his case is being tried. In the end, the Macapagal-Arroyo government opted to transfer Estrada and his son, San Juan mayor Jinggoy Estrada, from their detention cell in Camp Crame, to an army training camp in Santa Rosa, Laguna. The military quarters where the Estradas are now being kept is furnished with modest amenities including an air-conditioned bedroom.

xxv Interestingly, Estrada's ouster was viewed as the consequence of "too much corruption in his government" by 54% of the C, 33% of the D and 36% of the E respondents in Pulse Asia's 3-5 February nationwide survey.

REFERENCES AND DATA SOURCES

Alba, M. 1997. "The Structure and Possible Sources of Inter-agency Wage Differentials in the Philippines." in *Employment, Capital and Job Security: Recent Perspectives on the Philippine Labor Market*, edited by E. Esguerra and K. Itoh. Tokyo: Institute of Developing Economies.

Almario, A. "Estrada and the Unfinished Revolution." *Philippine Graphic.* June 15. 1998

Arroyo, D. 1990. "The Usefulness of the ABCDE Market Research System. A Means to Check Social Welfare and Class Attrributes." *Social Weather Bulletin* 90-11/12 Double Issue June.

Bautista, C. 2001. "The Filipino Middle Classes and People Power 2."

Bautista, C., L. Angeles and J Dionisio. 2000a. "Asian Responses to the 1997 Financial Crisis: Social Safety Net Programs in the Philippines" in Ms Gee, T. and S. Scott. *The Poor at Risk: Surviving the Economic Crisis in Southeast Asia.* Final Report Submitted to the Canadian International Development Agency. Institute of Asian Research, University of British Columbia.

Bautista, C., T. Rivera, A. Tabunda and J Arguillas. 2000b. "Exploring the Middle Classes of Metro Manila. Survey Report Submitted to the Academia Sinica and the UP Center for Integrative and Development Studies."

Bautista, C.B. 2000c. "Images of the Middle Classes in Metro Manila." *Public Policy* Vol III. No. 4 October-December.

Bello, W. 2001. "The Shakedown State: The Mafia as Government in the Philippines." *Dyaryo Akbayan.*Special Congress Issue, January.

Carroll, J. 1994. "Glimpses Into Philippine Political Culture: Gleaninigs from the Ateneo Public Opinion Survey Data." *Pilipinas* No. 22 Spring:47-61.

Casiño, T. 2001a. "View from the Streets: Different Folks, Different Strokes (First of 3 parts)." in *Philippine Daily Inquirer.* February 5.

Casiño, T. 2001b. "View From the Streets: No Group Could Have Done It Alone-All or Nothing (Second of three parts)." in *Philippine Daily Inquirer.* February 6.

Casiño, T. 2001c. "View from the Streets: Uprising must be brought to Palace Gates." in *Philippine Daily Inquirer.* February 7.

Couples for Christ 2001. "The Miracle of EDSA 2, the Couples for Christ Story." *Ugnayan* vol. X11 No. 1 January-February

David, R. 2001 "The Third Time As Farce." in *Philippine Daily Inquirer.* April 29.

David, R. 2000a. "Do The Poor Still Support Erap?" *Philippine Daily Inquirer.* November 26

David, R. 2000b. "A Question of Trust." *Philippine Daily Inquirer.* February 6.

De Dios, E. 1999. "Can He Do It? Assessing the Estrada Administration's Anti-Poverty Programme". Paper read at the Philippine Political Science Association Conference, Balay Kalinaw, University of the Philippines, July 23, 1999.

Doronila, A. 2000. "The Betrayal of the Poor." *Philippine Daily Inquirer.* October 18.

Doronila, L. 1989. *National Identity and Social Change.* Quezon City: University of the Philippines Center for Integrative and Development Studies.

Fabella, R. 2000. "The J2K Crisis and the Economy: The Broader Context." in *Forum (Unibersidad ng Pilipinas).* Quezon City.

Flores, P. 1998. "The Illusions of a Cinematic President." *Public Policy* II, No. 4 October-December:101-119.

Institute, La Liga Policy. 2001. "Poor People Power: Preludes and Prospects." April 29.

Karaos, Anna Marie 1999. 'What Went Wrong with Erap's Pro-Poor Act' *Intersect,* August.

Laquian, A. and E. Laquian. 1998. *The Centennial President.* Vancouver and Quezon City: Institute of Asian Research University of British Columbia and College of Public Administration, University of the Philippines.

Locsin, J. 1998. "'Centennial President' Likens Self to Andres Bonifacio'." *Philippine Star.* May 30.

Magno, A. 2001. "Insurrection 101: Direct Democracy Action in the 21st Century." in *Paper presented at the Seminar on Assessing People Power 2: Part II.* Department of Political Science, University of the Philippines Diliman. Forthcoming in *Public Policy*, vol. 4.

Mangahas, M. 2001. "Acceptance of Gloria is Nationwide." *Manila Standard* February 14.

Manlapaz, R. 2001a. "The Movie in Erap's Mind: Part III Gotterdammerung. Unpublished notes."

Manlapaz 2001b. "The movie in Erap's Mind: Part II." *Forum, Unibersidad ng Pilipinas*: January 28.

Manlapaz, R. 2000. "The Movie in Erap's Mind: Part I." *Forum, Unibersidad ng Pilipinas.* November.

Pertierra, R. 2001. "People Power 2-Miracle, Middle Class or Moro Moro.": Unpublished communications.

Philippine Daily Inquirer. 2000 "Class War" Editorial October 21.

"President Thanks Masa in Pasig Ultra Assembly." *Manila Bulletin, December 2, 2000.*
Pulse, Asia. 2000. "Ulat ng Bayan December 2-15, 2000 Nationwide Survey."
Pulse, Asia. 2000. "Ulat ng Bayan July 14-28, 2000 Nationwide Survey."

Pulse, Asia. 2000. "Ulat ng Bayan October 17-30, 2000 Nationwide Survey."

Pulse, Asia. 2001. "February 3-5, 2001 Thames Nationwide Survey."

Reyes, R. March 2001. "A People Powered Entry to the New Millennium." *Political Brief* 9 No. 3.

Rivera, T. 2000. "The Middle Classes and Democratization in the Philippines: From the Asian Crisis to the Ouster of Estrada," in Embong, Abdul Rahman. The Southeast Asian Middle Classes: Democratization and Social Change. Universiti Kebangsaan Malaysia.

Social Weather Stations, Inc. 2001. "January 6-9,2001 SWS ABS-CBN Survey."

Social Weather Stations, Inc. 2000. "Cronyism Perceived to be Serious in the Estrada Administration." *SWS Survey Snapshots.* Vol 1 No. 2 February.

Corruption and the Fall

EMMANUEL S. DE DIOS

THE CENTRAL ROLE CORRUPTION PLAYED in the downfall of the administration of Joseph Ejercito Estrada is both obvious and immediate. Perceptions of widespread corruption beginning as early as 1999 among the business sector were already a major reason for the steep decline in investor confidence. This directly affected the country's rate of economic recovery since the beginning of the Asian crisis and imparted an economic urgency and universality to what would later develop into both a moral and political crisis. More directly, corruption was at the heart of the entire impeachment process: unexplained wealth in real estate and ownership of corporations; illicit intercession on behalf of cronies; diversion of public funds; and payoffs derived from criminal activities. In turn the events leading to the end of the impeachment process was the immediate reason for EDSA 2 and the erosion of Estrada's loss of the capacity to govern.

Still, corruption—the misuse of public resources for private gain—is nothing new in Philippine politics and economy. It is regarded as a "fact of life", especially among business people dealing with government, and has been a feature of most administrations. Indeed, disingenuous defenders of Estrada maintained that he was no great innovator in these matters. Some even cynically argue that Estrada's problem was not that he was the most corrupt president the country ever had, but that he was simply too transparent in going about it. The April-May reaction, which saw public demonstrations and rioting in the wake of Estrada's arrest, showed that a large segment of the population still has not understood the reasons for his downfall. Indeed, an implicit argument by those who participated in the so-called "EDSA 3" was not that Estrada was not corrupt, but that he— among other corrupt presidents—was singled out. What remains to be explained, therefore, is exactly how and why Estrada provoked such a powerful popular reaction against his administration that led to its downfall, and what this may portend for the future of Philippine politics.

Corruption: The Garden Variety

WHEN HE CAME TO POWER, Estrada professed a pro-poor stance and promised to turn a new leaf on corruption in government (as witness, Estrada's now ironic-sounding inaugural speech about *walang kamag-anak, walang kaibigan*). Almost immediately, however, indications of corruption under the new administration cropped up. While not always showing clear links to the president, they showed at least the involvement of some presidential relatives and associates. During senate investigations into an attempted bribe for the release of funds for textbook contracts in early 1999, the role in influence peddling of a presidential "cousin"[1] was revealed in information volunteered by the education secretary himself. Subsequent incidents that similarly attracted public attention involved the controversial results of bids on fire-engines and the irregular disposal of items seized at customs to benefit "charitable" projects favored by the first lady, Ma. Luisa Pimentel Ejercito.

For all the public furor they caused at the time, however, these cases were remarkable for somewhat different reasons. First, the sums involved, while not exactly negligible, were not so spectacular as to unmistakably warrant the term "grand corruption" and fall somewhat short of "plunder". The supplier involved in the textbook scandal was in fact only medium-size, with the contract running into tens of millions of pesos, certainly a far cry from the celebrated cases of corruption from previous administrations, such as the PEA-Amari deal, or the Centennial project, both of which continue to be subjects of investigation by the *Tanodbayan*.

A second notable aspect of these early cases was that they appeared to involve a species of corruption that could be easily found to exist in most other administrations—that is, they involved old niches of bureaucratic corruption that have traditionally been taken over by changing political factions. Unless an administration makes a point of being particularly upright and even-handed, routine government purchases, imports, and bids may always be expected to contain ample opportunities for graft. The use of bureaucratic influence or discretion as a means to extract rents from agencies exercising discretion is well-worn corruption technology. Bids for textbooks and fire-engines, rice and sugar imports, the spiriting out of smuggled goods, and regular public works contracts fall under this classification. Upon a change in administration, such rents are simply reassigned to the new "gods".

In this respect the Estrada administration merely followed its predecessors by taking over old niches and simply appointing handpicked acquaintances and loyal camp followers—many obviously barely qualified—to do the president's bidding and to enjoy the largesse from the boards of agencies or corporations controlled by government. The self-evident and almost cynical nature of this situation was crystallized by a showbiz appointee, who upon being questioned about his qualifications, retorted: "Weather-weather *lang 'yan*"[2] [*pana-panahon*], a slang term referring to the variability of political fortunes, which indicates the self-evident-ness of redistributing the spoils among loyal camp followers. (In this connection, it should also not be forgotten that among the important revolving-door "spoils" redistributed early on by Estrada was the reaffirmation of outstanding claims by his major political financiers, particularly Eduardo Cojuangco Jr. and Lucio Tan. The election of Cojuangco as president of the country's largest conglomerate, San Miguel Corporation, followed immediately as a matter of course Estrada's assumption of the presidency[3]. Similarly it was no surprise that multimillion tax-liability cases pending against Tan were subsequently dropped by the Department of Justice.)

The controversies also focused attention on a system, newly instituted under the Estrada administration, that required prior clearance with the Office of the President for all contracts worth P50 million or more. This added a new layer to the regular process of approving contracts, modifying a previous trend toward allowing agencies discretion in approving contracts.[4] Whatever its other purposes, this system would ultimately present a serious bottleneck in the approval and implementation of projects. Both theory and experience show that additional layers of approval add to corruption, since each indispensable signature may always be leveraged to extract rents. Such a system, if it exists, is even more inefficient than even a monopolistic system of rents [Shleifer and Vishny 1993], since it effectively raises the demanded "take" on each deal. A point was reached when foreign lenders and donors complained formally about unseemly delays in projects and the unevenness. In similar fashion, contract-rich agencies in the Department of Agriculture, such as the National Food Authority in charge of grain importation, were placed directly under the Office of the

President. Government-controlled financial corporations, as well as the Securities and Exchange Commission, were also transferred from the supervision of the Department of Finance and brought directly under the Office of the President.

These initial exposés of the involvement of the president, his wife, and mistresses in various businesses did not immediately raise hackles, since they seemed to involve nothing more than a logical extension of the dealings of a small-town boss. Most of the businesses listed in the Securities and Exchange Commission (but not declared in either statement of assets and liabilities of either the president and his mistresses) dealt in real estate and vaguely defined consulting firms that seemed geared toward exercising influence or obtaining contracts with regulatory agencies. If at all, what seemed new and somewhat surprising was that a head of state should involve himself with deals that at times seemed almost trifling. The apparent garden-variety nature of the cases that first came to light momentarily sustained the perverse rationalization that corruption under the Estrada administration was inept and ham-handed—and therefore not particularly virulent.

In this respect, however, it should not be forgotten that illegal gambling payoffs in exchange for protection are themselves built on an old corruption niche. The pyramid of *jueteng*-related bribe-takers, from members of the police and the armed forces to municipal mayors, governors, members of Congress, reaching finally in Estrada's case to the president of the republic himself, is one of the most established and customary sources of corruption and political financing. Gov. Luis Singson in October 2000 revealed that in August 1998 Estrada took a share of *jueteng* protection payoffs by assessing a 5% take on the imputed revenues of known gambling lords.[5] Estrada's share of *jueteng* payoffs was said to have run from P32-35 million a month beginning in August 1998. The direct involvement of the country's highest elected official in a protection racket was a novelty indeed. While it was no surprise that local politicians would be involved in such schemes almost as a matter of course, it was hitherto presumed that national officials, particularly at the level of the president, would steer clear of these, either because of the risks of exposure involved or because much larger amounts were available from more sophisticated corruption ventures. Singson would conjecture that someone like Marcos, for example, would not have bothered with *jueteng* given the richer pickings involved in larger-scale government contracts and foreign loans.

Estrada's involvement betrayed the attitude of someone for whom "the presidency is the mayoralty writ large" [Coronel 2001:33], as well as an audacity borne of the sense of power attached to the office.

"Old-niche" corruption persists even as political leadership changes. Bureaucratic practices and organization change only slowly, so that the rents to be earned from these also persist. The technology and modus operandi in rigged bidding for regularly occurring public works projects will hardly change, and major payoffs will always flow upward as long as these are allowed[6]. Another obvious example is lucrative or influential board directorships in government corporations, which are awarded as a matter of fact to loyal followers of the faction in power. Pre-existing corruption niches are vacated and simply re-occupied by new personalities. In an earlier literature, the availability of such regular rent opportunities were part of what was termed the "spoils system", first noted under the revolving-door two-party system under the 1935 Constitution. Other things equal, such niches will be easy to occupy, since the available rents are for the taking by the clique in power almost by definition, and their existence is tolerated by business as a modus vivendi, being euphemistically termed "hidden costs".

The characteristic of old-niche corruption peculiar to the Estrada administration, however, was the sheer number of those who deemed themselves holders of corruption franchises. These seemed to include not only members of the immediate official family but also mistresses, bastard children, denizens of show-business, gambling partners, business partners both established and obscure, not to mention the underworld. A bounty-hunting system appeared to be in place, where enfranchised deal-cutters competed over who would be first to interpose themselves between approving authorities and private contractors. The effect was something akin to a feeding frenzy, as members of this privileged swarm sought to secure niches for themselves. Anecdotal information suggests that the "take" was cranked up to levels that were almost unsustainable, since interlopers demanded cuts on top of the accustomed bureaucratic corruption. Hence, although the amounts involved were not always spectacular, the sheer pervasiveness of this additional layer that laid itself down actually or potentially on all transactions with government had a particularly numbing effect on business.

Corruption Innovations

THE UBIQUITY AND CONSPICUOUSNESS of old-niche corruption under Estrada at first obfuscated the fact that larger, more important deals were in the offing. New areas of corruption arise as new institutions or strategies are introduced. Compared with corruption niches that are customarily lodged in the performance of bureaucratic functions, innovative corruption is typically distinguished by its grand scale and its new "objects of transaction". These niches differ from the first category in that their existence cannot be taken for granted but are premised on the introduction or continuation of some institutional novelty. Under Ramos, moves toward liberalization and privatization saw the advent of contracting under the build-operate-transfer (BOT) law, as well as the privatization of government-held assets through initial public-stock offerings (IPOs). A widely held (though still-unproven) suspicion then was that—in a form of insider-trading—blocs of IPO stock were initially assigned to important politicians. Rents could then be earned on capital gains realized through the equities market. Such maneuvers were, at any rate, well within the realm of the probable. Similarly, if as is widely suspected, corruption attended the "build-operate-transfer" ventures during the Ramos period, it was possible to do so only because the BOT avenue itself allowed private firms to participate in public works projects.

Indeed the Estrada administration inherited some of this largesse. The Caliraya-Botocan-Kalayaan (CBK) power deal left over from the Ramos period was, according to former finance secretary Edgardo Espiritu, "the first among many allegedly anomalous transactions" under the Estrada administration. The controversy involved the provision of a government guarantee (a so-called "performance undertaking") to a private foreign corporation Impsa's[7] unsolicited bid to rehabilitate a power-plant project under a BOT scheme. Government agencies such as NEDA and the Department of Finance originally advised against such guarantees, apprehensive that these would unduly favor the proponent and be disadvantageous to the government. In the end, however, presidential pressure led to the signing of an agreement that deviated significantly from the original recommendations of the relevant agencies, in violation of existing procedures for approval.[8] (See PCIJ [2001] for details.) A timely exposé of this particular deal led to its suspension and review, though not without its own cost: although the media merely reported Estrada to be an "unwitting" sponsor to an anomalous transaction, Estrada launched a personal vendetta against the Gokongwei-owned *Manila Times*, which ultimately forced the latter's closure and sale to a crony, Mark Jimenez.[9]

More than bureaucratic niches, innovative corruption is inherently difficult to detect. In the first place, owing precisely to their novelty, such deals will typically run ahead of the public's access to information and comprehension of complex transactions. That the object of the corrupt transaction in the Impsa deal, for example, was a "performance undertaking", i.e., a contingent liability that involved no visible or immediate outflow from public coffers, was probably abstract to the "common *tao*", or even the FX-riding middle classes, for that matter. Similarly arcane are the techniques of stock-price manipulation and corporate takeovers (which seemed to stump even lawyers in the impeachment trial). A second reason for the ambiguity of these innovations is the absence of benchmarks against which to measure performance. They often pertain to large scale, one-of-a-kind deals involving executive discretion and are connected with major policy decisions, thus making it hard to distinguish between mistakes resulting from a legitimate exercise of authority and anomalies arising from a breach of public trust [De Dios and Ferrer 2001]. While the overprice of school books or fire-engines may be easy enough to detect through comparison with open-market prices or competing bids, it is more difficult to pronounce whether stock purchases by SSS or GSIS in the open market by themselves are patently anomalous even if they should lead to losses—they may simply have been mistakes. In the same manner, favors to cronies were often dressed up as legitimate judgment calls in overall policy. The most blatant example of this type of "policy for sale" includes the disastrous air-dispute with Taiwan that was designed to preserve the monopoly of Lucio Tan's Philippine Airlines [Lim 2001].

Estrada contributed his own innovations to grand corruption, a new element of which was the leveraging of government assets and authority to undertake deals that were ultimately mediated by markets. This went beyond simple kickbacks on public contracts, since the rents to be earned did not directly originate from the usual exercise of bureaucratic functions (e.g., government procurement, auctions, etc.) but arose or were realized through the workings of markets or what would appear to be autonomous private-sector decisions.

The first instances of market-mediated corruption under Estrada involved the use of government-controlled financial institutions, particularly the pension funds, Social Security System (SSS) and the Government

Service Insurance System (GSIS) to implement private strategies for corporate takeovers. Headed respectively by Carlos Arellano and Federico Pascual, both handpicked appointees of the president, these institutions were actively used to facilitate the takeover or purchase of corporations owned by favored private individuals.

The purposes appear varied. In the purchase of PCIBank by the much smaller Equitable Bank (forming Equitable PCI, the country's third largest bank), the aim appeared to have been to facilitate the takeover of a target corporation by a favored crony. The directed purchase of shares by SSS and GSIS ultimately gave them respectively a 23-percent and a 12.5-percent share in the merged bank, which, together with the Go family's 30 percent stake, was sufficient to support the election of Jaime Go. Based on the assertions of Mark Crespo (alias Jimenez), a similar leveraging of presidential power and persuasion accompanied the sale of the Philippine Long Distance Telephone (PLDT) company from the Antonio Cojuangco interests to the First Pacific Group of Manuel Pangilinan. In both cases, the cost of entry would have been higher for the interested parties without the intervention of people in authority. For example, it would have been more costly for the interests allied with Go to buy enough shares to gain control of PCI Bank on their own. The use of government-controlled funds to buy huge blocks of shares effectively lowered these entry barriers. Corruption rents could easily arise from the value thus created for private interests, since their control of the targeted private corporations could not have materialized without the exercise of public power. Aside from commissions, of course, control by cronies of such institutions could prove valuable in other ways: PCI-Equitable, it will be recalled, became the host of the "Jose Velarde" accounts and an important conduit for laundering illicit gains.

More recently, testimony has been volunteered before the *Tanodbayan* that SSS and GSIS funds were also used to purchase shares of various corporations owned by or assigned to Mr. Estrada [Tirol 2001]. Among the companies mentioned were Belle Corporation, the real-estate developer of Tagaytay Highlands controlled by Jaime Dichaves, and Waterfront Philippines, associated with hotels owned by William Gatchalian. GSIS bought more than P1 billion worth of Belle shares, while SSS bought P784 million worth. In these instances, the probable intent of the participation of the pension funds was to bid up the value of shares owned by the vested interests, thus creating gains for their owners in the market. Newspaper reports cite sources who estimate that Estrada received a net profit of P1.14 per share for the 250 million shares bought by SSS alone [Batino, Dacel, Nocum 2001]. It is readily apparent that this was the same principle used in the BW Resources price-manipulation scam, namely, to create artificial value for the privileged owners of the stock. Indeed it has been asserted that the rents thus created were meant to compensate for the losses to Estrada arising from the BW Resources fiasco[10] [Tirol 2001].

The emergence of the stock market as a source of corruption rents coincided with the boom beginning in 1995, when the country's capital account was liberalized, Philippine economic growth picked up along with the rest of the region, and foreign portfolio investors took note of the Philippines as a "new emerging market" for equities. This episode, however, would be cut short by the onset of the Asian economic crisis in 1997.

Owing to the impeachment proceedings, the best-documented example of market-mediated corruption under Estrada was the BW stock-price manipulation scam. Estrada stood accused of conspiring to use the government's plans to legalize gambling in order to artificially push up the value of an otherwise obscure stock. He was also accused later of seeking to cover up the matter through direct intervention in the actions of the regulatory authorities. The source of rents, therefore, was not the national treasury itself, but seemingly autonomous and non-manipulatable markets. Corruption, weak regulation, and the collusion of important agents in the private sector, combined to perpetrate a scheme that preyed on the gullibility of an unsuspecting public [Pascual 2001].

As an innovation in corruption technology, the BW Resources stock scam was interesting in raising the possibility that an old corruption niche could be parlayed (at least in form) into a market-mediated one. BW Gaming and Entertainment Corp. (BWGEC), a corporation owned by Dante Tan, had been granted a franchise by the Pagcor to operate Bingo Online in December 1998. On the other hand, the subject of the scam was a different corporation listed on the stock market, originally named the GRC, but whose name was changed to BW Resources (or simply BW) after Tan acquired a large amount of its shares, in obvious reference to BWGEC. "Rumors spread to the effect that BW was an 'Erap stock', and 'the' gaming stock of the market" [Pascual 2001]. BW's press releases and declared "plans" continuously referred to intended entry into legalized gambling operations[11], all of which of course was meant to enhance the market's appreciation of its value. Questions will always remain over whether the

BW scam was a "legitimate" attempt gone wrong to securitize a gambling franchise, or whether it was planned as a scam from the beginning. Regardless of original intent, however, the collapse of the stock-market sentiment owing to the Asian crisis made that much more difficult to exploit the stock market legitimately, it made a natural "rise" in the stock less possible, leaving price-manipulation as the only avenue for gain.

In general, old-niche corruption is based on blatant deviations from market valuation, and competitive price benchmarks are easily seen to have been violated. In market-mediated corruption, however, the apparent intercession of markets conceals the irregularity of the act. Part of the problem market-mediated corruption has prospered is that, to begin with, markets in developing countries are imperfect and themselves prone to manipulation. The truth of this assertion is seen most clearly in the BW Resources scam. Even before and without the incidence of political intervention, the equities market left to itself was already scandal-ridden and prone to abuse by industry insiders. Government regulation was weak or captured. It is no wonder, therefore, that such a market was lent itself easily and almost willingly to the machinations of Estrada's coterie, whose depredations showed a difference in degree and audacity, but not in kind from what this market was accustomed to.

Jueteng-Gate—Beginning of the End

THE LIMITS OF USING MARKET-MEDIATED CORRUPTION have already been alluded to. The withdrawal of foreign portfolio players took the wind out of the sails of the private equities and credit markets, preventing the large-scale leveraging of corrupt deals through markets. The stock-market bubble burst, the period of easy foreign credit was over, and private banks were in distress owing to the past stock of bad loans, with a good number being inherited even from the previous administration. Given the Estrada coterie's strong appetite for accumulation, however, this circumstance left only the customary government niches to turn to.

Singson's testimony suggests that Estrada's participation in the *jueteng* rackets for over two years beginning in August 1998 continued along the customary lines of collecting a fixed take from established *jueteng* operators, an arrangement in which the latter acquiesced. What was later to provoke resistance and lead ultimately to exposure (most crucially by the insider Singson himself) was the attempted monopolization of the *jueteng* business by Charlie 'Atong' Ang around the second half of 2000, a move apparently undertaken with Estrada's blessings. Working through a Pagcor consultancy contract, Ang effectively obtained the authority to award franchises for "Bingo 2-Ball", the legalized version of *jueteng*, at the same time that police began to crack down on the older, unauthorized versions of the game. The latter included those run by Singson himself, while the legal franchise was given to his estranged brother, a political adversary.

A thought-experiment might be considered. If these franchises had simply been awarded to incumbent gambling lords, no further repercussions would likely have resulted: *jueteng* would have been effectively legalized (over the objections of the churches, no doubt) and the matter would have ended there. From the viewpoint of collecting rents at the center, however, this would have been less satisfactory, since larger collections could probably be made if fewer agents were legalized than the original number of *jueteng* lords. The issue of the legalization of *jueteng* was secondary. Regardless of *jueteng*'s legal status, at bottom what mattered was whether the incumbent operators would be allowed to continue.

In the event, Estrada and Ang selectively violated their implicit contracts with pre-existing operators and used the Bingo 2-Ball franchises to realign rights in the gambling rackets unilaterally. Much as gangs quarrel over turf, this squeeze-play predictably provoked an extreme reaction—namely defection and exposé by the aggrieved insider, Singson. A similarly desperate violent reaction, one will recall, was also the result in the only other time property rights were realigned through the overweening power of the executive, namely Marcos's campaign against certain factions of the elite (namely Lopezes, Jacintos, and the Osmeñas). What is most difficult is to occupy niches that are already occupied, which is why corruption and cronyism directed at arbitrarily redefining or reallocating rights are bound to confront the highest entry barriers and will only be engaged in extraordinary circumstances. The major Philippine experience has, of course, been under Marcos regime, when prominent families such as the Lopezes and the Jacintos were effectively dispossessed.

Gambling payoffs are an old bureaucratic-corruption niche. Estrada flirted with various attempts to turn it into market-based or white-collar corruption, through legalization and (in the case of BW Resources) even leveraging gambling through the equities market. The drying up of possibilities for market-mediated corruption will have caused the Estrada gang to revert to more primitive means of enlarging its shares of rents through centralization and reassignment. The *jueteng* affair, which ultimately brought down the regime, is a grotesquely fascinating illustration of the use of the entire gamut of corruption: from the takeover of customary bureaucratic niches, to attempts at innovative market-mediated deals, and finally a reversion to a simple grab of pre-existing claims.

Historical Perspective

EXCEPT FOR THE AUTHORITARIAN MARCOS PERIOD, corruption in the Philippines may be considered to be generally decentralized. Relatively routine corruption prevails among the tenured bureaucracy, and this is more or less tolerated and often even utilized by politicians and political appointees. It is lamented but also countenanced as a "fact of life" by the business sector. The variable and novel element has always been political corruption, especially in the presidency, where the degree of discretion is greatest.

The centralization of political corruption reached its peak under the Marcos dictatorship. At the same time bureaucratic corruption was suppressed to the extent that it was autonomous and did not fall in line with the requirements of the cronies and the ruling families (for example, the Bureau of Customs gained a reputation for a degree of professionalism under the Marcos dictatorship). The focus on the decline in bureaucratic corruption is largely the basis for the surprisingly favorable assessment of that type of regime (e.g., by Shleifer and Vishny [1993]), though they neglect the enlargement of the scope and scale of political corruption.

In the pre- and post-dictatorship democratic regimes (apart from the Estrada administration), on the other hand, political corruption also became more decentralized, given the obvious checks and balances and risk of exposure entailed by the separation of powers, checks and balances, and freedom of the media. As a result, one may hypothesize political corruption as being more modest and selective in such regimes relative to the years of dictatorship, even as the dilution of central power gives an opportunity for bureaucratic corruption even at the local and lower levels to gain more autonomy. This, of course, has its own economic consequences. *Selectivity* nonetheless entails that the corrupt deals politicians enter will be larger in magnitude (to attain scale economies), novel in character (to avoid detection), or both. Under the Ramos administration, for example, asset privatizations (including the IPOs of government controlled corporations), BOTs, joint venture contracts, and foreign loan syndications were new areas where potential rents could be obtained, but the very novelty of these areas made rents difficult to detect.

It was a unique feature of the Estrada administration that it failed to conform to the imperative of corruption-selectivity normally imposed on a non-dictatorial regime. The internal organization of the Estrada circle was effectively one of awarding bounty-hunting franchises to a number of individuals, consisting of cronies, kin, wives, and mistresses. (This arrangement was implemented partly by the formal requirement that all contracts in excess of P50 million be reviewed by Malacañang.) The peculiarities of Estrada's personal circle meant that this was a large number of persons, indeed, clearly indicating "excessive entry".

This arrangement was superimposed on pre-existing bureaucratic corruption. Anecdotal evidence suggests that on top of 10-15 percent bureaucratic markups on contracts, additional 10-15 percent "fees" were being required for franchised political facilitators. Under the Marcos dictatorship, by contrast, bureaucratic corruption had been reduced by some measure, leaving some slack for cronies and family to take over. The Estrada system put a strain on the system it had not been subjected to before and possibly contributed to its breakdown.

The *carte blanche* given to a large number of rent-hunters meant an open invitation to expand the sphere of extraction of fees and commissions. This clearly went against the selectivity in political deals that had been the accustomed trend in all previous post-dictatorship administrations. Besides the amounts involved, the sheer pervasiveness of sanctioned corrupt deals in the government proved to be an onerous burden on the program implementation.

Some writers have suggested that competitive corruption is in fact most conducive to welfare, to the extent that rents are bid down to zero by bounty-hunters competing with each other to nail down commissions. Hence, if a contractor finds the commission demanded by "facilitator" A exorbitant, why might he not transfer custom to facilitator B? This did not occur under the Estrada arrangement, however, since in the first place entry was not free (not just everyone could be a bounty hunter), and second, since the competition among franchise holders was not with respect to price, but one arranged as a race, with the first mover getting the prize. For this reason, rents to these bounty-hunters did not shrink to zero but were obtained at the expense of the markups of bureaucrats and private interests themselves, putting a strain on the system. Indeed, one will note how in a sense Estrada's fall from power was caused by the very failure of the arrangement. Singson turned his back on Estrada when his exclusive "franchise" was challenged by another franchise holder, Ang. From the viewpoint of the industrial organization of corruption, therefore, Estrada's system of corruption carried the seeds of its own destruction: it was an oligopoly with overcapacity.

Public Understanding of Corruption and Its Consequences

THE REVELATION OF ESTRADA'S EXCESSES may yet become a watershed in the country's long struggle against corruption and the reform of Philippine politics. Corruption had until then been lamented but ultimately accepted as a part of social life; poor and rich could cope in their own way with the various parts of the immutable system that affected them. On the one hand, the petty corruption of cops, local officials, and minor functionaries has been most onerous to the masses, although it is a corruption through which the very rich could always buy their way, and which they pass on as part of "hidden costs". On the other hand, many businesses have themselves often benefited in no small measure from the grand corruption that attends spectacular government contracts; these same deals, however, were incomprehensible and far-removed from the experience of ordinary people, who therefore had little motivation to condemn them. Rich and poor, therefore, have never really been united on what the issue means. The rich are hardly bothered by petty corruption; nor do the poor have anything to do with grand corruption.

To Estrada's lasting credit, his universal rapacity and indiscriminate pursuit of all corrupt avenues unified large sectors of the public in a convergent understanding of corruption in all its forms. Opprobrium first focused on Estrada's extravagant lifestyle and on his accumulation of wealth that was incongruous with his position and unreported in public declarations of his net worth. Real-estate and various corporations owned by Estrada, his legitimate and supposititious families, and dummies, were the first and most incontrovertible public evidence of primitive accumulation

[Chua, Coronel, and Datinguinoo 2001: especially Tables 2-4]. The acts and images from the impeachment that scandalized the crowds who massed at EDSA 2 were among the most elemental: the president signing an account under a false name; the president summoning people and making personal calls to head off an investigation into a fraud; the president involving himself in payoffs from known gambling lords; the president and members of his family receiving diverted public monies at their home— all were acts obviously unworthy and a betrayal of the office. These revelations involved well-worn modes of corruption, familiar even to the simple townsfolk, and confirming public suspicions about Estrada's unfitness for office.

More than this, however, the impeachment trial and the investigations in its wake served as an initiation to the very arcana of corruption for the millions who followed them. The very logic of the trial compelled viewers to understand the intricacies of fraud and betrayal of trust. Hence, to understand the significance of Estrada's personal intervention in behalf of Dante Tan in the BW affair, one had to fathom the fraud that lay behind "wash sales" and other forms of stock-price manipulation. Following the trail of funds leading to the Boracay mansion meant understanding the intricacies of shell corporations formed by law offices and the use of accounts under fictitious names. And so on and on. For the first time, all strata of society had a front-row seat to see and hear from operatives themselves exactly how different modes of corruption functioned. The trial created a remarkable juxtaposition of names—what would the banker Clarissa Ocampo normally have to do with the likes of a gambling lord like Chavit Singson, or the numbers-racketeer Ang with the government regulator Yasay? Yet, there they all were, in person or in print, a collective testimony to Estrada's catholic belief: *pecunia non olet.*

A less noticed but perhaps more fundamental consequence of the impeachment trial was how it exposed the extent of the rot in many of the nation's institutions. It was perhaps no surprise that corruption existed in government. But the evidence damned not only Estrada and the government, but indirectly also the other social institutions whose parts or representatives had proved only too malleable and obsequious to the demands of corruption. Thus, for example, the integrity of the banking system itself became open to suspicion, since—until the time of the trial—it became evident that some of its prominent representatives had countenanced money laundering and deception. Topnotch lawyers and law firms were revealed to have been willing accomplices to the concealment of ill-gotten gains. Heads of government financial institutions, who came from supposedly impeccable professional and private-business backgrounds, were seen to kowtow to very unprofessional demands to invest in speculative shares. Stock brokers—though apparently not for the first time—put themselves at the service of stock-price manipulators and defrauders of the public. Then there were the government bureaucrats, quaking in their shoes, forever agonizing and close to tears, but largely silent until the impeachment and EDSA 2 gave them the chance to confess and recant. Finally, of course, as a last straw, the senate itself—and indirectly the political system—failed palpably as an institution in the people's eyes by collectively refusing to allow the truth to be revealed, rendering itself party to the system of corruption.

For such institutions and individuals, it might be contended, Estrada's impeachment and popular indictment provided too easy an "out". By depicting Estrada as the perversion, the weakness and failure of these institutions could be excused as an aberration. The appeal to unusual harassment and fear might then be used to conceal the true picture, namely that the moral fiber was weak, that professionalism was insipid, that commitment to public interest was vacuous to begin with, and that personal gain could not be ruled out.

Much has been written juxtaposing "versions" 2 and 3 of EDSA. At bottom, EDSA 2 expressed a hope that Estrada's indictment and fall would herald a more thoroughgoing clean-up of other ailing social institutions. On the other hand, if anything was valid about what became known as EDSA 3, it was a cynical one—that Erap could not be judged alone because he could not have acted alone. A good part of society acted with him. Despite their frequent juxtaposition, therefore, the two EDSAs ironically proceeded from the same message, although one was grounded in hope, the other in cynicism.

The more radical critique, therefore, is not that Estrada was aberrantly corrupt, but that he merely took the institutions of society at that time for what they were—namely, like himself. Estrada's gargantuan appetites were remarkable, to be sure, but he was also the product and logical culmination of political and social institutions that had been long permeated by corruption and the betrayal of the public. The veneer of these institutions had worn thin and Estrada believed that he and many others read their true grain accurately. The tragedy was that, whenever Estrada acted upon this interpretation, he was not often disappointed. As in Andersen's fable of the emperor's new clothes, the sharpest indictment is ultimately directed not at the emperor's vanity, appetite, and gullibility, but at the degeneration of the court and society that could for so long tolerate a blatant fraud.

REFERENCES

Batino, C., R.Dacel, and A. Nocum [2001] "SSS admits P8 billion loss under Estrada watch", *Philippine Daily Inquirer*, Tuesday 17 April.

Chua, Y., S. Coronel, and V. Datinguinoo [2001] "Estrada's entrepreneurial families", in S. Coronel, ed., pp. 59-70.

Coronel, S., ed. [2001] *Investigating Estrada*. Quezon City:Philippine Center for Investigative Journalism.

Coronel, S. [2001] "Weather-weather", in S. Coronel, ed., pp. 2-14.

Coronel, S. [2001] "The Jueteng Republic", in S. Coronel, ed. pp. 26-37.

de Dios, E. and R. Ferrer [2001] "Corruption: a framework and context", Transparent and Accountable Governance Project, Philippine Center for Policy Studies (MS).

de Dios, E. and H. Esfahani [2001] "Centralization, political turnover, and investment uncertainty in the Philippines", in J. E. Campos, ed., *Corruption: the boom and bust of East Asia*. Quezon City: Ateneo de Manila University Press.

Fabella, R. [2000] "The J2K crisis and the economy: the broader context", University of the Philippines School of Economics, Discussion Paper No. 0012, December.

Pascual, C. [2001] "The BW Resources Scandal", Transparent and Accountable Governance, Philippine Center for Policy Studies (MS).

Shleifer, A. and R. Vishny [1993] "Corruption". *Quarterly Journal of Economics* 108(3):599-617.

Tirol, V. [2001] "SSS, GSIS losses traced to Estrada", *Philippine Daily Inquirer*, Monday, 16 April

[1] The person in question, Celia de Castro, originally introduced herself to former education secretary Andrew Gonzalez as a "sister" of the president but was later described as a "cousin". That she had some standing was seen in her official appointment as a presidential assistant.

[2] Coronel [2000] writes: "[W]hen under criticism recently for appointing assorted buddies to various government posts, Estrada was incredulous, feeling that he was, again, unfairly being targeted by a trigger-happy press. Neither could his friends understand what the furor was all about. Their collective reaction was best summed up by Rolando T. Meyer, known in the movie world as a sidekick of action star and presidential pal Fernando Poe Jr. In a television interview after taking his oath as a member of the board of the government-owned casino company, the Philippine Amusement and Gaming Corp. (Pagcor), a post that carries with it some P2 million a year in director's fees, Meyer said, nonplussed: *Weather-weather lang 'yan*'.

[3] Estrada's defenders point to the fact that it was the holdover Ramos appointees, using the government-sequestered shares, who actually voted'Cojuangco president on the eve of Estrada's assumption of office. Even so, however, this at most testifies to these appointees' psycophancy and desire to ingratiate themselves to the new leadership—which proves the point about revolving-door corruption. The point is that Estrada's own board appointees subsequently never saw fit to reverse this decision.

[4] This was not the only example of apparent centralization. Another layer of organization was the "flagship committee" headed by R. Aventajado. Also a part of the centralization of functions was the takeover by the Office of the President of important offices such as the SEC and the NFA. The SEC as it turns out became pivotal in the later scandal over the BW Resources. The NFA, on the other hand, was in charge of rice importations, which is known to pay generous commissions to private procurers.

[5] The detail that the take was based on an *assessed* or *imputed* revenues would explain why the recorded payoffs consisted of fixed amounts, notwithstanding the admitted variability of actual revenues. This was a point of some confusion in the defense's cross-examination of Governor Singson during the impeachment hearings.

[6] During the Aquino administration, a newly appointed education secretary received checks regularly "sent up" by private companies using the government payroll system to collect insurance premiums from public school teachers.

[7] Industrias Metalurgicas Pescarmona Socieded Anonima

[8] It should be remembered that this was not a new project but a carry-over from the Ramos administration, and it is not far-fetched that payoffs were also made during the previous administration, although the "goods" were not delivered, making payoffs to the successor administration necessary as well . This additional uncertainty

introduced by regular political turnovers is a characteristic that makes corruption in the Philippines particularly costly and pernicious [de Dios and Esfahani 2001].

[9] As a postscript to the CBK deal and a testimony to the durability of lobbying efforts, it should be reported that the Arroyo administration now appears to have approved the deal, nonetheless. (See PCIJ [2001].)

[10] Interestingly enough, this mode of generating corruption rents also fits well into the Estrada administration's idiosyncratically narrow rhetoric regarding what constituted a breach of public trust, namely, actual theft of public funds (*pagnanakaw sa kaban ng bayan*). But only self-deception and an inherently warped moral compass would allow such absurd distinctions.

[11] These announced plans included among others: a merger with BWGEC, which it will be recalled held a bingo-online franchise; the acquisition of Bingo Bonanza; a buy in by gambling magnate Stanley Ho; participation in Ho's Jumbo Floating Restaurant, etc. Pascual [2001] notes, however, that none of these schemes pushed through and therefore regards them as being merely part of a PR blitz to raise stock prices artificially.

Reflections on the Role of the Military in People Power 2

CAROLINA G. HERNANDEZ

Prologue

ON THAT FATEFUL DAY of January 19, 2001, the UP Department of Political Science faculty met its students in an alternative class before they all marched to the EDSA shrine. I remember expressing at that meeting my own concerns over the still contested role of the military in that first "People Power", in February 1986, and my hope that this time the military would stay neutral. This, I explained to them, would close the debate on an issue that had refused to be resolved for 15 years; it would also insulate Joseph Ejercito Estrada's political successor from excessive and unwarranted influence from the military hierarchy, at the same time help promote the institutionalization of democratic civilian control in government over the long term.

The issue was whether People Power would have succeeded in 1986 even if those reformist officers, represented by Gregorio "Gringo" Honasan, former Defense Secretary Juan Ponce Enrile, and the armed forces vice chief of staff, General Fidel V. Ramos, had not broken with the Marcos regime; or whether, without the support of the civilian population that kept vigil on EDSA on February 22-24, 1986, these three men with their scant followers holding out inside Camp Aguinaldo, would not have been destroyed by the Marcos loyalists, headed by the chief of staff, General Fabian Ver.

That issue remaining unresolved, the military elements dissatisfied with the successor government of Corazon C. Aquino became emboldened to mount coups with civilian partners from July 1986 to December 1989, reversing an incipient economic recovery, eroding international confidence in the government, and delaying the transition to democracy.

For these reasons, I now had to share with the students my concern and my prayer that the military would stay neutral. But it did not; instead it was persuaded by retired generals to withdraw support from Estrada, thereby hastening his departure and paving the way for his successor— Gloria Macapagal-Arroyo. What can be said about the role of the military in People Power? What are its implications for the Macapagal-Arroyo administration's ability to be free of military influence in making non-military-related policies? Its implications for the institutionalization of democratic civilian control in the country? For democracy itself? These issues have been raised by domestic and foreign observers (Burton, 2001), and these are the issues this essay seeks to address.

Comparing People Power 1 and People Power 2

THERE ARE SIMILARITIES AND DIFFERENCES between the two instances of People Power. The most obvious similarities are 1) the context in which they occurred, 2) the role of the church, particularly that of Jaime Cardinal Sin, 3) the spontaneity of the people's outpouring of support for what they thought was the right thing to do, 4) the quick and peaceful way of removing a corrupt president, and 5) the withdrawal of support from the government by the military.

People Power 1 and 2 took place amid popular indignation over what people thought were blatant attempts by the government itself to thwart constitutional processes. In 1986 it was the Marcos government stealing victory in the snap presidential elections from the opposition candidate. In 2001 it was the perceived attempt on the part of the government to ensure that the impeachment process against Estrada would lead to an acquittal, regardless of compelling evidence of guilt. Before the 1986 snap elections, a vigorous boycott movement including non-exercise of suffrage, despite legal and punitive consequences, had been mounted to protest the rigging of earlier elections to perpetuate Marcos and his cohorts in power. When it became apparent that it was all happening again, a civil disobedience campaign was launched. Companies owned by the Marcos cronies were boycotted, for instance. The boycott had begun to tell on the sales of these companies, and crony banks had begun to suffer significant withdrawals by the time the military broke with Marcos.

A group led by Gregorio Honasan, the maverick colonel, and Defense Minister Juan Ponce Enrile hatched "God Save the King", a plot to wrest power from Marcos (The Final Report, 1990), arrest all the opposition leaders and set up a junta led by Enrile. When the Marcos government discovered the plot, it prepared to arrest those involved, General Fidel Ramos, the vice chief of staff, and, again all opposition leaders. But the military breakaway and People Power preempted it all. Civilians came either in response to the call of Cardinal Sin and Butz Aquino, the younger brother of the slain Sen. Benigno Aquino Jr., or on their own cognizance of the need to forge solidarity with all anti-Marcos forces to oust the dictator. Four days later, Marcos fled to Hawaii.

There is a similarity between People Power 1 and 2 in the sense that in both cases people had been at first prepared to take the constitutional route. In 1986 they went to the polls hoping that this time fair and honest elections could be had that, with volunteer poll watchers of the National Citizen's Movement for Free Elections (Namfrel), Marcos could not cheat. But the constitutionally mandated government bodies—the Commission on Elections (Comelec) and the Batasan Pambansa (National Assembly)— were controlled by Marcos. By Enrile's own account after the breakaway, they were subverting the constitutional process of political succession with the intention of giving Marcos a fresh mandate to govern. The people then took to the streets even before the military reformists could themselves take significant action. More than a million were estimated to have joined this demonstration, claiming victory for Cory Aquino and condemning the fraudulent counting of the election results.

People took to the streets once again in January 2001 after it became clear that the impeachment process would not be fair and just. Eleven senators identified with Estrada preempted the chief justice of the Supreme Court who was presiding over the impeachment trial, by voting against the opening of an envelope containing damning evidence. The defense provided the legal ruse that content was not relevant to the original four articles in the impeachment charge. The 11 make up more than the required number to acquit in the end.

When the trial closed for the day, people poured out on to the streets crying, "Enough of this impeachment!"

In both People Power instances, the role of Cardinal Sin and his Church was crucial in mobilizing popular opposition. While Butz Aquino played a critical role in mobilizing people to come to EDSA in 1986, in 2001 it was Cory Aquino who joined the cardinal's call for the resignation of Estrada when the *jueteng* scandal broke out. In pursuit of the social role of the church as defined by the second Vatican Council, it engaged in a public information campaign, in mobilizing the faithful to join in the protest action, and in providing the moral basis for political protest.

Contrary to the portrayal of People Power as a form of "mob rule" undermining democracy (Spaeth, 2001, Mann, 2001, Estrada, 2001), both instances of People Power were peaceful. Those who went to EDSA were disciplined, responsible, and orderly in their expression of opposition to the sitting presidents. They demonstrated the best elements of the Filipino character—giving, self-sacrificing, generous, kind, hospitable, spiritual, and responsible. Violence would have broken out easily had they been less so, given their numbers. In fact, it was the far thinner ranks of pro-administration groups that became violent. People Power was a demonstration of democracy in action, in which unfit and corrupt leaders, themselves prostituting the constitutional processes, were removed in a peaceful popular action.

Finally, the military played an important, although different role in 1986 and in 2001. The civilian protests were already under way in both instances when the military broke away from the administration. However, in 1986 the breakaway faction was at risk of being killed by the loyalist forces. In 2001, the military withdrew their support from Estrada after being persuaded by a group of retired military officers and on the conviction that the protest movement against Estrada had become "irreversible". In 1986, the military became divided. In 2001, the military hierarchy broke away to avoid dividing the military, among other reasons.

The two instances are different in significant ways. People Power 1 did not include the Left, and the majority consisted of the middle-aged. People Power 2 represented the cross section of the political spectrum, including various factions of the Left. An estimated 80% of the crowd were young. The people's mood also differed—fearful and uncertain of the consequences in 1986, indignant and more certain in 2001, perhaps because they have become empowered by the earlier experience. Telecommunications technology facilitated the gathering of huge numbers in 2001 as hand phones were the main means for mobilizations.

As already noted, the two demonstrations of People Power were also different in that the military was divided in 1986. They were apparently united in 2001, largely due to the "persuasive" tactics used by the retired generals over the defense secretary, the military high command, and the police hierarchy. Moreover, the military was protected in 1986 from the loyalist forces by the civilian population consisting of nuns, priests, civil-society actors, families, business people, students, workers, and others. In 2001, the civilian throngs on EDSA did not have to protect the military that came to join them when its hierarchy, led by armed forces chief of staff, Gen. Angelo Reyes, realized that "the trend [apparently referring to the success of People Power 2] was already irreversible…that it was going to happen within 24 hours, or 48 hours". (*Far Eastern Economic Review*, February 15, 2001). In short, the withdrawal of support was driven by the apparent impending success of People Power 2.

The Role of the Military in Philippine Politics

THE MILITARY'S ROLE in politics has been described as either one of military influence, military participation, military control with civilian partners, or military control without civilian partners. (Welch, 1976). Its role in Philippine politics has shifted over time from military influence to military participation. This shift began in the 1950s with the appointment of Ramon Magsaysay as secretary of defense (Hernandez, 1979). Subordinated to a civilian president who was commander-in-chief of the armed forces, the military participated in politics as it became a partner of the authoritarian administration under Marcos from September 1972 to February 1986. From 1946 to 1972, the principle of civilian control embodied in institutions exercising oversight functions over the military governed civil-military relations. These oversight functions included those over military appointments and promotions, the military budget and expenditures, as well as investigative powers in the case of alleged military irregularities. In addition, an independent judiciary and media supported civilian supremacy over the military.

However, the exigencies of the communist insurgency from the late 1940s to early 1950s prompted a reorganization of the military. The Philippine Constabulary, originally under the Department of the Interior, became part of the defense establishment. Counterinsurgency also facilitated the recruitment into civilian positions officers both retired and on active duty. When Marcos came to power in 1965, he initiated a policy that made the military a partner in national development, giving its officers a chance to acquire civilian-oriented skills through graduate education in civilian universities. In 1972, Marcos imposed martial law using the military as its administrator and partner in governance. This undermined the oversight functions of civilian institutions over the military. It also led to the further politicization of the military. (Hernandez, 1979)

A combination of many factors led to the military breakaway in 1986. Favoritism and personal loyalty considerations for assignment and promotion provided a selfless rationale. Suspicion about the failing health of Marcos and the scramble for power among those around him, however, could not be discounted. Enrile was himself facing an uncertain political future. He had been eased out of the center of power by Gen. Fabian Ver, the armed forces chief of staff, whose influence was rising, and by Marcos himself, who doubted Enrile's loyalty. Finally, there loomed as a real prospect—Cory Aquino's victory in the snap elections. Enrile's own chances at succession were greatly diminished. Conversely, the prospect of his being answerable for human rights violations by the police and the military, possibly including members of the Reform the Armed Forces of the Philippines Movement (RAM), his own partners, was increased (McCoy, 2000). With their plot against Marcos revealed, Enrile and Honasan had no choice but to break away.

This background is useful in analyzing the role of the military in People Power, because the military by the time of People Power 1 was no longer a political innocent. By February 1986, the military had become highly politicized, subordinated no longer to civilian institutions but to the person of Marcos; it enjoyed considerable political, economic, social, and other non-military powers. Short of ruling the country, its officers were part of the limited circle of the political governing elite during the authoritarian rule of Marcos. Since the restoration of democracy in February 1986, the military in fact has continued to enjoy considerable political influence, if not outright political power. In spite of the division between the coup makers and the constitutionalists in the military, it still had an advantage over the civilian government in its control over the legitimate use of force, its hierarchical structure, its continuing role in combating communist insurgency and Muslim separatism, and the continuity of its organization and the survival of most of its officers. Its role in People Power 1 gave the military a boost in public image, although this was undermined by the series of coups that plagued the early years of the Aquino government.

The Role of the Military in People Power

CLEARLY, THE MILITARY PLAYED an important role in the two instances of People Power. But whether its role turned the tide against the incumbent presidents or not is now a rhetorical question. In the first instance, the military breakaway hastened the fall of Marcos, while civilian protection for the breakaway group prevented bloodshed. The military officers ordered to come to EDSA could not fire upon unarmed civilians that included families some of whom might be their own. The aftermath of People Power 1 was a string of coups perpetrated by losers in the redistribution of power under Cory Aquino. The military could not trust the woman in yellow who led those who had stood on the other side of the barricades against Marcos. She was also the widow of the man assassinated under military custody in 1983 and a person seen as bereft of any political experience. Finally, she had close advisers seen as anti-military and Left-leaning (Hernandez, 1987). Consequently, removed from the center of power and without a leader, Marcos loyalists from both the military and the civilian sectors tried to unseat Aquino. The RAM that originally planned the "God Save the King" plot with Enrile were eased out of power soon after the Aquino government was organized. They had an interest in ousting her from the presidency and forming a junta (The Final Report, 1990). The Young Officers Union (YOU), a group of idealistic junior officers, joined the RAM in the two most serious, though failed, challenges to the Aquino government—the coups of August 1987 and December 1989.

Claiming credit for the People Power success against Marcos, Enrile and some of the RAM boys felt betrayed by what they saw as a vindictive Aquino administration. Others did not, and still don't, share this view, however. At any rate, those who did, having been eased out from power first by Marcos and now Aquino, plotted to overthrow her government. They reckoned that the decline in Aquino's popularity over time would win them popular support. They were wrong. Public opinion surveys conducted after the coups revealed an overwhelming rejection of the coup as a means to transfer power (See various SWS Surveys, 1986 to 1990).

Not that the coup plotters gained nothing at all. They in fact got a total approach to armed insurgency and separatism, salary increases and other material benefits, and the removal of Cabinet officials perceived as anti-military and Left-leaning. The restoration of democratic civilian control and military professionalism were implemented through reorientation and value-reformation programs undertaken by the military (Hernandez and Ubarra, 2000) and the rebuilding of civilian institutions with oversight functions over the military. And during the Ramos administration, peace talks with armed opponents of the government, including military rebels, were conducted to put an end to armed conflict that discouraged investments, trade, and business in general. The Aquino approach of reconciliation with justice that did not yield any tangible results was replaced by the policy of unconditional amnesty to officers and men implicated in the plots against the Aquino government. Consequently, the Ramos and Estrada administrations went unplagued by coups.

The issue that needs to be raised is the implications of unconditional amnesty for the long-term professionalization of the armed forces and the institutionalization of democratic civilian control. The policy of unconditional amnesty is a utilitarian one. It could not have been so easily adopted by a civilian leader; but perhaps, the military background of Ramos made the difference. Unconditional amnesty bought peace for the government that provided the environment for economic recovery and development. But the lessons in discipline that the policy left to young officers in the military are fuzzy at best. It can encourage military misbehavior in the future since those who violated the Constitution went unpunished. Some of them were even elected to public office, including Honasan, now a senator, though on suspicion that he had benefited from an electoral fraud called *dagdag-bawas* (literally add-subtract). By giving the rebel military a stake in the restored democracy, they were encouraged no longer to engage in armed military intervention in politics. Moreover, during the Ramos administration, some 150 retired officers were appointed to strategic and sensitive positions in the national government and in corporations owned or controlled by the government (Hernandez, 1997). This led analysts to view the military as having emerged as a new set of political force (Doronila, 1997) despite a number of reforms undertaken from 1987 up to the presidency of Ramos to restore professionalism in the armed forces (Hernandez and Ubarra, 2000).

Long before the impeachment process against Estrada began, there already had been rumors of a military coup. The occasion was the perceived unfitness of the incumbent president to govern. The company he kept, his lifestyle, his management style (or the lack of it), the absence of an overarching program of government, the Cabinet intramurals—these are only some of the most often cited complaints against Estrada. Responsible opinion leaders were quoted as being open to a coup in their desperation for a leadership change. Fortunately, the usual suspects—the RAM—appeared no longer to have neither the appetite nor the capacity for it. Having learned their lessons and become probably more mature for the experience, their leaders have been in fact speaking against coups as a means toward political change. It was also thought that the military has reconciled itself to the new constitutional order, wherein the civil institutions have control over the military, and the police are separated from the armed forces. Furthermore, it was thought that the military lacked a charismatic leader, such as Honasan probably had been. If there was any danger of armed action against the government, it was likely to come from the police. The Philippine National Police (PNP) took in the young rebel officers after their unconditional amnesty had been given.

Ramos had also been a staunch critic of the Estrada government for good reasons. Having presided over the economic recovery and development that made the country the latest of Asia's rising tiger economies before the financial crisis of 1997 and having earned for the country a respectable place in the region and the world, he could not but extend unsolicited advice to his successor, whom he saw as an unworthy one. Estrada in turn accused Ramos of graft and corruption in connection with some controversial deals done during the Ramos presidency, such as the PEA-Amari and the National Centennial Park scandals. Subsequent investigation, however, exonerated Ramos.

Estrada's civilian defense secretary, Orlando Mercado, also clashed with the military almost soon upon taking office. He accused the vice chief of staff, Gen. Ismael Villareal, and some retired officers, including the former armed forces chief of staff, Gen. Lisandro Abadia, of wrongdoing in connection with a military retirement fund. The replacement of military officers by Mercado's own people in the defense-department positions traditionally occupied by military officers also did not sit well with those replaced. The creation of the Presidential Anti-Organized Crime Task Force (PAOCTF) under Estrada's trusted lieutenant in the Philippine National Police (PNP) was also silently opposed by a number of police and military officers who thought not only that it was an unnecessary bureaucratic layer in law enforcement but that it overstepped into existing units organic to law enforcement and tended toward abuse of authority. There were allegations, too, that police and military officers outside of the pro-Estrada circles were either being demoted or put in the "freezer" or reassigned to hardship posts. A group of battalion and brigade commanders came out questioning the promotions process in the armed forces that enabled his chief of security to bypass more senior and more qualified officers.

When public protest over the bribery and corruption scandal broke out and civilian calls for the resignation of Estrada were made under the leadership of Cardinal Sin and Cory Aquino, retired generals also joined in. Some of them even raised the prospect of military intervention. Estrada made the mistake of brushing this threat aside, calling the retired generals spent forces. In response, they formed a group that allegedly networked among active duty officers in both the police and the military, all of whom their juniors, and persuaded them to withdraw support from Estrada. Thus, the military became a partisan player in People Power 2 as well.

What role did the military play this time? The retired military capitalized on their fraternal ties with active-duty officers. Together with the defense secretary and the police, the military high command defected in the last hours of People Power 2. By the admission of the chief of staff himself, General Reyes, this occurred through the persuasion of the retired generals and his own assessment that Estrada's fall or the success of People Power was "irreversible". The defection was an additional factor to the eventual triumph of People Power. Perhaps it avoided bloodshed; perhaps it avoided a coup; perhaps it shortened the process. The fact is the people on EDSA swelled by the day, and more were preparing to come from distant provinces on January 20. The fact is that the civilian population, either organized or not, were on the way to victory in ousting Estrada when the military and the police joined in. The fact is that these nameless masses were the ones that ensured the success of People Power 2 (*Today*, February 21, 2001, p. 8).

Retired military officers also helped the United Opposition in mobilizing a multisectoral group, organized into task forces to help frame the program of government of Estrada's political successor, especially for its first 100 days. Among these retired officers was Gen. Renato de Villa, later appointed as President Gloria Macapagal-Arroyo's executive secretary. The military was in the minority in this group and civilian conscripts with expertise in diverse fields lent their wisdom and their experience to the formulation of the program of government later adopted by the Cabinet. An area where a military interpretation might have prevailed is in treating the peace process as part of the total approach to insurgency and secessionism and in making the department of defense the lead agency for its implementation. President Macapagal-Arroyo's program of government, in any case, is not one overly influenced by the military.

Implications of the Military's Role in People Power

ALL THE SAME, how free can she be of any military influence in non-military areas of public policy in the long term? That will be determined by her ability to meet the popular expectations she raised in her inaugural speech, and actually deliver on her promise in the first 100 days, which in turn will determine how much public support she can muster and how long she can keep it. Surely she very well knows that undue military influence in politics is encouraged when civilian political leadership and institutions are weak, unstable, and have a low level of popularity and/or legitimacy and/ or when the military feels an overwhelming sense of power. The first months of the Macapagal-Arroyo presidency, therefore, are crucial because expectations are not yet met, a program of government has yet to be put in place, the political institutions of governance are still fragile, and the military still feels powerful.

President Macapagal-Arroyo enjoys popular support on the following expectations, among others: that the fight against poverty will be won within the decade; that moral standards in government and society will be improved and made as a foundation for good governance; that a politics of party programs and process of dialogue with the people will replace the politics of personality and patronage; and that she will lead by example (Macapagal-Arroyo, 2001). To achieve all this will definitely require official team effort as well as the cooperation and support of civil society and private business. The members of the government coalition, starting with President Macapagal-Arroyo's own People Power Coalition, must demonstrate this new politics in ways that can be seen by the people so that examples are set. She has good leaders in the National Anti-Poverty Commission and the Department of Social Welfare and Development. They originated from civil society and had worked with the people at the grassroots level. They understand the people's needs and fears. But the president has also traditional politicians around her to whom, like the military, she feels beholden. To what extent she would be able to lead by example remains to be seen.

The legitimacy of her assumption to power has been questioned by

Estrada and his die-hard supporters and even by some foreign critics. But there appears general acceptance among the citizenry, and by other nations and by international and regional organizations. The fact of her occupation of the Office of the President can no longer be changed. Her continued occupation of the position will depend, however, on popular support, which will be decided by performance.

The military's image has been enhanced by the war in Mindanao initiated by Estrada. Now this image is enhanced by its role in People Power 2 as acknowledged again and again by no less than President Macapagal-Arroyo herself. This must be the reason behind the measures she took upon assuming the presidency. Since her inaugural speech, she has continuously heaped expressions of gratitude on the military and police hierarchy for withdrawing their support from Estrada on the last hours of People Power 2. These expressions have also been transformed into material benefits, despite the huge budget deficit, she has extended to the military, such as increased pay, new livelihood opportunities, and housing, and others. The practice of appointing retired military and police officers, even in positions having nothing to do with traditional military and defense matters, has continued under the new administration. There is also public perception that many appointees to top government positions are linked to Ramos or De Villa, raising the concern that they may not be her own people and that, therefore, she can count on them to push her program of government. Some have even advanced the view that her Cabinet is not a Macapagal-Arroyo Cabinet since its members are more closely identified with other leading political personalities than with her.

Moreover, retired military officers appointed to non-military related positions are bound to bring their own military-oriented practices, ethos, and values into their offices. It is likely that they would bring their own coterie of consultants, advisers, and other confidential personnel. The appointment of a retired military officer into a civilian position has that sort of multiplier effect. The practice also tends to exclude equally competent, if not more competent, civilians from public service. It also extends the shelf life of retirees by recycling and prevents the entry of more vigorous new blood for the renewal and reinvigoration of the bureaucracy. It discourages the growth of meritocracy as fraternal links tend to outweigh achievement. All in all, it limits the perspective of policy making.

The legal argument that retired military officers become civilians begs the basic issue that habits of mind bred by professional training in a profession and inculcated by practice last beyond retirement. They also do not fade away when the person no longer performs in that profession. In this regard, anti- or non-democratic military practices, ethos, and values (Huntington, 1957) are likely to be brought into the civilian agency headed by a retired military officer, making the long term institutionalization of democratic civilian control even more challenging. Of course, in every generalization there are exceptions. One only hopes that the exceptions include those in President Macapagal-Arroyo's government.

Implications for Democracy and Democratic Civilian Control

THE MILITARY'S ROLE in People Power 2 did not take the form of a coup d'etat. In fact, it supported the popular call of the civilian population for the ouster of Estrada. It justified its action with the constitutional provision that defines the function of the country's armed forces as "the protector of the people and the State" (Article II, Sec. 3). The people's welfare would have been at risk if extremists from both Right and Left had been allowed to exploit the political impasse. The people's welfare would have been at risk had the huge anti-Estrada forces clashed with the small group of Estrada partisans clustered near the presidential palace. By joining People Power 2, the military averted these prospects.

The military pledged its support to the new president, Estrada's constitutional successor who is also the new commander-in-chief of the armed forces. The new president will serve only the remaining portion of Estrada's term, or until 2004. The democratic constitution of 1987 was not suspended, nor a state of emergency declared. The offices of government have remained intact.

Whether the role of the military in 2001 or even until 2004, would undermine democracy depends on what the military would do in the event that the new government failed to perform. If it tries to grab power either for itself or for another group, it would undermine democracy. But its role in People Power 2 would not have been the cause of such misbehavior. As noted earlier, the seeds of military intervention in politics had been sown much earlier than 2001 or even 1986. The seeds were sown in the creeping enlargement of the military function, the weakening and destruction of democratic institutions that reached their peak during the authoritarian rule of Marcos. The role of the military in People Power can only enhance the leverage of a military already inclined toward intervening in politics whenever the opportunity arises. Effective governance that enjoys wide popular support is a necessary and effective antidote to this dire prospect.

To institutionalize democratic civilian control, it is necessary to strengthen the civilian political institutions that exercise oversight powers over the military. These are the legislative bodies that deal with defense and security issues, such as the budget and military appointments and promotions. Those that oversee defense and security matters must be knowledgeable about them. Otherwise, the military's advantage would remain unchallenged. Indeed, civilian capacity building in this area is critical. This capacity building must extend to civil society groups, and the media that also serve as watchdogs for democracy.

It is equally important to put the defense department, the national security and intelligence agencies under the leadership of civilians who are defense and security specialists. Today, one of the strongest justifications advanced by the military, both on active duty and retired, to the need to appoint retired military officers to head these offices is that they are better informed. The response to this argument is to develop equal competency among civilians.

Concluding Remarks

IT IS UNFORTUNATE that the military did not maintain its neutrality in the political crisis that led to the ouster of Estrada. Had it remained neutral, People Power would have been a singular, unadulterated, and incontrovertible achievement of civil society functioning in a democracy in a situation where constitutional institutions and processes were being undermined by the political leadership. This would have avoided the debt of gratitude felt by President Macapagal-Arroyo to the military leadership and expressed in material rewards to the military and in appointments to civilian positions. This would have enabled her to form her own Cabinet that must pull together with her to deliver her program of government, and this would have saved her the resources she now must use to manage the constraints that the military defection from the Estrada administration had caused. The specter of coups that haunted the Aquino administration continues to haunt the nation, just as People Power 2 enhanced people empowerment that marked People Power 1. A more empowered citizenry can only be harnessed to protect democracy from military intervention in politics if the government delivers. This is the real challenge to the government of Gloria Macapagal-Arroyo.

REFERENCES

Burton, Sandra (2001). People Power Redux. *Time Magazine*, January 29

Doronila, Amando (1997). Military: New Political Elite. *Philippine Daily Inquirer*, April 20

Editorial (2001), "Hair on Palm" *Today*, February 21

Estrada, Joseph (2001). Viewpoint. If this Can Be Done to Me, Who is Safe? *Time Magazine*, February 19

Final Report of the Fact-Finding Commission that Investigated the Failed Coup of December 1989 (1990). Makati: Bookmark Publishing Co.

Hernandez, Carolina G. and Ubarra, Maria Cecilia T. (1999). Restoring and Strengthening Civilian Control: Best Practices in Civil-Military Relations in the Philippines. Institute for Strategic and Development Studies, Inc., December 31

Hernandez, Carolina G. (1997). The Military and Constitutional Change: Problems and Prospects in a Redemocratized Philippines. Public Policy Volume 1 No. 1 October-December 1997

Hernandez, Carolina G. (1987). Towards Understanding Coups and Civil-Military Relations. Kasarinlan 3(4th Quarter)

Hernandez, Carolina G. (1979). The Extent of Civilian Control of the Military in the Philippines: 1946-1976. Ph.D. dissertation, State University of New York at Buffalo

Huntington, Samuel P. (1957). The Soldier and the State: The Theory and Politics of Civil-Military Relations. New York: Random House, Inc.

Inauguration Speech of President Gloria Macapagal-Arroyo (2001). A time to heal, a time to build. *Philippine Daily Inquirer*, January 21

Mann, Jim (2001). A Risky Move by Filipinos. *Los Angeles Times*, January 24

McCoy, Alfred W. (2000). Lives at the Margin: Biography of Filipinos Obscure, Ordinary, and Heroic. Quezon City: Ateneo de Manila University Press

Spaeth, Anthony (2001). Oops, We Did It Again. *Time Magazine*, January 29

Sheehan, Deidre (2001). Duty-Bound (Interview with Gen. Angelo Reyes), *Far Eastern Economic Review*, February 15

Social Weather Station (1986-1990). Various public opinion surveys on the coups during the Aquino administration

Welch, Claude E., Jr. (1976). Civilian Control of the Military: Theory and Cases from Developing Countries. Albany: State University of New York Press

A Crisis of Political Leadership
From 'Electoral Democracy' to 'Substantive Democracy'

JOSE V. ABUEVA

What are the implications for democracy of President Estrada's impeachment by the House of Representatives and trial by the senate, and of his removal from office through "People Power and his trial in court"? How did Estrada impact on the nation's values, on political leadership, on various institutions and sectors of society, and on the consolidation of democracy since EDSA 1, or People Power 1, in 1986? What do all these reveal about the weaknesses and strengths of Filipino democracy and its institutions, the crisis of leadership, and the imperative to rise from "electoral democracy" to "substantive democracy"?

Answers to the above questions are offered by Dr. Abueva, U.P. Professor Emeritus of Political Science and Public Administration, former U.P. president, and now president of Kalayaan College at Riverbanks Marikina, a new school founded by U.P. professors.

I. People Power 2 was an Exercise in Direct Democracy

JOSEPH ESTRADA became the 13th President of the Philippines on June 30, 1998, having won over his five serious rivals by obtaining nearly 11 million votes, or almost 40% of the total cast for president. He was deposed by the people on January 20, 2001, after only 31 months in office, five months before the middle of his six-year term under the 1987 Constitution.

Estrada, Marcos's Heir

BY THE REASON for and manner of his repudiation and removal, Estrada shares with the dictator Ferdinand Marcos the ignominy of being driven out of Malacañang by an outraged citizenry because of unbridled corruption and abuse of presidential power. While Marcos lasted more than 13 years as an authoritarian leader, following almost eight years as an elected president, Estrada's early and swift ouster took place in a restored democracy 15 years after the EDSA Revolution, now also known as EDSA 1, that ended the Marcos dictatorship.

Marcos was overthrown in EDSA 1 and forced into exile in Hawaii in February 22 to 25, 1986, soon after he had stolen the presidential election from Corazon Aquino and three years after her husband, former Sen. Benigno 'Ninoy' Aquino, had been assassinated in the custody of the military at the Manila International Airport. Since Marcos and Estrada were deposed in popular uprisings named after the place where the tumultuous but peaceful events took place—EDSA, for Epifanio de los Reyes Ave., in Metro Manila—these are now etched in the nation's memory as EDSA 1 and EDSA 2, respectively. Actually, EDSA 2 might better be recognized as People Power 2 or EDSA People Power 2, because the main political event at EDSA was accompanied by "Erap resign" rallies in several major cities. It is important to stress the people's spontaneous assertion of their sovereign power over their abusive, corrupt, and oppressive presidents.

Although different in many ways, Marcos and Estrada shared certain similarities. They were both charismatic and likable persons who could sway other leaders and people. They were masters in political communication and manipulation, patronage, and cronyism for their private gain. They were egregiously cynical, greedy, and corrupt. As president, each excelled in graft and corruption, destroyed political institutions, betrayed the public trust, corrupted public morality, and added immensely to the disrepute of government and public office.

In a sense, Marcos was worse than Estrada not only because the former had wielded and abused presidential power much longer. As dictator, Marcos was much more destructive of democracy and the economy, a greater plunderer, and far more abusive of human rights. But in a way, Estrada is no less to blame. Disregarding the values and promise of EDSA 1, Estrada followed Marcos's evil ways and caused serious havoc on the nation in only 31 months as president. The fact that Marcos and Estrada were elected and reelected and rose to the highest public office makes Filipino elections and democracy problematic. The fact that People Power 2 was necessary should make Filipinos ponder what had happened to their restored democracy and to governance after EDSA 1.

Estrada's Investigation and Impeachment

EARLY IN 2000 some citizens and Senate Majority Leader Teofisto Guingona began calling for the resignation of President Estrada for bad governance, suspected corruption, and the worsening economy. In October his political ally and buddy, Gov. Chavit Singson, testified before the senate Blue Ribbon committee, charging the president with receiving millions in protection money as "lord of all *jueteng* lords" and kickbacks from excise tax payments on tobacco. Public criticism rose that the president had actually neglected, if not betrayed, his basic constituency—the poor *masa*—grossly enriching himself at their expense.

On November 13, 2000, Estrada became the first president to be impeached by the House and thereafter tried by the senate—for bribery, graft and corruption, betrayal of the public trust, and culpable violation of the Constitution. On December 7 the impeachment trial began with Chief Justice Hilario Davide Jr., as presiding officer. Despite mounting evidence of his guilt, his conviction on the Articles of Impeachment was practically impossible and his acquittal almost certain because his partisans in the senate were in the majority. It would take 15 of the 22 senators to convict him.

But, by a fatal miscalculation, the 11 pro-Estrada senator-judges precipitated a walkout of the prosecution lawyers, the resignation of Senate President Aquilino Pimentel, and an abrupt ending of the impeachment trial that triggered (EDSA) People Power 2 and Estrada's ouster. Instantly, the people's trial of Estrada took over from the failed impeachment trial by the senate and the people rendered their irreversible judgment of guilt, punishable by his removal and replacement by Vice President Gloria Macapagal-Arroyo.

Perhaps, the apparent impunity and visible staying power of the Marcos family and Marcos loyalists after their years of plunder, abuse in office, and disregard of the people's interest have taught the likes of Estrada that corruption and abuse in office pay. For did not President-elect Estrada decide that the late dictator Marcos should be given a national hero's burial at the *Libingan ng mga Bayani* (the National Heroes' Cemetery)? Estrada relented only after the deafening protest against the proposed desecration. As it turned out, Estrada, the Marcos loyalist since his years as mayor of San Juan, was really Marcos's heir as president.

Perhaps, citizens who by and large were demoralized and confused— many of whom are also impoverished—have been inured to the wayward habits of the powerful who lead them. In a way, yes, but the combined disapproval of Estrada shown in the 1998 presidential election despite his victory by an impressive plurality and the reasons for EDSA People Power 2 may be saying otherwise.

Estrada was Deposed by People Power 2

ESTRADA WAS DEPOSED, or induced to resign, in four days of People Power 2 (January 16 to 20). In his departure statement from Malacañang he said in effect that he was leaving to avoid bloodshed and for the good of the nation.

The popular uprising began right after the failure and adjournment of the impeachment trial on its 24th day, on account of the suppression by the 11 senator-judges of crucial evidence on the president's secret bank account of P3.2 billion. Citizens who had enthusiastically joined the rallies demanding Estrada's resignation and the millions more who watched or followed his impeachment trial on television, radio, and the print media for several months, had become familiar with the issues raised against the president, and with the Articles of Impeachment and the evidence disclosed by the prosecution lawyers and an array of witnesses. Moreover, they fully witnessed how the legal system and the impeachment process work, revealing how defense lawyers and the pro-Estrada senators collaborated to conceal the truth about the president's corruption and betrayal of the public trust.

Spontaneously, more and more people gathered along EDSA, from Ortigas Ave. to Camp Aguinaldo, from the night of January 16. Vice President Macapagal-Arroyo's negotiating team had given Estrada until the morning of the 20th to leave Malacañang, but the embattled president wanted five more days. In the afternoon of January 19 Defense Secretary Orlando Mercado, AFP Chief of Staff Angelo Reyes and other top generals, and the deputy head of the Philippine National Police joined the mammoth crowd at EDSA to announce the withdrawal of their support from President Estrada.

In the morning of the 20th, several hundreds of demonstrators marched to Malacañang to pressure the embattled president to resign. Shortly after noon Vice President Macapagal-Arroyo took her oath as president of the Philippines before Chief Justice Hilario Davide Jr. This prompted the deposed president to leave the palace with his family and return to his home in San Juan.

Popular Participation and Acceptance of People Power 2

A WEEK AFTER ESTRADA'S OUSTER and President Gloria Macapagal-Arroyo's oath-taking as president, on January 27, 2001, the Social Weather Stations (SWS) conducted a survey of voters in Metro Manila. In the words of the SWS, 70% of those interviewed said that People Power 2 expressed the sentiment of the majority of the voters and not just a few of them. For the upper-class (AB), the middle-class (C), the lower-class (D), and the poorest class (E), the percentages were 70, 76, 66, and 77, respectively. Significantly, proportionately more (77%) of the poor, the so-called Estrada *masa* or basic constituency, agreed that his ouster and the succession of President Macapagal-Arroyo reflected the sentiment of the majority of the people and not only of a few.

There was great public interest in the impeachment trial as an unprecedented political event and the best-ever television and radio soap opera. In particular, 86% of Metro Manilans had watched the live telecast on January 16 when the senators voted 11-10 not to open the "second envelope" supposed to contain records of the Equitable-PCI Bank deposit of President Estrada under an alias, Jose Velarde. Eighty percent called the suppression of the evidence "an unjust decision". Rumors had been rife that senators were partial to the president because they had been paid handsomely for their support.

The SWS survey report goes on to say: "The sudden bursting out of People Power thereafter can be explained as due to the betrayal of the common trust, among a very great majority of citizens, whether pro-conviction, pro-acquittal, or neutral, in the fairness of the impeachment trial process. This commonality was the main finding of the January 6-9 ABS-CBN/SWS survey." People Power 2 in Metro Manila alone, not counting the rallies in other cities, was an impressive show of civic participation. "Thirteen percent of those surveyed, all voting-age adults, had attended rallies from January 16 to 20. This corresponds to some 840,000 persons, of whom 770,000 were angry about the 11-10 vote. They were accompanied by youth from 8 % of all households in Metro Manila, or an estimated 175,000 households."

The national ABS-CBN/SWS survey of February 2 and 3 showed that people nationwide had generally the same views as the people in Metro Manila. Sixty percent of Filipinos viewed live on television the impeachment trial on January 16 when the 11-10 vote blocked the opening of the second envelope, and 12% heard it on radio. Seventy percent of the nation said it was unjust. Three percent, all adults (about 1.2 million), said they had personally joined rallies. Nearly 4% (at least 1.7 million) said some youth from their households joined the rallies. Seventy-one percent said People Power 2 expressed the sentiment of the majority, compared to 28% that said it represented only that of a few.

Fifty-six percent said that Gloria Macapagal-Arroyo's right to be president is based on People Power; 23% on the Supreme Court's ruling of a vacancy; 20% on the Catholic Church's support; and 18% on the withdrawal of the military and police of their support from the deposed president. By pointing to People Power and the Supreme Court's ruling as the main reasons for the right of Vice President Macapagal-Arroyo to be president the people underscore her legitimacy as president and the justness of President Estrada's removal from the presidency. Only 9% said Macapagal-Arroyo had no right to become president.

Moreover, 53% agreed and only 21% disagreed with the statement "Even if the military and police had not withdrawn support from former President Estrada, People Power would still have succeeded in removing him." Estrada's loss of legitimacy and effectiveness is further shown by the agreement of 55% with the statement "Even if Joseph Estrada had stayed in power, he would no longer be able to lead the country effectively, because very few citizens would obey him"; only 21% disagreed.

It can therefore be said that People Power 2 was a massive exercise in direct democracy after the institution of impeachment had failed because of the inability of the senator-judges, and the senate as an institution, to act with the integrity, impartiality, and wisdom that the people had expected of them. People Power 2 manifested from January 16 to 20, 2001, was an extraordinary assertion of popular sovereignty that resulted in the incapacity of President Estrada to govern, his peaceful removal from office, and his succession by Vice President Macapagal-Arroyo.

The validity and legitimacy of People Power was demonstrated in a number of ways. As the SWS surveys revealed, People Power reflected the sentiment of the majority of the people and not just that of a few. On January 19, most Cabinet members resigned and the Armed Forces of the Philippines and Philippine National Police withdrew their support from the beleaguered president. On January 20, amid nearly a million people at the EDSA shrine and beyond, Vice President Macapagal-Arroyo took her oath as president before Chief Justice Davide. The Supreme Court had authorized the chief justice to administer the oath. Representing the senate and the House of Representatives, respectively, Senate President Aquilino Pimentel and Speaker Arnulfo Fuentebella participated in the oath-taking ceremony. Through the diplomatic corps and the messages of heads of state, the international community gave its recognition to the Macapagal-Arroyo presidency.

Immediately the peso appreciated, the stock market revived, and public and business optimism replaced pessimism. These were additional economic and psychological indicators of the legitimacy of People Power 2. A few weeks later the senate and the House of Representatives approved President Macapagal-Arroyo's nomination of Sen. Teofisto Guingona as vice president.

Criticism and Justification of People Power 2

DESPITE HIS DEPARTURE LETTER admitting the end of his presidency, Estrada and his partisans would insist that he had been forcibly removed by People Power 2 and that this was unconstitutional and unjust. In what appeared as an antedated letter to the senate president, the deposed president said that he had taken a leave from the presidency and that President Gloria Macapagal-Arroyo was holding her office only as acting president. Estrada and his lawyers would assert and maintain this view as the ousted president faced criminal charges of plunder, graft and corruption, and perjury, among others, and as more of his cronies and former associates in high office offered to testify against him. If the Supreme Court would rule in his favor, Estrada would invoke his immunity from criminal prosecution as the incumbent president.

In a *Time* magazine article (February 19) carrying his byline, the ousted president referred to People Power 2 as "mob rule", "a lynching", and "a very dangerous precedent". He referred to the Arroyo government as "illegitimate" and said: "We face a constitutional crisis that impairs not just the presidency, but the rest of government and its democratic institutions." He continues to ignore the truth about himself and the nation he has betrayed.

Foreign criticism of People Power 2 was voiced by correspondents and commentators in *Time, Newsweek, Far East Economic Review*, and other periodicals. People Power 2 was described by the critics as mob rule, a constitutional coup, an assertion of military power, a coup by the rich and powerful against the poor who supported the deposed president, a bad habit of changing an undesired president, and disrespect or violation of the Constitution and its provision for removal of the president by impeachment.

To this criticism Filipino leaders and media commentators responded by recounting the long, open, popular, and participatory process of exposing and investigating President Estrada's alleged abuse of presidential powers and acts of corruption, culminating in the investigation by senate Blue Ribbon committee, and the aborted impeachment process. Unknown to many, the SWS surveys in late January and early February would disclose how the people had believed all along in upholding and observing constitutional rules and democratic practice in determining the innocence or guilt of President Estrada. Moreover, they had justified the validity and legitimacy of People Power 2 in the ways described in the analysis above.

Far from being weakened by People Power 2, Filipino democracy has been strengthened by it and given a new beginning and opportunity to reform itself and work for the common good.

Before continuing with the assessment of the implications for Filipino democracy of the impeachment trial and the ouster of President Estrada and his replacement by President Gloria Macapagal-Arroyo, it is in order to consider the larger context of these events in the re-democratization of the political system and the consolidation of democracy since People Power 1 in 1986.

II. Re-Democratization and Consolidation of Democracy (1986-1998)

ESTRADA'S RISE TO THE PRESIDENCY and his downfall should be put in the context of the transition from Marcos's authoritarian rule to the re-establishment of democracy under President Corazon C. Aquino and President Fidel V. Ramos. More deeply and broadly, that context includes some basic and chronic problems of the country and the systemic problems of democratization and political consolidation to undo over 13 years of authoritarianism.

That context included certain problems the Philippines shared with other newly restored democracies since 1974: (1) major insurgencies (communist, Moros); (2) ethnic-communal conflicts apart from the insurgencies; (3) extreme and widespread poverty; (4) severe socio-economic inequality; (5) chronic inflation; (6) substantial external debt; and (7) terrorism.

Following EDSA-People Power 1 and Marcos's exile, President Aquino began dismantling the authoritarian regime by discarding the 1973 Constitution that had institutionalized the Marcos dictatorship. Ironically, she had to set up a revolutionary government under her Freedom Constitution in order to start rebuilding democracy. Even as she restored political rights and civil liberties, she made law by executive fiat until a new Constitution could be written and then ratified by the electorate in February 1987 and the members of Congress elected three months later. Elections for local officials would follow.

The 1987 Constitution established a democratic and republican state with its separation of powers and checks and balance, safeguards against the resurgence of authoritarianism, a strengthened bill of rights, provisions for participatory governance and local and regional autonomy, and many other progressive features. The independence of the judiciary was being restored. Constitutional commissions for the conduct of elections, for the civil service, and for government audit were given back their autonomy. Principles and policies encouraged the institutionalization of democracy under the rule of law.

The democratic space invigorated the newly freed press and broadcast media. It gave rise to thousands more people's organizations and NGOs (non-government organizations) in civil society demanding and achieving participation in public decision-making and programs. Monopolies were broken up, and the economy was liberalized and deregulated. Several public corporations were privatized. The Presidential Commission on Good Government sequestered the enterprises and assets of Marcos and his cronies and initiated the recovery of his ill-gotten wealth. A comprehensive agrarian reform program was instituted. Peace talks were held with the Moro National Liberation Front and the Cordillera People's Liberation Army on the one hand, and with the National Democratic Front on the other. Congress implemented constitutional provisions promoting regional autonomy for Muslim Mindanao, devolution, and local autonomy.

The politicized military had to be reoriented to its professional role in a democracy under civilian supremacy. But from 1986 to 1989 its Right wing faction would stage six coup attempts to overthrow the Aquino administration and newly restored democracy and thus set back the government's economic recovery. The national police was separated from the Armed Forces and placed under the Department of the Interior and Local Government. Remarkably, after all the coup attempts had been put down the military and the police were effectively reoriented away from their powerful roles as partners and guarantors of the Marcos dictatorship. The military rebels were extended amnesty and some of their leaders sought power through elective office. One of them became a senator.

Elections have been largely free, honest, and credible even if marred by some irregularities, and occasional violence, vote-buying, and fraud. The senatorial election in 1992 was compromised by the so-called *dagdag-bawas* (adding and shaving) of votes in the official canvassing for certain candidates. Still, the integrity of elections as a primary institution of democracy has been considerably restored compared with their sham practice during the authoritarian rule. In the 1998 presidential, congressional and local elections 88% of the voters regarded the voting in their precinct as clean and free, according to a survey of the Social Weather Stations. Yet in some regions political warlords continued to dominate the political scene.

At the same time, the cost of political campaigns and elections and staying in office have been rising, putting increased pressure on elected officials to recover their expenses and prepare for the next election by raising funds through corruption, patronage, and political favors. The pressure on politicians to inform the public and keep a good public image induces some of them to corrupt susceptible media practitioners.

For the consolidation of the newly restored democracy the holding of the fairly free and fair presidential election in 1992 was crucial. Despite allegations of cheating by a defeated presidential candidate, most people regarded that election as credible. Fidel Ramos won with a narrow plurality over his closest rival, Miriam Defensor Santiago. Ramos had the support of President Aquino, who wanted to ensure the defeat of two candidates most identified with Marcos: Eduardo Cojuangco and Imelda Marcos herself.

President Aquino's legacy to the nation included the dismantling of the Marcos regime, the restoration of democratic institutions, the jump-starting of the economy, the taming of the Rightist military, the strengthening of civil society, and the holding of presidential, senatorial, congressional, and local elections. She set a personal example of a decent, honest, accountable, and dedicated president as the opposite of the unlamented dictator.

For his part, President Ramos appreciably advanced the country's economic recovery and favorable image to investors and tourists, its political stability and infrastructure development, and democratization. He also succeeded in signing a peace treaty with the Moro National Liberation Front and persuaded its leader to seek election as governor of the Autonomous Region in Muslim Mindanao and head a Mindanao peace and development council.

'Electoral Democracy'

IT WAS UNDER the formally restored and operating democracy after EDSA 1 and under the 1987 Constitution that the popular former movie idol and municipal mayor, Joseph Estrada, became senator in 1987, vice-president in 1992, and president in 1998. Where Eduardo Cojuangco and Imelda Marcos before him had failed, Estrada succeeded in becoming president. As a Marcos loyalist, he was the lucky beneficiary of the rebuilding democracy and recovering economy albeit with their imperfections and inadequacies.

On the basis of a critical and comparative (international) assessment, however, it must be said that Filipino democracy is more of what political scientists call an "electoral democracy" or a "procedural democracy", rather than a "substantive democracy". The former is one in which the principal leaders are chosen through regular and relatively fair, honest, and peaceful elections, and in which the major parties alternate in power. In addition to this, a "substantive democracy" enables most of the people to realize and enjoy not only their political and civil rights but also their social and economic rights—to achieve a decent level of living and social security under the rule of law. The chronic problems of mass poverty, unemployment, inequity, rebellion, and ineffective governance are indicators of the lack of "substantive democracy" in the Philippines. And even its "electoral democracy" admittedly suffers from certain flaws.

However, it should be recognized that since 1986 Filipinos have defended their restored democracy against several coup attempts and peacefully ousted two presidents who had become notorious for their massive corruption and grave abuse of power. There seems to be a greater awareness of the urgent need to effect basic reforms to reduce poverty, improve governance, and hasten development.

III. Estrada's Impact on Politics, Government and Society

Estrada's Election as President in 1998

FROM THE OUTSET of the presidential campaign Vice President Joseph Estrada was perceived as the candidate to beat. He scored high in all political surveys, way ahead of all the possible and actual rivals. His widespread popularity was based on his image as a former leading movie hero, his captivating campaign slogan, "*Erap para sa mahirap*", and his persona as a simple and unsophisticated college dropout, and a down-to-earth, approachable leader. Most people called him Erap, an inverted spelling of the Filipino word for *pare* (*compadre* or buddy). Hilarious Erap jokes at his expense made him a household name. To many, his being the vice president made him a credible aspirant to the next higher office.

His opponents and critics derided him as *babaero* (womanizer), *lasinggero* (heavy drinker), *sugalero* (gambler), and *bobo* (ignorant and unprepared). But these qualities made many ordinary people identify with, if not fantasize about, him. What qualifications Erap obviously lacked he said he would make up for by seeking the advice of experienced leaders and needed experts. More to his advantage, his several rivals would divide the votes he would not get. Consequently, rich businessmen, especially

Chinese-Filipino, filled up his campaign chest, making him the richest candidate by far.

Erap's popularity, superior resources and resulting bandwagon—*Jeep ni Erap*—proved inexorable and to many irresistible. His rivals share of the votes said it all: As against Estrada's 39.86%; Speaker Jose de Venecia got 15.8%; Sen. Raul Roco, 13.83%; Gov. Lito Osmeña, 12.44%; Manila Mayor Alfredo Lim, 8.71%; Secretary Renato de Villa, 4.86%, and the five other minor candidates a combined total of just over 4%. Estrada obtained 10.7 million votes against the 4.3 million of his closest rival, De Venecia. "The most striking characteristic of the 1998 election," according to the SWS, "is how Joseph 'Erap' Estrada was rejected, by a small but significant margin, by the ABC or middle-to-upper classes, but nevertheless won easily due to mass support among the D and E classes."

For vice president, Sen. Gloria Macapagal-Arroyo won by even more votes and a higher plurality than Estrada. Macapagal-Arroyo got 12.6 million votes, or almost 50% of the total votes cast, as against Sen. Edgardo Angara's 5.6 million votes, or 22%. Reflecting the edge enjoyed by celebrities like Estrada, from showbiz, or from sports, were the four top senatorial candidates: Loren Legarda-Leviste, Rene Cayetano, Vicente Sotto III, and Robert Jaworski.

The 1998 elections underlined the worsening problem of "money politics". Campaign contributions and spending by the millions and a few billions were corrupting the practitioners, beneficiaries and benefactors alike: Estrada, some of the candidates and supporters he financed, the voters who cashed in on his campaign money, and the big donors themselves who expected and later demanded their reward after his election as president. Time and again, President Estrada would return the favor of his big contributors and ask government officials to help them get what they wanted. In the impeachment trial, star prosecution witness Chavit Singson testified that the president's liaison man with media received P2 million a month from the *jueteng* protection money for help and bribes to media practitioners.

The Revised Election Code and related laws and rules and the Commission on Elections were simply not equal to the task of regulating campaign funding and other excesses. Worse, President Estrada felt compelled to pay back his enormous debts to his financiers. He also deepened his dependence on some of them as allies in making big and easy money through various scams, as revealed in the impeachment trial.

Estrada's Character Flaw and Lack of Work Ethic

DURING THE PRESIDENTIAL CAMPAIGN Estrada's rivals and critics, and particularly religious leaders led by Jaime Cardinal Sin, emphasized that Estrada's immoral private life (his several mistresses, gambling, and drinking) disqualified him from election to the highest office. His supporters, particularly, the so-called *masa* or the poor who make up a majority, and some intellectuals, opted to overlook these moral shortcomings as essentially a private matter; they wanted to believe that his preferential option for the poor, if you will, was genuine and it compensated for his private immorality. His opponents did not present any evidence concerning his involvement in graft and corruption during his 40 years of public service.

For him and his supporters it seemed to be the time for trying a presidential leadership of a different kind: unsophisticated and pragmatic and eminently pro-poor, charismatic, and popular. This would be a departure from the leadership of well-educated, professional, and experienced presidents that had nonetheless failed to change the condition of the majority of poor citizens. Estrada was even compared by some to Ramon Magsaysay, a simple man who loved the people and was loved by them, a leader who dedicated his presidency to the amelioration of poverty and to good government.

Estrada's presidency and impeachment trial proved his critics and rivals right and his supporters wrong. His gross private immorality easily became public immorality in the face of great temptations to corruption and unprecedented opportunities for personal enrichment. In the case of Estrada, as with Marcos, ingrained personal immorality, a serious character flaw, inevitably impacted on his presidency with grave public consequences. This is why Jaime Cardinal Sin, who predicted that an Estrada presidency would be disastrous for the nation, was credible in his call to Estrada to resign soon after Gov. Chavit Singson testified in the senate on Estrada's enrichment through bribery and corruption involving *jueteng* money and income from excise tax on tobacco.

As it turned out, Estrada had no work ethic either. Some of his close associates would admit that he did not devote as much time to his duties, to reading papers and reports, and holding consultations with different groups. Given his deficient background and knowledge, he was handicapped as president and chief executive. Consequently, he liked to assert his superior status as president by reminding others of his power and by bullying them. *"Sino ba ang presidente?"* *"Mag-presidente muna sila."*

In the midst of the senate hearings on Singson's revelations and then his impeachment trial, Malacañang tried to project the image of a reinvented Estrada working hard, abolishing his Midnight Cabinet, abstaining from drinking, and moving around the country to attend to the people's needs and problems. To shore up his eroding base with the poor, his office publicized his distribution of public housing and land titles to his constituents. More than ever, he tried to validate his commitment in his slogan, *Erap para sa mahirap.* He mobilized his *masa* supporters by portraying the calls for his resignation and his impeachment as a conspiracy of the rich against him and the poor, led by the Makati Business Club.

Erap's *Barkadahan* and Personalism Weakened Institutions

ESTRADA WAS INTENSELY PERSONAL in his perspective, perceptions, and relationships. This quality endeared him to his friends and associates and supporters as the mark of a very human and humane person. However, in its excesses this personalism and *barkada* syndrome would often get in the way of perceiving, understanding, and dealing with problems and relationships in terms of policy and institutions. The latter the president must do if he is to extend the scope and reach of his power and authority to benefit large constituencies and the nation as a whole.

Estrada's intense personalism meant that he had little understanding and appreciation of the importance of institutions, and his duty as president of working with and through institutions the better to improve and strengthen them. He was most comfortable with and preferred small, informal groups that related to him personally. He was at ease in small meetings with leaders, technocrats and businessmen. He was most comfortable and happy with his Midnight Cabinet, reportedly consisting of his drinking, gambling buddies, and business partners. They had common interests and dislikes and they were bound by personal ties of reciprocity and shared secrets.

For one of his limited intellectual grasp and executive experience, the large official Cabinet overseeing various departments and agencies of the national bureaucracy was difficult to lead and manage: its meetings involved complex issues and problems and institutional interdependence that would test his understanding and responses. Preferring to deal with individual legislators, he discontinued the institutionalized collaboration with the senate and the House through the Legislative-Executive Development Advisory Council (Ledac) that enabled President Ramos to get legislative support for the smooth enactment of his reform legislation.

President Estrada's irregular, if not illegal, interventions in certain government agencies violated their integrity and autonomous operations. The media reported various instances where the president favored his biggest campaign contributor, Lucio Tan, including his acquiring the majority interest in the Philippine Airlines and the Philippine National Bank, getting a loan of P600 million for the Philippine National Bank with inadequate collateral, and evading full payment of his taxes on his tobacco company. The president's impeachment trial disclosed that he was a business partner of Dante Tan's BW Resources that made billions in insider trading, and that the president interfered in the investigation of Tan by the Securities and Exchange Commission, a quasi-judicial agency. He had also transferred this agency to the Office of the President to increase his control over it.

Moreover, on his orders and allegedly for his private gain, pension funds of the Government Service Insurance System (GSIS) and the Social Security System were invested in big business acquisitions and mergers and behest loans of the Philippine National Bank. By his interventions, Estrada directly contributed to the collapse of the stock market through the local and foreign investors' loss of confidence in its operations, in the government, and the business environment in general. He revived the crony capitalism in Marcos's time and undermined the efforts of President Aquino and President Ramos to dismantle monopolies and ensure a level playing field for business. He also contributed to the laundering of ill-gotten money by the banking system and allegedly some questionable acts of the Central Bank as well.

President Estrada tended in other ways to regard public office as his private and personal preserve. In the impeachment trial the prosecution showed that he used Malacañang and his official residence in the many corrupt deals that enabled him to amass his enormous ill-gotten wealth. His wife and their son, San Juan Mayor Jinggoy Estrada, directly intervened in the allocation of resources and ambulances to various recipients. Elected chairman of the League of Municipalities because of his father, Jinggoy would have his name painted on the ambulances. His brother

Jude once used the presidential plane in a trip to Mindanao. When the media criticized this improper behavior, the president virtually justified it. Apparently, his mistresses were enormously enriched through his influence; they built mansions, expanded their businesses and displayed luxurious lifestyles.

A Disgraced and Weakened Presidency

IN THE VARIOUS WAYS DESCRIBED, Estrada compromised, weakened and disgraced the presidency in a manner that only the dictator Marcos could match or exceed. It will take a great deal of exemplary conduct and superior performance for President Macapagal-Arroyo and succeeding presidents to rehabilitate this primary institution of constitutional democracy and governance.

The Constitution and laws may have to be revised to prevent presidential abuse and corruption. The extreme difficulty of removing an unworthy president by impeachment may gain support for a shift from the traditional presidential system to the parliamentary system. Hopefully, enlightened voters, civil-society organizations, and political parties will examine more carefully and critically the character and record of candidates for public office. There will be increasing demands for reforms toward a "new politics" of character, competence, policies and programs, and responsible and committed parties; and away from the traditional politics of personality, popularity, patronage, corruption, and unprincipled parties and party hopping, as exemplified by so-called "tradpols" or "trapos".

Damaged Congress

DESPITE SUBSTANTIAL GAINS in regaining their independence from the executive and performing their legislative functions and instituting reforms mandated by the 1987 Constitution, the House and senate suffered setbacks under the Estrada presidency. Not one who understood the importance of institutions, the president tended to look at senators and congressmen more as individual political leaders to be won over and kept friendly and beholden to him by personal relations of reciprocity with each of them. He relied heavily on satisfying them through personal favors, pork barrel, and gifts that amount to bribes. Nor, again, did he relate to legislators as party members or through the Legislative-Executive Advisory Council (Ledac).

The 11-10 vote to suppress the truth and obstruct justice in the impeachment trial disillusioned and angered the people and turned them against the pro-Estrada senator-judges. The insensitivity and arrogance of partisan power manifested in the senate damaged its reputation as the supposedly more statesmanlike chamber of Congress and training ground of future presidents. The apparent incompetence of certain senators who had been elected mainly because of their popularity as movie or television entertainers or athletes diminished the stature of the senate. Consequently, future revision of the Constitution may favor the abolition of the senate and the shift to a unicameral legislature.

Earlier on, in gagging Governor Singson as he testified in its hearings, the House betrayed its extreme partisanship and its indifference to the pursuit of truth regarding the alleged wrongdoing of the president. Recurring reports of irregularities, mediocrity and abuse of power by some representatives, and of the frequent waste of scarce resources allocated to public works, have tarnished the image of the House. The record of the House suggests the advantage of electing many more legislators by using the party-list method, which would better assure the selection of competent leaders committed to party policies and platforms.

Enhancing the Independence and Integrity of the Judiciary

WHILE THE JUDICIARY and the Supreme Court had lost their integrity and independence during the Marcos dictatorship, much has happened in reforming them during the Aquino, Ramos, and Estrada presidencies. This was made possible by reforms mandated by the 1987 Constitution, through legislation, and by improvements introduced by the Supreme Court. Chief Justice Davide's sterling performance as presiding officer of the senate in its role as impeachment court elicited the nation's admiration and this added to the prestige of the Supreme Court. This will serve him and the high tribunal well in pushing for more judicial reforms. To his credit, it was President Estrada who appointed Chief Justice Davide.

From 'Electoral or Procedural Democracy' to 'Substantive Democracy'

IMPORTANT AND DESIRABLE as they may be in themselves, reforms and improvements in the structures and functions and operations of the electoral system, the presidency, Congress, the judiciary, the bureaucracy, the military and police, and local governments—the crucial test of Filipino democracy is the test of policy and program performance to benefit all the people. It may be added that "substantive democracy" in the Filipino context means free and credible elections, plus the rule of law and the fulfillment of the vision of "the good society" (*ang magandang lipunan*) as may be discerned in the provisions of the 1987 Constitution and the people's aspirations.

The Filipino "good society" is one that is free, peaceful, pluralistic and united, prosperous and progressive, egalitarian, just, and humane—achieved through a dynamic political, economic, social and cultural democracy, and one that is "God-centered", loving and truthful (*maka-Diyos, mapagmahal, makatotohanan*) as described in the Constitution and affirmed in national social surveys.

A Crisis of Political Leadership

THE SO-CALLED EDSA 3 or "Poor People Power" that sent thousands of poor people on a violent march to Malacañang on May 1, 2001, was organized by leaders loyal to the ousted president, several of whom were senatorial or local candidates in the May 14 elections—in hopes of restoring him as president. The alarming rampage to seize the president's office and residence was viewed by millions of Filipinos on their television screen, even as its instigators disclaimed participation in the uprising. Although it was eventually put down by army reinforcements of the presidential security and the police, the uprising was a powerful warning that the nation's legions of poor people, once sufficiently empowered, may finally rise against a society and political system they judge to be hopelessly unjust and oppressive.

If EDSA 1 gave the nation it's second chance for the restoration and consolidation of Filipino democracy, EDSA 2 is the nation's third chance to reform its "electoral democracy" and seriously bring about "substantive democracy". Failing at this time, it may take a very long while for the Filipinos to emerge from anarchy, misery, and a resurgent authoritarianism in the midst of a revolution.

Looking at the larger picture, with historical hindsight, the nation is in the grip of a crisis of leadership. President Gloria Macapagal-Arroyo, the senate, the House of Representatives, and local government officials must summon the political will to do together what must be done to reverse course. The Filipino people must move toward the national vision of "the good society"—"a just and humane society"—embodied in the 1987 Constitution.

Hopefully, through nationalistic and determined leadership and unrelenting hard work the lofty purposes and practical objectives of People Power 2 will be gradually achieved. In this way Filipino democracy will be consolidated and its vitality, creativity, resourcefulness, and viability ensured. This will require understanding and learning the lessons of People Power 1 and 2, and making People Power 3 unnecessary.

Did the Estrada Administration Benefit the Poor?

ARSENIO M. BALISACAN

Introduction

POVERTY REDUCTION as development initiative was not unique to the Estrada administration. While centerpiece programs of past and incumbent administrations differ, poverty-reduction goals have always been a feature of development planning during the postwar period. But the Estrada administration may be considered the most vocal about its intention to reach out to the poor. As soon as Joseph Ejercito Estrada assumed the presidency in 1998, he declared that he would work for the eradication of poverty in the Philippines, beginning with the poorest of the poor.

The Estrada administration's slogan, *Erap para sa mahihirap*, was seen and heard ostentatiously everywhere in the country. It became a battle cry of government. The catchy phrase, along with the way former President Estrada spoke and ate with the poor, reinforced his pro-poor image. The poor, the *masa*, saw themselves in him. Erap gave them hope. It is thus no wonder he enjoyed strong support among the poor.

But did the deposed president live up to this pro-poor image and translate his pronouncements into action and more importantly, results? What exactly did his administration do to ease the lives of the poor who voted and supported him? Are there fewer poor people now than before he became president? These are some questions that need answers notwithstanding former President Estrada's aborted term. The intention is to examine the myths, facts, and policies of the Estrada presidency vis-à-vis poverty reduction and, in so doing, draw lessons for future anti-poverty programs.

The Poverty Alleviation Program of the Estrada Administration

THE ESTRADA ADMINISTRATION came to power with lavish pro-poor agenda. It recognized the imperative of *bringing broad-based rural development, led by agriculture, to win the war against poverty*. Its Medium-Term Philippine Development Plan (MTPDP) 1999-2004 identifies the main elements of development strategies required to spur growth and sustainable development in rural areas. The plan, for example, envisages an aggressive delivery of basic social development services, removal of policy and regulatory distortions inhibiting resource allocation efficiency and equitable outcomes, sustained development of rural infrastructure, improvement in governance, and macroeconomic stability.

In practice, the Estrada administration's front line initiative for poverty alleviation was the Lingap Para sa Mahihirap Program (hereafter referred to simply as Lingap) coordinated by the newly organized National Anti-Poverty Commission (NAPC). The program aimed to deliver a range of services and interventions through six national government agencies to 100 poorest families in each province and city. Assuming that there was no leakage of program benefits to the non-poor, the program would be able to benefit about 16,100 families, or a mere 0.4% of all poor families in 1997.

Lingap was built upon the institutions, particularly local networks, set up by previous administrations, such as the Social Reform Council of the Ramos administration. The local government units (LGUs) played a key role in the implementation. NAPC provided overall coordination and implementation monitoring. The Department of the Interior and Local Government (DILG) meanwhile assumed the role of facilitating linkages with the LGUs. It was also given the responsibility in identifying the 100 poorest families in each province and city. Regional directors, governors and mayors were assigned to identify 100 poorest families from four or five poorest *barangays* in their respective jurisdictions based on indicators such as minimum basic needs (MBN), human development index (HDI), location, occupation/nature of employment, and primary resource base. The senators and congressional representatives also played a key role, particularly in the disbursement of the Lingap funds.

The General Appropriations Act (GAA) for 1999 appropriated P2.5 billion to the program. NAPC reports show that as of December 2000, or after about two years of implementation, the six Lingap agencies disbursed a total of P2.48 billion and were able to accomplish the following: 1) establishment of deepwells in 390 *barangays* and 200 rural waterworks system; 2) establishment, repair, and improvement of day care and crisis centers, and provision of protective services including educational assistance to 6,968 families; 3) processing of health insurance for more than 16,000 families, upgrading of equipment of government hospitals and health centers, and implementation of several packages of Sustansya para sa Masa Matching Grant; 4) house improvement or land purchase of more than 14,000 families; 5) establishment of more than 4,000 Erap sari-sari stores nationwide, rice subsidy, and emergency relief assistance due to the Mayon volcano eruption and the conflict in Mindanao; and 6) revolving fund grants for the livelihood projects of cooperatives and the 100 poorest families.

How did the Estrada administration's approach and funding support to poverty reduction differ from that of the Ramos administration? First of all, the Ramos administration focused on raising the level of overall economic growth through improvement in economic efficiency and global competitiveness of local industries. At the same time, it put in place a social reform program aimed at lifting the socioeconomic conditions of lagging areas or regions. This program, dubbed the Social Reform Agenda (SRA), constituted a package of government interventions aimed at addressing poverty in the country's 20 poorest provinces and target groups. These priority provinces and groups were chosen based on gravity of poverty, existence of armed conflict, and isolation and special development needs. As shown elsewhere (see Balisacan et al., 2000), for any given amount of budget for poverty reduction, this approach is far superior to the Estrada's Lingap initiative. Moreover, the amount allotted for direct poverty reduction was much smaller under the Estrada administration (P2.5 billion for 1999 compared with an average of P3.0 billion a year). And of the Lingap fund of P2.5 billion, about 68% was under the direct control of national and local politicians—the area, project, or activity had to be identified by them. The Lingap budget was thus largely a pork barrel, which Joseph Estrada had promised precisely to do away.

Poverty Before and After Erap

IN 1997, or one year before the Estrada administration was installed, poverty incidence in the country stood at 32%. This means that there were about 4.6 million households (or 27.3 million people) below the official poverty line. The Estrada administration, as indicated in the MTPDP, intended to bring down poverty incidence to 25-28% by 2004, or a reduction of at least four percentage points. President Estrada himself, however, declared a more ambitious target, to reduce poverty incidence to 20% by the end of his term.

Despite its resounding rhetoric for the war against poverty, the Estrada administration failed to lower poverty incidence to its target. By the end of 2000, "best estimates"—based even on the highly unlikely situation that the changes in aggregate income from 1998 to 2000 was distributionally neutral—suggest that poverty incidence could have fallen by at most one percentage point between 1997 and 2000. To be sure, poverty incidence could have increased to 33.0% in 1998, when per capita income declined by 2.6% owing to a combination of the El Niño phenomenon and the Asian crisis. The drought that year caused agricultural output to contract by 6.7%. Then poverty incidence could have fallen to 31% following a recovery, albeit minimal, of economic growth in 1999 and 2000. But since population continued to increase at 2.1% a year, the number of poor people could have even increased from 27.2 million in 1997 to 28.3 million in 2000.

Official poverty estimates indicate that poverty declined by an average of one percentage point a year during 1985-1997. Another set of estimates—one in which consistency in poverty comparison over time is ensured—suggests a more substantial decline of 1.3 percentage points a year during this period (see Balisacan, 2000). By international standard, this rate of reduction is slower than that seen in East Asia and Pacific as a whole (1.6 percentage point a year), though comparable to that in China and Indonesia. Still this is remarkable considering that the growth of the Philippine economy during 1985-1997 (2.9% a year) was substantially lower than in virtually all developing East Asian and Pacific countries, especially China (7.8 % a year) and Indonesia (6.3% a year).

The difference in the rate of poverty reduction is even more stark if the comparison is between 1994-97 (Ramos years) and 1999-2000 (Estrada years). During these "Ramos years", when the country's output grew by about 5.0% a year, poverty incidence declined at an average rate of

2.4 percentage points per year (Balisacan, 2000). In contrast, the Estrada years saw poverty incidence declining at an average of only 0.75 percentage point a year and output growth hovering around 3.0% a year. Recall that the Ramos administration focused on accelerating the pace of economic growth by building on international competitiveness of domestic industries, reforming regulation of services and industry (mainly commercial banking, transportation, and telecommunication), and investing in basic infrastructure.

The Poor's Access to Basic Social Services

POVERTY HAS SO FAR BEEN SEEN only in terms of income. While income provides a fairly reasonable indication of the overall living standards of the population, it is usually also important to look at non-income indicators of well-being. Apart from directly influencing household incomes, governance—good or bad—may also influence the well-being of the poor through other channels. One of these is improvement in people's access to basic social services, particularly education, health, and nutrition as well as important amenities like electricity, water, and sanitation.

The country's performance based on these non-income measures could provide another meaningful gauge of whether or not the poor were made better off during Estrada's term. Results from the 1998 and 1999 *Annual Poverty Indicators Survey* of the National Statistics Office, the main source of nationally representative data for such indicators, have not been encouraging. (As of this writing, comparable data are not available for 2000.)

Access by poor pregnant and lactating women to nutrition and health services were worse in 1999 than in 1998. In fact, among families in the lowest 40% income group, the proportion of those with pregnant and/or lactating women members receiving iron supplements decreased in 1999. There was also a decline in the percentage of poor families whose pregnant or lactating married women were given at least two injections of *tetanus toxoid*. Moreover, during 1998 and 1999, more pregnant/lactating women in the higher income groups received iodine supplement than those women with lower incomes.

With respect to access to education, fewer families were able to send their children to school, elementary and secondary. Among families in the lowest 40% income bracket, there was a decline in the proportion of families with 6-12 years old members who sent their children to elementary schooling. In many cases, poor children have been forced out of school to work and help augment their family's income.

Access by the poor to electricity and sanitary toilets remained low although there were slight improvements. Of the lowest 40% income group, only about one-half had electricity and two-thirds had sanitary toilets.

One-third of Filipino families reported being worse off in 1999 than in the previous year. Majority, however, noted no change. The main reasons cited by those worse-off were increases in food prices and reduced income. To cope, many had to change their eating patterns, while others had to work longer hours.

By and large, while the economy rebounded in 1999 (expanding by 3.3% from a negative growth in 1998), this did not translate into improvements in people's welfare in terms of access to health, education and other social services. Worse, the year witnessed a deterioration of conditions for many of the poor.

Poverty and Agriculture

THREE OF EVERY FOUR POOR FILIPINOS live in rural areas. This indicates that poverty in the Philippines is still a largely rural phenomenon despite rapid urbanization in recent years. Moreover, majority of the poor households derive their main source of incomes from agriculture. This is not surprising since the large majority of the rural population rely on agriculture for employment and income.

Within the agricultural sector, among the poorest typically are: 1) farm workers in sugarcane, rice, corn, coconut and forestry; and 2) corn and "other crop" farmers, coconut farmers and fishermen. Rice producers normally have higher incomes and fewer members below the poverty threshold, but they contribute the bulk of overall poverty in the agricultural sector because of their huge numbers.

The traditional characterization of the poor is that the poorest of them are the landless and those depending mainly on wage incomes. This is not so. Poverty among the self-employed is at least as high as that among "wage" households. In agriculture, the poor self-employed heads of households include primarily lessees, tenants, and small owner-cultivators. They account for over one-half of the country's poor population [Balisacan, 1999].

Poor families in the agriculture sector are characterized by a high level of underemployment, partly because of the monsoon-dependent nature of agricultural production. They are also beset by inadequate access to or use of modern technology (mainly because of lack of credit) and weak access to social services, including health care and family planning. For the large number of poor owner-cultivator farmers, farm size is typically small and located in unfavorable areas (for example, outside of irrigated areas).

Any serious effort aimed at addressing the poverty problem in the Philippines must therefore grapple with the fundamental causes of under-development in agriculture and rural areas. Considering that about two-thirds of the population are dependent on agriculture, the pursuit of broad-based growth, one anchored on agricultural and rural development, is cen-tral to a strategy towards poverty reduction.

How the Agriculture Sector Fared

COGNIZANT THAT A LARGE MAJORITY of the poor live in rural areas and are dependent on agriculture and agriculture-based industries for livelihood, the Estrada administration declared agricultural modernization as one of its priority agenda in its war against poverty. In the MTPDP, it affirmed that a large part of the poverty problem could be traced to the low agricul-tural productivity. To address poverty, therefore, it aimed to accelerate ag-ricultural growth through a modernization program. It also aimed to pro-mote rural development through expansion of non-farm income-generat-ing opportunities for rural households. The Estrada administration tar-geted the agricultural sector to grow at an average of 2.6-3.4% a year.

The crafting and articulation of agricultural modernization as a weapon to fight poverty did not have to start from scratch. The Estrada adminis-tration ascended to power with a ready-made strategy for agricultural mod-ernization, thanks to the Agriculture and Fisheries Modernization Act (Afma) passed by Congress in 1997 after two years of extensive public consultations and studies—through the Congressional Commission on Agriculture—on the constraints and problems plaguing agriculture.

While the Department of Agriculture (DA) was—and still is—tasked to implement Afma, it has been hampered by serious funding con-straints, by the Estrada administration's own making. For example, in 2000, Congress appropriated P20.2 billion for the DA so that the latter could start implementing Afma, but Malacañang through the Department of Budget and Management released to the DA less than half of this amount (P8.0 billion). The department therefore has to contend with having much less than the resources required to install the foundations for agricultural modernization and enhance the quality of life of the rural population.

Nonetheless, the agricultural sector exhibited substantial growth during the Estrada administration. From a negative growth in 1998 traced largely to prolonged dry spell of the El Niño phenomenon, the sector rebounded by 6% the following year. This was led by rice production which posted an impressive growth of 38%. Sugar production posted about 24 percent, and corn production roughly 20%. Although the agriculture sector slowed down in 2000 to only 3.4%, this growth was still quite close to the target set in the MTPDP for that year (3.5- 4.1%). Overall, the average growth during the last two years was twice higher than the average for the 1980-97 period.

Considering the limited support for agriculture, its performance was truly impressive, thanks to favorable weather conditions. In 1999 and 2000, the country was visited by only about 15 to 16 typhoons each year, lower than the average number of typhoons that hit the country each year over the last two decades. Blessed by sufficient rainfall, the sector could have achieved even higher growth if support in terms of adequate irrigation, farm-to-market roads and other infrastructure, as well as stronger focus on research and development, were put in place. The presence of these support mechanisms, along with more equitable distribution of physical assets, increased public investments in physical and human capital, and sound macroeconomic and sectoral policies, could have led to a more substantial contribution by the agriculture sector in poverty reduction through its link to the growth of rural non-farm sector. In the absence of these interventions, the growth performance in 1999 and 2000 could not be sustained in the following years. Indeed, given its present state, the agriculture sector would simply get back to its long-term growth path—a mediocre growth of 1-2% a year.

To be sure, the DA, under the able leadership of then Secretary Edgardo Angara, implemented a number of measures in 1999 and 2000 to push agriculture to a higher growth path. These included an aggressive stance to R&D investment, application of modern science to agriculture (including biotechnology), investment in irrigation and farm-to-market roads, development of human capital in agriculture through trainings and scholarships, and bureaucracy restructuring to enhance efficiency, accountability, and transparency. However, these efforts could only go a little distance; they lacked strong and sustained support from the fiscal side. The bottom line was money to implement the Afma; the Estrada administration did not put its money where its mouth was.

How the Poverty Problem Could Have Been Faced

SUCCESS IN RURAL POVERTY ALLEVIATION requires the growth not only of agriculture but also of rural non-farm activities. In developing economies, where there is a high share of population in rural areas and where urban-rural links are nascent, the rural non-farm economy is very much linked to agriculture. In these economies, the main stimulus to rural industrialization-led poverty reduction is agricultural growth. Increases in agricultural productivity and farm incomes stimulate the growth of consumer demand for non-farm goods, thereby opening up employment opportunities for the poor, especially in rural areas.

Drawing from the Asian experience, broadly-based rural growth anchored on technological progress in agriculture holds the key to sustained poverty alleviation in the Philippines. This type of growth requires that the initial conditions of rural areas would have to be made more favorable than they were in recent years. Strong response of rural non-farm areas and, hence, of rural poverty to the stimulus provided by agricultural growth requires investment in rural infrastructure to lower transaction costs, removal of public-spending biases strongly favoring large farmers and agribusiness enterprises, improvement in access to land and technology, and macroeconomic and political stability.

An examination of the recent performance of provinces in poverty reduction reveals that indeed initial conditions—those relating to infrastructure, distribution of physical and human assets, and institutions—significantly account for the differences in poverty alleviation [Balisacan, 2000]. In provinces where the implementation of the agrarian reform program was relatively rapid during the last ten years, poverty reduction tended to be likewise relatively fast, suggesting that beneficiaries of the Comprehensive Agrarian Reform Program (CARP) achieved higher household incomes than comparable households not covered by the program.

Similarly, in provinces where land quality improved (through, say, irrigation development), poverty reduction was faster. Moreover, provinces with initially favorable access to markets and off-farm employment tend to have faster poverty reduction. The result confirms the common assertion that public investment in rural infrastructure, especially rural transport, generates dynamic economic linkages critical to sustained growth and development of the local economy. Meanwhile, maintaining a favorable overall investment climate for local growth also matters a lot in hastening the speed of poverty reduction.

The agriculture growth-rural industrialization link was recognized by the Estrada administration, but, again, practice lagged way behind rhetoric. Investment in social and physical capital in rural areas was nowhere as dramatic under the Estrada administration as that under its predecessor.

Targeting the Poor

WHILE SUSTAINED GROWTH is necessary, it is not sufficient to address the poverty problem. This is because socioeconomic conditions and circumstances of households vary considerably. There are some groups who are unable to participate during episodes of growth or, who may be hurt by public decisions to move the economy to a higher and sustainable growth path. These groups may include: 1) individuals who do not have the assets, particularly skills, necessary to take advantage of the opportunities offered by growth; 2) households located in geographic areas bypassed by growth; 3) households whose entitlements are shrunk by public actions chosen to bring the economy to a higher growth path; and 4) households falling into poverty traps owing to the reinforcing effects of adverse shocks and inaccessibility to credit. There is strong evidence, for example, that the Asian economic crisis hit hardest the poorest groups in society.

Evidently, policy and institutional response to the poverty problem requires more than growth-mediated (i.e., long-run) poverty alleviation initiatives. The response should as well involve direct intervention to avoid transient poverty and escape poverty traps. To be effective, however, special programs for the poor should employ a well-designed targeting approach such that program benefits accrue only to the poor. The Estrada administration's Lingap program, while it is targeted, is a poorly conceived program. What is even more surprising is that the program was launched without any regard to lessons learned from vast experience in targeted pro-poor interventions, both in the Philippines, particularly the SRA, and in many Asian countries.

Efficiency in the use of resources for poverty alleviation underlies the principle of targeting wherein benefits are channeled to the highest priority group that a program aims to serve. Targeting requires identification of the poor as distinct from the non-poor, as well as monitoring of program benefit flows to intended beneficiaries. Since it is costly to screen the poor from the non-poor—especially if this involves hundreds of thousands, if not millions, of households—a universal subsidy might be a preferable scheme to alleviate poverty. In a universal subsidy scheme, everybody in the population, regardless of income, receives a subsidy. Universal subsidy, however, is costly precisely because of the leakage of subsidies to the non-poor and excessive amounts required to alleviate if not eliminate income shortfalls of the not-so-poor.

A general food price subsidy, such as the one commonly employed by the National Food Authority (NFA), to effect poverty alleviation, is not a cost-effective scheme. NFA's rice price subsidy has a substantially high leakage of the benefits to the non-poor whose consumption account for a large share (over one half) of the total rice consumption. Clearly, if the objective is to reduce national poverty, then the general rice price subsidy is unlikely to work. [Balisacan, 2000]. To be sure, beginning early this year, the NFA has moved to refine its subsidy scheme by progressively limiting the rice subsidy only to poor areas of the country, including depressed or resettlement areas in major urban centers.

Recall that the Lingap Program of the Estrada administration applied *uniform* targeting, in the sense that it was aimed at 100 poorest households for each province and city in the country. Although this approach could have low leakage of benefits to the non-poor, it failed to reach a large percentage of the poor. Indeed, as noted earlier, the Lingap Program could cover not even 1% of the poor. Worse, the leakage to the non-poor was high.

One would also note that while the Lingap program targeted the poorest families, many of the interventions were provided at the community level rather than at the household level. While this approach contributed to higher outreach, it resulted in too much dispersion and high program cost.

Designing a Targeted Anti-Poverty Program

A TARGETED anti-poverty program must be incentive-compatible. This means that the unintended beneficiaries do not have much incentive to preempt program benefits while the intended beneficiaries do. This requires that either the cost of participation for the non-poor is high, or the channel used to transfer benefits is available and attractive mainly to the poor.

A prerequisite in designing an anti-poverty program is to identify who the poor are, where they are, and understand why they are poor. It should respond to specific needs of poor individuals and households. In some households, for instance, the intervention may lean more towards basic food needs involving, say, food stamps.

An anti-poverty program has to be clear whether its goal is to address chronic poverty (long-term) or transient (short-term) poverty. If the objective is to address transient poverty, the instrument must be directed toward the sources of vulnerability of certain households to shocks. On the other hand, if the objective is to reduce chronic poverty, then the program will have to address the distribution and quality of household entitlements—land, physical capital, human capital, financial capital, etc. A program that best applies to addressing one may not be suitable for the other, although there may be instances when a program addresses both (e.g., food-for-work program in drought-stricken rural areas).

Another consideration in designing an anti-poverty program is, of course, funding. It is unrealistic to assume that very generous fiscal resources are available for direct poverty intervention, especially during a period of macroeconomic adjustment. As noted, in reducing aggregate poverty to a certain level, a universal (untargeted) income transfer program has substantially higher fiscal costs than a targeted program employing easily observable information about potential beneficiaries. It is far less costly, for example, to reduce poverty if the anti-poverty program is intended for areas where the poor are geographically concentrated.

Monitoring and Evaluation of Pro-Poor Programs

FAILURES OF PAST pro-poor programs, including the Lingap, are in part attributable to the lack of an appropriate, credible, and responsive beneficiary impact monitoring system. Indeed, in virtually all rural development initiatives during the Estrada administration, there was no in-depth evaluation of the impact of such initiatives on welfare outcomes.

A beneficiary impact evaluation needs to be able to gauge welfare changes (or proxy indicators of such changes) attributable to the program. To be credible, it should be conducted by those persons not in any way involved in the implementation of the program.

As the results of a rapid appraisal of pro-poor programs in select rural areas suggest (see Balisacan et al., 2000), LGUs could play a critical role in the implementation of pro-poor programs. They provide the linchpin around which a number of other institutions—national government agencies, NGOs and POs—converge. It is therefore imperative that their energy and potential be harnessed in the implementation of any poverty alleviation program. Unfortunately, in the case of Lingap and many rural development programs, this has not been the case. Most LGUs have been bypassed altogether and made simply implementors of programs conceptualized at the national level. Consultations (mostly token) have been made with them only when the programs were about to be implemented. Consequently, ownership of the programs by the local governments has not been generated. This is unfortunate considering that local governments do have the proper institutional mechanisms and processes at the local level that could effectively house and customize pro-poor programs. Also, local level decisions on targeting is considered effective because typically communities have more information than central authorities.

The same rapid appraisal done at the local level also showed that the participation of intended beneficiaries has been lacking. Ideally, the participation should have involved, at the very least, consultation vis-à-vis identification of their needs and of intervention instruments.

Challenge for the Macapagal-Arroyo Administration

IN THE WAR against poverty, the Estrada administration had set high expectations which it failed to meet after more than two years in power. While it was able to reduce the proportion of the population deemed poor, the rate of reduction (less than one percentage point a year) was so slow that there are more poor people now than in 1997. On an annual basis, the rate of reduction was slower than that achieved in 1985-1997, especially in

1994-1997. Among the major Asian countries, the Estrada administration's track record in terms of poverty reduction was quite pathetic.

The major challenge for the Macapagal-Arroyo administration is to put in place good governance, restore favorable investment climate, and push the economy to a higher growth path. Contrary to common claims, the Philippines is not an exception to the usual story about growth and poverty reduction in East Asia. As in East Asia, poverty in the Philippines has been responsive to economic growth. The main reason for the relatively high poverty in the Philippines is primarily the short duration of growth and the slowness of this growth. What the relatively fast growth—sustained for over 20 years—in East Asia (especially China, Thailand, and, prior to the Asian crisis, Indonesia) means is that these countries were able reduce absolute poverty by more than half in a relatively short period of just two decades. This is a remarkable achievement unprecedented in recent history (and not eroded by the region's financial crisis).

Economic growth sustained over a long period is the key to the poverty problem in the Philippines. This growth, especially if it is broadly based, mediates the development of human capabilities for meeting basic needs. Indeed, where chronic poverty is pervasive owing mainly to the failure of the economy to generate productive employment opportunities, it is hard to imagine a more enduring solution to the poverty problem than one requiring policy and institutional reforms aimed at enhancing the economy's capacity to grow and generate these opportunities.

Priority should be given to sustaining growth in agriculture, thereby broadening the impact of growth on poverty. The effort should involve developing rural infrastructure, investing in agricultural R&D and human capital, applying modern science and information technology to agriculture, and maintaining a pricing policy regime favorable for agriculture and small- and medium-scale industrial development. As the East Asian experience demonstrates, investment in land quality and in access to land and infrastructure, together with sound "fundamentals" (i.e., fiscal and monetary restraints), are critical to the building of initial conditions for broad-based growth and development.

Growth is, of course, not enough. There are usually some groups in society whose full participation in the growth process is constrained (e.g., lack of skills required by the rapidly growing sectors). Some groups are likewise more vulnerable than others to policy and institutional reforms necessary to restore growth or to bring the economy to a higher, long-term growth path. For these groups, access to safety nets is critical to ensuring growth-with-equity outcomes. The design of these safety nets must be informed by lessons from past anti-poverty programs, including those of the Estrada administration. It is costly to the society, especially the poor, to repeat the mistakes—and follies—of the Estrada administration.

* The writer is grateful to Gemma Estrada, Magdalena Casuga, and Sharon Faye Piza for their technical assistance in the preparation of this article, but takes sole responsibility for it.

REFERENCES

Balisacan, Arsenio M. (1999). "Poverty Profile in the Philippines: An Update and Reexamination in the Wake of the Asian Crisis." Report prepared for the World Bank, Washington, D.C.

Balisacan, Arsenio M. (2000). "Growth, Redistribution, and poverty: Is the Philippines an Exception to the Standard Asian Story?" *Journal of the Asia Pacific Economy*, Vol. 5 (1/2), pp/ 125-140.

Balisacan, Arsenio M., Rosemarie Edillon, Alex Brillantes, and Dante Canlas (2000). Approaches to Targeting the Poor. Manila: United Nations Development Programme and National Economic and Development Authority.

The Detrimental Role of Biased Policies
Governance Structures and Economic Development

JOSEPH Y. LIM

THE POLITICAL AND ECONOMIC CRISIS facing the Philippines during the twilight days of the Estrada administration showed the clear link between weak institutions and governance structures and the poor economic performance of the country. This has been a known fact long before the Estrada scandals, but its significance and importance have not been felt so palpably and strongly as then. If any lessons should be derived from this episode of our country's history, it is that careful and more historically rooted studies should be done in analyzing the role of institutions, governance structures, and the state in the economic development of the country, and how the nature of these institutions and structures, as they evolve over time, affects economic development.

The objective of this study is to find out how biased policies, meant to benefit narrow vested interests at the expense of national interests, impact negatively on the economy. The hypothesis is that such policies are more damaging: 1) the more they are inconsistent with the main economic program of the government, 2) the more they impair the capacity and credibility of important regulatory bodies which enforce property rights, ensure fair competition and/or address "market failures" in the economy, 3) the stronger the adverse feelings of the public with respect to the unfairness of the policy, 4) the more social cohesion is broken and the more key economic players withdraw their cooperation due to the adoption or disclosure of such policies.

It would be beneficial if we come up with some loose framework that will situate biased policies within the institutions and governance structures of the country. In particular, the first part of this paper will give some discussion of how institutions and governance structures are vital to the economic development of the country. The second part will try to show

how the state transitions in the Philippines, as they historically unfolded, had not sufficiently strengthened these institutions and governance structures, and had not displaced the dominant clientelist type of relationship in the state bureaucracy and institutions. Thus biased policies not based on transparent and accountable processes continue to persist and allow short-run vested interests based on personalistic patron-client ties to dominate long-term national ones, and eventually to sabotage economic development. The next section will look at and analyze within the above context "hot" issues involving the Estrada administration. The last section will tackle the political possibilities of correcting the governance structures of the country in order to effect economic development.

The Role of Institutions, Governance Structures, and the State in Economic Development

IT IS NOT VERY PRODUCTIVE if we study biased policies (that lack transparency and accountability) in a vacuum, isolated from the institutions, governance structures, and economic programs of the country.

There is a growing literature (Rodrik, 1996 and 2000, Stiglitz, 2000)) emphasizing the necessity of strengthening institutions and governance structures in order to achieve economic development, especially under a regime of economic liberalization. These are due to the following prerequisites for economic development:

Efficient and adequate physical infrastructure. Competition in the domestic market and, more importantly, competition in the world export market, necessitate productivity and efficiency of domestic production. Thus good physical infrastructure and facilities, and efficient provision of transportation, public utilities and ports become vital. Governance structures and bureaucracies that are either inept or whose criteria for awarding projects are not performance-based (such as the case with many corrupt governments) will, most likely, not provide these infrastructure and facilities adequately and with the appropriate quality. This will result in higher overhead costs in transportation, power, utilities and the like, thereby reducing the competitiveness of the country's products.

Ascription of clear property rights and enforcement of contracts. Both Adam Smith and Douglas North (1984) point to the important role of the capitalist state to ascribe clear property rights and enforce contracts. This is important for market operations so that firms and households have clear control of their assets, profits and income in order to continue their participation in the economic processes and so that there are incentives to increase productive capacities, introduce innovations and improve human capital.

Enforcement of labor contracts, business contracts, debt contracts, rental contracts is important so that economic activities can be made with some assurance of a modicum of security and predictability. The great economist John Meynard Keynes has always said that contracts and "conventions" are required to cope with uncertainty and volatility, and this allows the capitalist system to survive as it faces an unknown future.

The set of institutions and practices in the executive, legislative and judicial branches as well as informal sources of power and authority is crucial in the ascription of property rights and enforcement of contracts. This includes activities related to: 1) the formulation of laws, rules and regulations that guide the protection of and limits to property rights, 2) the implementation and policing of these laws, rules and regulations, 3) the punishment of the breakers of these laws, rules and regulations.

The granting of special franchises or licenses to undertake specific economic activities and earn corresponding profits (such as franchises for construction of physical infrastructure, for managing and operating public utilities, for forest or gambling concessions) is an important aspect of ascription of property rights. Institutions and governance structures dominated by vested interests and personalistic relations would prefer the proliferation of such franchises (which can be captured by those close to the powerful authorities) and would give them to the dominant faction or cronies of those in power.

On the other hand, stronger institutions and governance structures might not be completely bereft of corruption but would: 1) limit these franchises only to areas of natural monopolies and special cases where franchises are really necessary, and 2) for these areas, require the winner of franchises to subscribe to a minimum performance standard and to revoke the franchises in case this standard is not reached, or important rules and requirements are broken.

Even if this prerequisite of ascription of property rights and contract enforcement has always been taken for granted by most (neoclassical) economic studies, the fact stands that many states of developing countries—including that of the Philippines—lack the capacities and political will to ascribe correct property rights, and enforce legal contracts needed for capitalist development.

Market regulation. Markets do not exist in a vacuum; they are part of the social and political milieu of a particular country at a particular time. The quality of the market and its performance therefore is only as good as the quality of the social and political institutions and governance structure wherein it is situated (Polanyi,1957)).

Apart from the ascription of property rights and enforcement of contracts, the state and economic institutions should ensure that good competitive policies are being followed and that anti-competitive and fraudulent behavior should be checked and punished. This is not only important to get efficient production and allocation of resources (as neoclassical theory would take great pains to prove) but also to assure social cohesion and cooperation of key economic players in the development process.

Furthermore, the latest economic literature points to the importance of governance structures in dealing with "market failures"[1]. Market failures arise because of: 1) adverse results of market processes that cannot automatically be corrected by the market itself, or 2) the need for additional provision of resources, information, or technology that will make the economic system improve its performance but that the market itself cannot adequately supply. Important examples of the positive effects of regulation or interventions in the market are:

1) regulation or taxation of firms to prevent them from degrading the environment and natural resources,

2) regulation of natural monopolies and public utilities to protect the consumers from unfair pricing and substandard services,

3) quality control and ensuring health standards for consumer products,

4) prudential regulation and supervision of the financial system to avoid over-risky transactions, which may cause self-fulfilling crises and runs,

5) regulation and policing of the stock market to prevent "insider trading" and other fraudulent activities,

6) regulation of market activities that may have adverse social effects, such as cigarette smoking, alcohol drinking, gambling, etc.,

7) the requirement of regular and honest information from firms, banks, and individuals to ensure transparency and accountability, and the processing and dissemination of such information,

8) provision of quality education and research and development infrastructure to improve human capital and technology of the country.

A cursory look at the list above—plus the need to ensure fair competition and prevent fraudulent activities—would bring out the importance of the efficiency, capacity, and integrity of institutions and governance structures in dealing with market regulation and related activities.

Provision for social insurance. It should be emphasized that one of the major reasons the world capitalist system did not degenerate into chaos or become socialist (as Marx predicted) was that capitalism, after uprooting people from feudal and kinship ties, eventually had to provide social insurance and minimum standard of living to the mass of unemployed and poor people. This involved successful economic and social programs for poverty alleviation as well as efficient and fair systems of safety nets for the unemployed and the poor.

The Asian financial crisis has made it clear to the stronger East Asian economies (South Korea, Malaysia, and Thailand) that social insurance and safety nets should be institutionalized in order for their economies to become even stronger and more resilient.

Social cohesion and conflict management. Successful handling of all of the above contributes to social cohesion and social cooperation (at least by key economic players) in the development process. No doubt the above are necessary but not sufficient to ensure social cohesion and cooperation from key economic players. Many societies have strong divisions and rivalries along ethnic or religious lines. Others have different factions of the business and landed elite vying for both political and economic power. In economic and market activities, even with the best rules and regulations, there will bound to arise areas of conflicts over policies, property rights, or the sharing of the economic pie (e.g. labor vs. capitalists, farmers vs. real-estate developers, indigenous peoples vs. mining firms and builders of power plants or dams). Even if conflicts are not especially prominent, there will also be coordination failures (another new literature in macroeconomics) wherein individual actions of the various economic players do not contribute to the overall welfare of the economy.[2]

All the above require an astute state, which has the respect of the key economic players in order to effect compromises and solutions during times of conflicts, and coordinated collective action during times of possible co-ordination failures. Social institutions will also have to be such that some minimum level of social cohesion and social cooperation in national de-velopment is achievable. This means that there has to be a workable social contract in dealing with areas of tension and conflict (such as divisions due to ethnicity, religion, ideologies, property rights claim and policies).

Macroeconomic stability. For securing strong investment and produc-tion potential from both domestic capital and foreign capital, there is a need to generate political and socio-economic stability that will instill con-fidence in the economy.

Macroeconomic stability includes many diverse things but is tradi-tionally restricted to minimal up-and-down volatility in output, employ-ment, and prices (which means of course increasing or accelerating output and employment and low inflation), low fiscal and external deficits, and a modicum of political stability (and social cohesion). Achieving macroeco-nomic stability—what the International Monetary Fund (IMF) insists as conditionalities during crisis and recession periods—is not simply a result of "correct" economic policies but a result of institutions and governance structures that include bureaucratic institutions and institutions and gov-ernance structures for social cohesion and conflict management.

Economic and political stability implies some confidence in the eco-nomic system and some level of social cohesion and cooperation, which in turn implies some acceptance of the power of the state and the rules it imposes.

Sustained low inflation implies a labor-management arrangement that does not lead to destructive wage-price spirals (very much an institutional and governance problem), just as it implies appropriate exchange rate and aggregate demand policies. Similarly, the size of the fiscal deficit is itself a partial reflection of the state's capacity to collect revenues (which depends on the bureaucracy of tax and customs bureaus and related institutions). It is also a reflection of the capacity, willingness, and cooperation of the business, propertied, and labor sectors to be taxed (which most likely will be low during crisis and recession periods). It is also a reflection of the state's spending priorities and capacities (such as whether they put more priority in provision for basic social services, pump priming the economy, or sustaining government "fat" for corrupt officials). These are not independent of the institutions, governance structures, social contracts and relationship between the state and its people, and the nature of the state itself.

History has confirmed the theories of Marx, Keynes and the new institutional economists (using "market failure" approaches in the real and financial sectors) who said that the market system by itself does not automatically bring about a situation of equilibrium and full employment. In fact, uncertainty, changing moods, and varying confidence levels bring a lot of volatility and instability to the system. And globalized world markets often create these volatilities and instabilities, as proven by the East Asian crisis (not to mention all other previous economic and financial crises) and the impending world recession due to the dire prospects on the Japanese and U.S. economies.

Thus managing the instabilities and stirring up and maintaining confidence in the system is another big task for the state. Again its capacity and capability becomes a critical factor.

It is this need for strong institutions and governance structures that provide the framework of the study. The ability of vested interests, patronage politics, clientelism and personalistic power relations to thwart and distort policies through non-transparent and non-accountable mechanisms sabotages the credibility, consistency, capacity and commitment of institutions and governance structures to deliver the important functions described above.

This either puts in doubt the capability and fairness of regulatory bodies needed badly in an increasingly liberalized economic and financial setting and/or breaks the social cohesion and cooperation of key economic players needed by government to push the economy forward. This in turn negatively affects investors' confidence, investment inflows and economic efficiency and productivity. The extent of negative public perception contributes to the depth and gravity of the impact. This brings about efforts from civil society to undertake watchdog activities and, in extreme circumstance like the recent People Power uprising, to organize massive protests and rallies. This in turn leads to offsetting moves from affected government officials to tame public outrage and to avoid punishment, oftentimes using legalities and technicalities. The uncertainties and potential dangers (military coups, bombings, a "wag the dog" war, social unrest following an impending acquittal amidst overwhelming evidence) we just experienced (and, hopefully, ended) further decrease investor, lender, producer, and consumer confidence and brings the economy into further jeopardy and distress.

Patronage Politics and Clientelism

THIS SECTION ATTEMPTS, in a quite amateurish way, to give a political analysis of the Philippine state and power relations so as to shed light on the nature of 'biased policies not based on transparent and accountable processes'. It follows Hutchcroft's (1996 and 1997) approach in analyzing corruption in the Philippine context. His thesis is that the main reason why corruption in the Philippines (particularly during the Marcos regime) had been more malignant and deleterious than corruption in other East Asian countries (with the possible exception of Suharto's Indonesia in the nineties) is that patronage politics and clientelism (or to use another phrase of Hutchcroft, booty capitalism) dominate state institutions and relations, and account for much of the pernicious effects of corrupt policies.

A strong manifestation of this fact is, according to Hutchcroft, that, in areas of governance where clientelism and personalistic ties dominate, informal networks have stronger authority than formal structures (e.g. Mafia-type networks of drug lords or kidnapping gangs have stronger authority or have stronger hold over local police). In this case, corruption tends to be more prevalent and more malevolent.

Furthermore, in areas of governance dominated by clientelism and personalistic ties, patron-client networks do not "coincide with formal lines of authority" and "constitute competing source of orders and inducements"[3]. This would result in more variable and more unpredictable forms of corruption and therefore would yield more pernicious results. Good examples of this are the cases Estrada was involved in. If the charges against President Estrada are true, then his informal circles of friends (through the authority of the presidency) flaunted the rules and regulations of the

Philippine Amusement and Gaming Corporation (Pagcor) and the Civil Aeronautics Board (CAB), and more seriously, the Philippine National Police (PNP), and the Department of the Interior and Local Government without any possible resistance from the formal authorities. President Estrada also allegedly attempted to do this less successfully with the Philippine Stock Exchange (PSE) and the Securities and Exchange Commission (SEC).

To further explain this point, we again lift from Hutchcroft (1997, p. 231-2):

> In the former (pre-1980s) Thai bureaucratic polity, for example, formal bureaucratic authority was well developed and informal networks of power and formal status overlapped to a large degree; in such a system, businesspersons were likely to have a good sense of whom to approach and what to expect from one transaction to another. In the Philippines, by contrast, lines of formal authority are weaker and the disjuncture between authority and power is often quite pronounced. In this loosely structured system, where patrons are as often found outside formal structures of authority as within them, there is likely less regularization of corruption from one case to another....[In this sort of] disorganized bureaucracy, the official chain of command is unclear and constantly shifting and the decision-making criteria are similarly arbitrary and unknown.

We have two things to add to this insight of Hutchcroft:

1) The unpredictability is aggravated by the fact that, because of elections, there are periodic changes in the local and national political leadership and heads of executive, legislative, and judicial branches. If clientelism and personalistic ties predominate, different factions with different interests alternate with each other and the more "decision-making criteria become arbitrary and unknown".

2) It is not just unpredictability that is causing the problem because of the above processes. The volatility and instabilities are often more importantly caused by periodic shattering of social cohesion and the withdrawal of key players in cooperating with the perceived "unjust" arrangements.

The gist of the above is that patron-client and personalistic relations dominating governance structures in the Philippines result in the dominance of very narrow vested interests over national interests. Since vested interests are varied and changing, predictability and consistency of policies are lost and investments and economic confidence are reduced. Furthermore, vested interests become more malignant and rapacious as they become shorter in time horizon, since terms of office are limited.

The blatant "corruption" further destroys social cohesion periodically and leads to various non-cooperation from the aggrieved and bigger sector not benefiting from the "corrupt" practices.

No Qualitative Change

HUTCHCROFT'S PAPER concentrated on the clientelist state during the Marcos regime. Why are we still using the same framework in our analysis? The answer is clearly that the post-Marcos regimes failed to qualitatively change state institutions and governance structures and veer them away from patronage politics and clientelism.

To be sure, there had been substantial improvements in many respects from the Marcos regime. Institutions and state apparatus for repression and human rights abuses had been weakened and less consolidated and therefore less malevolent than during the Marcos period. More democratic processes also allowed watchdog activities, airing of grievances and exposés of wrongdoings to be widely practiced and to effectively check corrupt and harmful practices and policies. The general public's recollection of the Marcos days had made this a strong weapon against corruption and anomalous practices.

The Aquino administration also set up a new Constitution, which despite its flaws, allowed civilian rule to take over and to reduce military power and abuses.[4] The buffer Aquino provided against Right-wing military ambitions was a contribution not quite appreciated by many.

Still, the more radical sectors of our society would be correct in claiming that the break with the Marcos regime was not a revolution since the basic institutions and governance structures remained intact and the processes of clientelism preserved. The Aquino regime viewed the victory against Marcos as a vindication of the pre-Marcos regimes of democratic elections and alternating governance of different factions of the elite. This view saw the Marcos tragedy as caused by one man's or one family's greed and lust for power. Institutions of governance and systemic roots of corruption and bureaucratic inefficiencies were completely ignored and not dealt with.

The preservation of clientelism and personalistic power relations in the state bureaucracy and institutions of governance was a key disenchantment with the Aquino regime. The rise of certain power blocs identified with the regime was used by the Right-wing coup plotters as one of the reasons to sabotage the government. The rise of the political power of the Cojuangcos (with President Aquino's brother gaining leadership of the main political party and gaining hold of Tarlac province), the Sumulongs (uncle of the Cojuancos in Rizal province) and the Oretas (in-laws of the Aquinos in Malabon, Rizal) indicated a return of political clans in Philippine politics. Building genuine parties based on clear platforms and policies took a back seat to power politicking, first by the anti-Marcos faction of the elite, and later on joined in by the previously pro-Marcos faction.

Evidence of the preservation of patronage politics and clientelism (where personalistic ties and connections dominated formal rules and regulations) was best demonstrated in the dismal performance of the Presidential Commission on Good Government (PCGG), which was tasked to acquire and sequester ill-gotten wealth and assets of the previous regime. Marcos cronies were able to go into compromise deals, retain their assets and corporations (in what many consider to be corrupt deals) and return to the Philippines unscathed. Other institutions (Department of Justice, Bureau of Immigration, Office of the President of both Aquino and Ramos) cooperated in the rehabilitation and comeback of what were previously denounced as the country's looters. The most prominent of course is Eduardo Cojuangco who regained much of his former economic and political power, and was even a major presidential candidate who could have succeeded President Aquino. He also was able to capture his former prize, the country's top food conglomerate San Miguel Corporation, by the time President Estrada began his administration. The Marcoses themselves were allowed to enter the country under the Ramos administration and join in the power game of national and local politics.

The Ramos administration, though improving the style of management and leadership (and mixing it with some developmental vision), also did not basically try to eradicate the patron-client relations in state institutions and governance structures. In fact the biggest corruption case of the Ramos administration—the Public Estates Authority (PEA)/

Amari scandal—involves two possible personalistic ties: one involving George Triviño and then Speaker Jose de Venecia, and the other involving Justiniano (Bobby) and Agnes Montano and no less than President Ramos himself (see Coronel, 2000). Both independently used their connections to affect the result of the deal. The other big corruption case in the Ramos administration is the Expo Centennial, which involved questionable diversion of government funds for a Marcosian white elephant project and possible fund raising activities for the administration party (again see Coronel, 2000).

The alleged link of corruption cases in the Ramos administration and fund raising for the administration party is quite prominent. Rumors were that even the rise of kidnapping cases during this period was related to the funding of election spending. The corruption cases of the Ramos administration, even with the large amounts that were involved, were limited to questionable bids and contracts of large special projects and did not cause much disturbance and unhappiness from much of the big business players and the general public. They did not involve changing policies that would affect a large number of players[5], nor did they involve such known controversial personalities as to have caused a furor and a sense of unfairness from a large section of the public.

The fact that then Speaker Jose de Venecia, himself tainted with ill-gotten-wealth charges from the Marcos days, as the biggest king player and coalition builder in the Ramos administration, points to the choice of an expert in Philippine political maneuvering to effect important compromises and negotiations during the administration. To be fair, the result was positive as congressional support of key bills of the administration were assured and the legislative and executive branches seemed to have a common economic and political program. This increased the level of confidence and improved the economic performance during most of the Ramos period.

The achievement, however, was undertaken again without changing (and perhaps using) the basic nature of patron-client relations in Philippine state institutions and governance structures. The improved leadership and management achieved during the Ramos administration was more about good style and astute politics than about leaving a legacy of performance-based rules and conventions in state institutions and replacing personalistic and patron-client relations.

It is this legacy of patronage politics, patron-client relations and informal networks capturing formal structures of authority that was supposed to be used to the hilt by the Estrada administration.

Economic Liberalization: The Main Program

WHILE THE STATE INSTITUTIONS and governance structures did not qualitatively change, the post-Marcos governments went into high gear in qualitatively changing the economic program of the government into domestic and external liberalization, deregulation and privatization.

Lifting of import quotas was undertaken in the second half of the eighties, while in the nineties, the country locked itself into further trade liberalization and tariff reduction with its entry into the Asean Free Trade Area (AFTA), the World Trade Organization (WTO) and the Asia-Pacific Economic Cooperation (APEC). Simultaneously, deregulation of the oil, telecommunications and shipping industries were done in earnest. Deregulation and privatization of the water sector was done in the second half of the nineties while privatization and deregulation of the power sector is being planned. Capital account liberalization was undertaken in 1992.

The logic of these moves, pushed by multilateral agencies (the IMF and World Bank) and economic technocrats of the country, was precisely to replace the state with the private sector and with markets and to reduce possible areas of intervention by the state in the national economy, under the assumption that efficiency and productivity will be increased and that the temptation of corruption and the Marcosian cronyism is still ever present. The view that reducing the areas of state intervention, without initiating state and institutional reforms to reduce clientelism in governance structures, would at best be a valid short-term policy for a corrupt and inept state, but completely ignores the entire Section 2 discussed above. This type of economy (a liberalized economy with bad institutions and governance structures) would definitely fail in the medium and long term. As the latest charges on the BW Resource scandal and the air war with Taiwan show, even supposedly liberalized and market-determined areas can be badly affected by allegedly malicious interventions in the regulatory institutions charged to ensure competition and to prevent fraudulent activities. Similarly, inimical policies, even in the non-tradable sector of gambling, can cause large adverse effects on social cohesion and economic confidence in a liberalized economy.

In fact, economic liberalization actually puts more demand and pressures on the state to effectively enforce property rights and contracts, to ensure competitive and non-fraudulent market processes, to regulate the markets to avoid socially undesirable activities (pollution, over-risky transactions, monopoly and predatory pricing, low quality and standards of goods, etc.) and to undertake or promote socially productive ones (infrastructure, access to quality education, research and development). Liberalization and deregulation also require the cooperation of a bigger mass of domestic and foreign players who should at least feel confident and secure of fair play and adequate macroeconomic handling by the state.

Policies that promote the interests of a particular few at the expense of national interests, especially if they go against set policies already prescribed and attack the fair and unbiased management and relatively autonomous role of the state, will leave many players unhappy and unwilling to cooperate in the market processes that have supposedly been liberalized.

The growing role of clientelism in the state under the Estrada administration therefore directly clashed with the economic thrust of the post-Marcos governments and presented a major stumbling block to economic development for the country.

If the corrupt charges on Estrada and those close to him are true, then the Estrada presidential victory in 1998 should be seen as a takeover of a faction of the old elite, which viewed election victory as a feudal conquest that would put the state apparatus at the helm of the winning clique and their friends. This view would be substantiated by the alleged wanton and unabashed attempts by the president to influence various government agencies to give special consideration to his friends, many of whom allegedly turned out to be acting as his proxies.

The benefiting friends of President Estrada were varied ranging from big established businessmen like Eduardo Cojuangco (the coco levy fund issue) and Lucio Tan (the Philippine Airlines and Philippine National Bank issues), to bankers and stock market players (George Go and Dante Tan), to shady businessmen (Mark Jimenez, Lucio Co and Jaime Dichaves), to movie actor friends (the Paquito Diaz bid for firetrucks), to in-laws and relatives (textbook scam, use of government aircraft and vehicles, questionable funding of "Miss Saigon"), to known gambling aficionados (Luis 'Chavit' Singson and Atong Ang).

The *Jueteng* Scandal

WHAT BROUGHT ON the impeachment of the president was his alleged love and interest in gambling (the stock play of BW resources and the *jueteng* scandal) and his seemingly obvious connections and friendships with shady characters of the underworld. The alleged attempt to centralize in the national level the illegal *jueteng* payoffs, many say, proceeds from a small town mayor or "local boss" mentality. One common belief about local officials is that one of their methods of accumulating funds would be to consolidate proceeds from illegal activities in the local area. With clear loyalty from the local police chief and operators, this can be done smoothly and without much fanfare at the local level.

But once the small town mayor becomes the president of the country, and a feudal conquest mentality dominates, the ambitious attempt to centralize *jueteng* payoffs becomes a very risky move, especially if it involves siding with one faction of the syndicate and the attempt is leaked out in the national media.

The biggest evidence of informal networks and transactions (with personalistic ties and patronage system) dominating formal authorities and rules was the entire process followed in the scandal: from the alleged centralization of *jueteng* payoffs to the president from the various regional gambling lords of the country involving direct participation and complicity from the PNP and local government heads, to the alleged money laundering in the formal financial institutions, to the legalization of *jueteng* by the Philippine Amusement and Gaming Corporation (Pagcor) as Bingo 2-Ball but allegedly giving the franchise to a privileged crony of the president, to the alleged use of threats of violence to balking factions of the gambling world, to the alleged cover-up and blatant suppression of vital evidence by the 11 senator-judges in the impeachment trial. All these processes have led the Estrada government to be termed by some as a "mafia" government (Bello (2000)). True enough, a "mafia" government or "bossism" can only hope to succeed and thrive when institutions and governance structures can be "captured" via personalistic ties, bribes and acquiescence to requests via the sheer use of political (e.g. presidential) power and threats.

Let us look at some of the processes described above:

→ The alleged attempt to centralize the illegal *jueteng* payoffs and give the president a 3% share of all proceeds is perhaps the most blatant crossing of lines between illegal activities and formal authority lines. It is in a way a direct capture by a faction of the underworld of no less than the presidency itself. The temerity to organize an illegal gambling tax for the highest position in the country, and to centralize the collection and accounting of such proceeds, is the biggest corruption case to be exposed. It is even more scandalous given the facility of obtaining cooperation from the police as well as gaming and local authorities. Given that the scandal erupted only because part of the faction and a close presidential friend squealed on him, fears are raised that all these would have been undetected if the underworld friends did not quarrel. It also puts in the forefront the question everybody seems to be afraid to ask before as to how far up in the government hierarchy payoffs from drugs, kidnapping, and gambling have gone in the past and in the present.

→ The laundering of money documented so well in the impeachment proceedings involving at least one of the biggest banks of the country and the ex-president of that bank[6] exposes that close ties between powerful persons in government and powerful persons in the big financial institutions contribute to legal financial processes being bastardized into money laundering and accumulation of ill-gotten wealth. The issue here also exposes the use of bank secrecy laws and leniency in opening deposits and accounts in camouflaging illegal financial activities. This points to the twin need to correct financial rules and regulations and institute more transparent and accountable processes on one hand, and to remove clientelism and patronage systems in legal financial and big business dealings. The two should be done simultaneously, and may not be achieved simply by changing rules and regulations, if relations between bank officers and politically powerful people remain as personalistic, under-the-table and based on patron-client relations.

→ The otherwise correct policy of legalizing *jueteng* by Pagcor was completely sabotaged by giving the exclusive franchise and operation of the Bingo 2-Ball game to a close presidential friend and alleged head of a faction of the gambling underworld. Viewed by many as simply a continuation of the centralization of gambling proceeds via a more greedy attempt to give legal control of gambling funds to a favored gambling crony, this aspect of the scandal also shows how policies are distorted by informal networks and pressures, and how national interests are completely overshadowed by and subsumed to vested (in this case, criminal) interests. Regulatory bodies (such as Pagcor) become stooges of inimical policies.

→ The attempt to silence Ilocos Sur Gov. Luis 'Chavit' Singson in his exposure of the entire *jueteng* scandal based on his defiance of the new underground/presidential policy on gambling is a case study of 'Mafiosi' tactics as well as clientelism. The alternate tactics of using mutual friends and presidential relatives as intermediaries, promises of possible favors, the reversal of the policies that brought about the grievance in the first place, and finally (as Singson claims) the full use of the threat of violence to life and property are all reminiscent of strategies of Mafia-like gangs and local warlords. These same tactics would be used in the attempted silencing of former Security and Exchange Commission head Perfecto Yasay in his media war with the president and testimony at the Blue Ribbon committee and of former Finance Secretary Edgardo Espiritu in his testimony in the impeachment trial—both on the BW Resources scandal to be discussed in more detail in a later section.

Policy Flip-Flop

THE AIR WAR with Taiwan[7] demonstrates that when vested interests conflict with the liberalization thrust of a sector of the economy, regulatory institutions become susceptible to reversals and flip-flopping of policies that are damaging to predictability, efficiency, investor confidence, and, most importantly, mutual trust and goodwill required in bilateral economic relations. The issue is again aggravated by apparent presidential intervention in favor of a close friend.

The Air Liberalization Law (Executive Order 219) was signed in 1995 by then President Ramos. The law follows a gradualist approach and does not provide for a full open-skies policy. It envisages a phased progressive improvement of the air transport industry to world-class efficiency before full liberalization and deregulation is undertaken.

The Civil Aeronautics Board (CAB), the civil aviation policy-making body within the Department of Transportation and Communication (DOTC), was tasked with the regulation responsibilities and implementation of this law. In undertaking this task, its charter called for "taking into consideration the larger interest of the country, especially users of air services".

Under the law, the Philippines has been maintaining Air Service Agreements (ASAs) with several nations, which give their air carriers fixed passenger quotas in specific routes. ASAs with Taiwan and Hong Kong were signed in 1996. The quota given to Taiwan carriers was 9,600 passengers weekly. The ASAs also gave "sixth-freedom rights" to the countries' national carriers. The concretization of this in the agreement with Taiwan was that China Airlines and Eva Airways were allowed to recruit passengers from the Philippines and fly them, via Taiwan, across the trans-Pacific route to North America.

These ASAs were said to have effectively weakened Philippine Airlines' monopoly over certain air routes, particularly to North America. Other blows came when the CAB granted franchises to other domestic airlines in the local air routes, and designated at least one other Philippine flag-carrier (Grand Air[8]) to also serve international routes.

Despite perceptions that the CAB had been biased in its policies in favor of Philippine Airlines ever since Lucio Tan revealed his majority shareholdings and takeover[9] of PAL in 1996, it had to take a call from President Estrada in early 1999 to review the bilateral agreements after PAL blamed foreign competition for its poor showing. This "favor" to presidential friend Tan was apparently a response to Tan's agreeing not to fold up the country's flag carrier after being crippled by labor strikes. Few then expressed disapproval of the president's intervention, and many even praised him for saving the national flag carrier.

Following Estrada's intervention, CAB communicated to Taiwan aviation authorities the Philippines' desire to cut down the 9600 weekly seats flight quotas given to Taiwanese carriers to 4000 seats.

Because international practice and provisions in the 1996 agreement called for a 12-month cooling-off period before any attempt to abrogate the arrangement, the Philippines did not use unfair competition as the main reason of the break-off but invoked the one-China policy, which points to the extent that the administration was willing to risk productive economic relations to effect the change in policy. As expected invoking the one-China policy did nothing to make Taiwan come to heel and only offended it greatly.

On August 2, 1999, the Philippines decided to make a unilateral move: Taiwan must accept only 3000 seats or have all flights suspended by

September 30, unless a new agreement was reached before the deadline. The decision was relayed by Manila Economic and Cultural Office (Meco) chairperson Eva Estrada-Kalaw to the Taiwan Economic and Cultural Office (Teco). At the time the news broke, Philippine aviation authorities were also reviewing the bilateral agreements involving Korean Airlines, Asiana, Cathay Pacific, Singapore Airlines, Pakistan Airlines, Royal Brunei and KLM.

No agreement was reached before the deadline. On September 30, flights continued as both sides met and waited for President Estrada's final decision—whether to halt the route or extend it another month while negotiations were under way. Direct air links were severed the next day (October 1).

As early as October 3, 1999, *Taiwan News* said the Philippines stood to lose more than Taiwan from its decision. In mid-October there was still no impetus for renewal of talks. In late October, the Philippine government approached Taiwan for the resumption of direct flights. The analysis in *China Times* on October 27, 1999 added that apart from the losses to the Philippines in terms of Taiwan's investments, tourism and labor and product exports to Taiwan, the suspension has not helped PAL but proved a boon to charter flight operators and other airlines that link Taiwan and Philippines via third countries.

Taiwan set preconditions for resumption of talks, the main being reinstatement of the 1996 agreement. Taiwan also wanted talks to be official—being stung by Manila's earlier stress on the one-China policy, and having had a taste of Manila's inconsistent voices. And they specifically wanted no more unilateral cancellation.

After rejecting Taiwan's conditions in the media, Manila reinstated the 1996 agreement on November 3, 1999, on condition that talks should be completed by January 31, 2000 and that China Airlines (CAL) and Eva Air (EVA) give up their sixth freedom rights. Manila claimed Taiwan had earlier tried to employ delaying tactics and was abusing the sixth freedom rights by offering cut-rate prices to passengers bound for the US via Taiwan.

Taiwan's foreign minister received the Philippine CAB resolution the night of November 3, 1999, and criticized the Philippines for negotiating through the media. The minister said they would review Manila's offer before responding, although officials at Taiwan's Civil Aeronautics Administration (CAA) commented that the offer did not directly address Taiwan's demand that the 1996 pact be reinstated officially. Taiwan essentially took its time to respond to Manila's offer to resume flights.

Incidentally, Taiwan's labor market was opened to Vietnam on November 1, 1999. The Taiwan Association of Manpower Agencies shifted recruitment policies, gradually replacing Filipinos migrants with Vietnamese and Indonesian workers. This was with the endorsement of their Council of Labor Affairs, which advised them to prepare for the possibility that Taiwan might declare a ban on recruitment of Filipinos.

In mid-November President Estrada sent aides to Taiwan to negotiate for a preliminary air agreement. Manila said CAL and EVA could maintain their quota of 9,600 passengers a week provided they did not fly them to third country destinations via Taiwan. Estrada said—and Taipei denied—that Taiwan agreed to give up the sixth freedom rights. A planned trip by Taiwan officials to the Philippines was cancelled. The reason, according to CAA, was that the Philippines failed to put in writing that it was recognizing the 1996 agreement. The reason according to a Philippine official involved in negotiations was that CAA officials refused to sign a preliminary air agreement, which was supposed to be the purpose of the trip. By this time both sides were aware that the Philippine government was facing a lot of pressure from overseas workers in Taiwan who wanted to go home for Christmas. Adding to the pressure was the CAA's recommendation that charter flights not covered by the ASA be suspended before Christmas.

Another attempt at negotiations on December 14, 1999, again broke down on the issue of sixth freedom rights, which Taiwan said it would not give up, though might be willing to set a quota on it. The Manila representatives said they did not go to Taiwan to negotiate. Manila was pushing for an immediate resumption of flights, while Taiwan wanted the ASA to be cleared up first. The CAA announced that charter flights would be suspended by the end of the year, and rejected PAL's application to operate charter flights. The move was not expected to significantly affect Taiwanese charter flight operators, but will hurt tourism and overseas labor in the Philippines.

An interim agreement in the form of a letter of understanding was signed on January 28, 2000, setting the quota at 4,800 weekly. Flights resumed February 16, 2000.

CAL then applied for a Kaohsiung-Manila route where it expected to carry another 4,800 passengers monthly. CAB rejected the application. Taiwan retaliated by cutting PAL's flights by half and did not push through with a March 1-2, 2000 meeting for a new agreement.

In a letter to CAB on March 6, 2000, Meco Chairperson Kalaw advised CAB to disregard the January 28 understanding. CAB cancelled all flights. The CAA said they were informed late in the night of March 14, and an EVA flight, not informed, was refused entry to Philippine air space at NAIA. Taiwan responded by cutting all links, and the situation deteriorated again. And this time with a lot more ill will.

Meantime, the involvement of CAB in the Taiwan controversy prompted Japanese firm IASS Co. Ltd. to air its grievances against CAB at the Philippine Investment Seminar in Tokyo. CLA Air Transport, their joint venture with Filipino firms, had not moved forward because obstacles that had appeared only since Estrada assumed office.

Tourism Secretary Gemma Cruz-Araneta and foreign business groups had also come out with public disapproval of CAB's actions, which was seen as openly serving the interests of PAL, and Lucio Tan in particular. They were joined by Filipino overseas workers going to Taiwan, by local businessmen doing business with the Taiwanese, and the business sector in general which saw the policy as directly linked to the president's biased policies and protection of close friends and cronies. The overwhelming pressure to end the air war from various government officials and entities came not only from Secretary Araneta, but also from Trade Secretary Manuel Roxas II, the entire Economic Coordinating Council (made up of all the economic and finance secretaries) and the senate Foreign Relations Committee. The committee strongly recommended the resumption of flights between Manila and Taipei.

The principal author of the report, Sen. Francisco Tatad, a close ally of the president's, emphasized the positive effect that resumption of flights with Taiwan would have on reducing and correcting the perceived cronyism of President Estrada, whose public rating had gone through a see-saw—nose-diving because of perceived cronyism and scandals and recovering due to military victories against the Muslims in Mindanao.

By the end of September 2000, the president and the CAB succumbed. A new agreement was signed with Taiwan, which was almost a carbon copy of the abrogated 1996 agreement. It restored the 9,600 weekly quota to Taiwanese carriers, and allowed sixth-freedom rights to both countries' national carriers. The main difference with the 1996 agreement was that there was now an increase of 1700 monthly seats to Taiwan carriers on the Manila-Kaoshiung-Manila route.

The Costs of the Erroneous Policy

FIGURES 1 TO 4 give us the large costs to the Philippines of the air war in terms of losses in: Taiwanese tourists, overseas workers to Taiwan (and implicitly their remittances), foreign direct investments, and exports to Taiwan.

Visitor arrivals from Taiwan plummeted from 10,273 in September 1999 (the month immediately prior to the cancellation of flights) to 6,764 in October 1999, to around 5,000 by mid-2000. Overseas workers to Taiwan plummeted from 20,363 in the third quarter of 1999 (the quarter immediately prior to the cancellation of the flights) to 14,798 in the next quarter, remaining around this level until the resumption of flights. Foreign direct investments plummeted from P268.8 million in the fourth quarter of 1999 (the quarter when flights were cut) to P23.6 million in the next quarter to practically nil in the second and third quarter of 2000. Philippine exports to Taiwan plummeted from around $500 million (the highest level ever achieved) around September and October of 1999 (just when the flights were cancelled) to around half the amount between November 1999 to October 2000.

The salient points and insights from the air war are:

1) In this case, the dominance of vested interests (Lucio Tan or at best the Philippine Airlines) over national and bigger interests set into motion a process that contradicted and reversed economic policies and bilateral agreements. The counter-reaction, not only of the aggrieved other country, but of all other losers within the country (overseas workers, tourism, trade and economic officials, and businessmen, foreign and local), set also in motion a round of protests and countermoves to reverse the reversal. This costly process involved not only debates in the Economic Coordination Council but also a media war between tourism officials, businessmen, and overseas workers' organizations on one hand, and officials from Philippine Airlines, CAB, and the Office of the President, on the other. It also led to a senate investigation and recommendation contrary to the original reversal of policy. The final result was another reversal of policy, back to where it was in the first place. This costly process also entailed along the way huge losses of investments, exports, tourist receipts, overseas workers' remittances, and a significant souring of goodwill, which is irreversible despite the reversal of the reversed policy.

2) The irrationality of the government move was further emphasized by the fact that PAL was cutting costs and reducing the capacity of their flights, including those in the Taiwan routes, thus aggravating the difficulties of our overseas workers, tourists, exporters, and investors.

3) Again, the direct intervention of the president contributed to the gravity of the problem, as predictability and security were lost and possible reversals of policies became very genuine realities. The complaint of IASS Co. of Japan, after the air war erupted, precisely pointed to the perception that presidential interventions were causing business transactions to be arbitrarily halted or derailed due to vested interests. The effect of this on longer-term investments, not only from Taiwan, should also be considered here.

4) It should be pointed out that it was the intervention of people close to the president that reversed the reversal. These people were those with formal authority (Tourism Secretary Gemma Cruz-Araneta, Trade and Industry Secretary Manuel Roxas II, a close ally and party-mate Sen. Francisco Tatad's, other economic, Cabinet officials and party mates). Thus, informal personalistic ties caused the initial reversal of policy. Personalistic ties with people with formal authority caused the second reversal. This emphasizes the unpredictability the whole process generates, and the need to win over political allies of the administration in order to repair damages done by wrong policies in a system of patronage and clientelist politics.

5) There are still debates on whether Taiwanese carriers Eva and China Air Lines were actually undertaking "dumping" and "under-pricing" activities in the Philippines, which would have justified the Estrada administration's actions. Whatever the case, it appears that the Philippine government's actions did not give due importance to proving and demonstrating anti-competitive behavior of the Taiwanese airlines, and seemed by all indications mainly affected by the close relations between the president and Lucio Tan and the need to immediately return the dominance of Philippine Airlines over the Manila-Taipei route.

6) This is corroborated by the anger of Lucio Tan at the second reversal, which almost caused another crisis at Philippine Airlines. Lucio Tan threatened to sell his majority stake in PAL, demanded the return of the $200 million he used to recapitalize the ailing national flag carrier, and

called for the cancellation of all the guarantees he and his companies have extended to PAL to keep it afloat. Journalist Amando Doronila wrote: "Tan's terms of quitting PAL [were] so tough that these [would have] entail[ed] huge costs to the government, raising questions on whether the government would succumb to this blackmail and whether it could sustain a breakaway from a crony relationship."[10] The vehemence of Tan's reactions seemed to indicate that somebody in the government owed him a favor that had been promised and broken.

Damaged Governance Structures and Value System

THE PREVIOUS SECTIONS in various respects shows how weak our institutions and governance structures are and how they somehow failed to withstand the pressures of a particularly vicious type of paternalistic patronage politics that have gained authority and power. The Estrada administration had replaced key formal authority lines and rules with informal personalistic ties, favors and vested interest cuddling.

Nowhere was this more obvious than in the successful attempt of 11 senator-judges in the evening of January 16, 2001 to blatantly disallow (using an illogical technicality of "irrelevance and immateriality" to the Articles of Impeachment) conclusive evidence of ill-gotten and unexplained wealth. This was a clear case of the complete breakdown of the institution of the senate and of the impeachment process itself. It implies an initial condition of bias in favor of the president by a majority despite overwhelming evidence of guilt. This is remarkable given that the senate had been viewed most of the time as having more integrity than the Lower House. Again this subversion of the institution of the senate did not happen overnight as some people may think. It had been going on as cultivation of friendships (some literally using the "godfather" relation), personal favors and, as Jaime Cardinal Sin calls it, "envelopmental" arrangements between the patron and his clients occurred over time and finally paid off when crunch time came. It is also illustrative of how laws (no matter how well formulated) have arbitrary interpretations. More often than not, rulings by the justice system depend more on mere technicalities than on the real merits of the cases. We have to view this as part of clientelism and how it sabotages formal authority and formal rules and institutions. It is indeed intrinsic to the system of clientelism and the patronage system.

The rendering of the senate as a "damaged institution" (as Senate President Pimentel would call it before tendering his resignation) finally doomed whatever possibilities the state institutions, governance structures, and constitutional processes could have had in using the impeachment process to correct the rotten system that was developing. Extra-constitutional processes had to take place. This important fact was completely lost on the Lee Kuan Yews, *Time* and *Newsweek* magazines, and *International Herald Tribune* that followed the American obsession of law above humanity, constitutional processes before morality. They saw on television what seemed to be a fair impeachment trial, ignored the backroom deals and patronage system, and claimed that it was the Filipino people, not the Estrada administration, that subverted the constitutional processes.

The institutions and governance structures, even if weak and helpless in many respects, did allow some free flow of information and some freedom of expression and dissent, thanks in no small measure to the first People Power revolution, against Ferdinand Marcos's dictatorship. The strong counter-force and resistance to the Estrada administration was made up of a powerful coalition of big business and a sizeable portion of the elite, the established Catholic church, most Protestant churches and Muslim groups, former presidents, and practically the entire organized sector of trade unions, people's organizations, and non-government organizations, including the entire spectrum of the Left. This coalition, as in 1986, provided the strongest pressure for change in the system, and delivered the extra-constitutional processes needed to overthrow the corrupt government.

One thing will have to be emphasized. This is the often overlooked but important role of culture and the value system. Decades (and perhaps centuries) of clientelism and patronage systems, both inside and outside the state, have bred among many of us a value system that tolerates patron-client and personalistic relations even as they subvert national interests and thus views corrupt and unfair practices more acceptingly than we would admit. This point of view was the biggest ally of the Estrada administration since it either blinded people to the unfairness of corrupt practices or justified them on the pretext that everybody else (including past regimes) is practicing corruption. This view had been caricatured as one that tolerates corruption by a patron as long as the winnings are shared by the patron with his clients (*balato*)[11]. It allowed the established order to be able to organize its own mass rallies as long as favors and gifts were given. Together with the massive funds channeled to radio stations and other media outlets catering to the masses, this value system allowed the Estrada administration to muster temporarily mass support, which some opinion poll surveys lavished on the media.

But history provides important moments and conjunctures when events happen and the people and masses are forced to rise above vested, partisan interests, and fight for the common good and national interests. These are the moments of the Chavit Singson revelation, the Clarissa Ocampo and Edgardo Espiritu testimonies, and, finally, the senate vote not to open the sealed envelopes. When this happens, the moral conviction of the citizenry that decides to go to the streets and fight for a higher good would be far stronger and committed than any patron-client and "old boys' club" sentiment. Thus the number of people in the streets announcing their disgust of the Estrada administration, should be weighted—in terms of potential impact and effectiveness—much more than those who chose to stay in their homes. (This is not a one-vote-one-count situation. The opinion poll surveys therefore gave a wrong assessment of the political will of the people and a wrong reading of the political situation, which caused the Estrada administration to miscalculate the situation completely.) They would be able to stimulate the nationalist and patriotic sentiments as well as moral indignation from among even the staunchest friends and clients of the established order[12]. This was how both the 1986 revolution and People Power 2001 succeeded.

Institutional Reforms Necessary for Development

IT IS FINALLY dawning on us economists that extra-economic forces are important factors that make and unmake economies. Fortunately the trend in theoretical economics and new institutional economics talk of important needs to provide clear property rights, competitive and fair play, to tackle "market failures" and to ensure correct and enlightened governance and regulations, as we discussed in the first half of this paper. The old conservative school of economics had preached for many a decade that markets and private sectors, on one hand, and the state and its intervention, on the other, are competing entities that are incompatible. Hands-off policy by the state on economic matters had been the prescription for decades.

Now a more enlightened environment allows us not to blame all economic woes on state interventions per se, but to scrutinize good interventions from bad interventions, good governance from bad governance and good states from bad states. Equally important is the realization of the need for good governance and institutions as a precondition for economic development. Instead of making state/market and state/private dichotomies and promoting anti-statist policies, a more open and flexible model of state-market and state-private partnership and cooperation, not in production as economists fear, but in regulation and governance can now be adopted. Furthermore, economistic beliefs that economic liberalization, deregulation and privatization on their own automatically result in the rise of better institutions, governance structures and value systems have been refuted by the case of the Philippines[13] and most other countries.[14] Thus economists would have to work in a more interdisciplinary spirit and finally respect the other less 'exact' social and political sciences since human, social and institutional frailties, bounded rationality and outright irrationality (from an economistic viewpoint) are more the norm than the exceptions. In the end, we economists need the other social sciences more than they need us.

The Question Is, Who Will Do It?

THE MORE ENLIGHTENED new institutional economics theories would try to come up with rules, regulations and incentive structures to tackle the requirements for "market failures", regulatory needs, property rights ascription, and provision of a competitive and fraud-free environment and to ensure performance and merit-based criteria in order to reduce patronage and personalistic relations. If done well, these would be major contributions. One can have good policy papers on what programs to adopt to stop money laundering in the financial institutions, or what laws and procedures would be beneficial so that chances of identifying and punishing corrupt public official will be enhanced. One can even focus on important enforcers, regulators and instruments of justice such as the Office of the Ombudsman, Commission on Audit, the Securities and Exchange Commission and the judiciary. But there is something more basic than these.

First, no matter how good rules, regulations, and incentive structures are, they will come to naught if the regime in power is captured by vested interests that subsume national interests under theirs. This is illustrated in the cases that we have taken up in this paper. The *jueteng* scandal precisely broke clear rules and laws that prohibit top officials from participating in, and partaking of, the fruits of illegal gambling. The laws broken were clearly mentioned in the impeachment proceedings against Estrada. It also involved inappropriate granting of a gambling franchise. Similarly the air war with Taiwan was a questionable abrogation of a bilateral agreement and goes against the spirit of a very clear executive order. Thus in both cases there were clear rules and regulations, and existing regulators and enforcers. The bad policy was breaking or arbitrarily changing the rules in favor of dubious interests.

This brings to fore the related question, Who will choose, regulate and veto the regulators? A bad regime representing vested interests that are incompatible with national interests will obviously nullify the effects of good rules and incentive structures and neutralize good regulators and enforcers.[15]

Second, new institutional economics tells us that the dominant atmosphere countries face is one of uncertainty, "market failures", and bounded rationality. We cannot foresee all possible problems, volatilities, and dangers that confront the country and its economy. Thus good governance includes proper discretionary policies to meet unforeseen circumstances, which existing rules and regulations may not be able to tackle and deal with. Regimes captured by narrow vested interests will no doubt manipulate current problems and volatilities in the system for their own benefits, and not to the national interest.

A Relatively Autonomous State with a Vision

BECAUSE OF the two points—the need for a relatively autonomous state not captured by narrow vested interests and the inadequacy of existing rules and regulations to solve national problems—important questions such as, Will clipping the powers of the executive branch be beneficial? Will a switch to a parliamentary system of government be good for the country?, cannot be independent of the type of ruling coalition that is emerging in the country. Thus, they are secondary to the more important question: Is there the possibility of a political force and coalition committed to reform and economic development that can win power and eradicate patronage and personalistic relations and politics in government?

The histories of economic development of countries all point to the need for the ascendance of a ruling coalition that has a developmental and long-run vision for the country. These may be as varied as the originally imperialist and colonial ruling powers of the developed countries (which are now mostly made up of liberal democratic governments) to the strongly Right-wing authoritarian People's Action Party of Singapore, to the Communist-led government of China (which is strongly committed to a market economy). How these coalitions eradicated or neutralized the powers of vested interests are themselves the stories of development of these countries. They were achieved through means as varied as revolutions, civil wars, democratic elections, and elimination of rival groups in the same parties or coalitions. Not all the governments are likeable ones and many are still authoritarian and repressive. But what they do have is some recognition of national interest, a relatively autonomous state that punishes vested interests that go against national interests. Some have been horrendously tyrannical governments—such as the Pinochet government of Chile and the Park Chung Hee government of South Korea—which over the decades were eventually replaced by more liberal and democratic regimes.

In the Philippine context, since we want this done democratically and with as little repression as possible, the only option is to ensure a reformist government voted in strongly by the electorate for a substantial period of time[16]. This is of course easier said than done. To be effective the reformist government will have to be strongly developmental in the sense of having a long-run vision of economic development for the country, free of inimical vested interests and strongly pro-poor in orientation. This is almost asking for a miracle since all past governments in our less than six decades of independent rule have been narrow and short-term in vision, and controlled and manipulated by powerful interest groups (from landlords to business cronies to mafia-type syndicates).

Most importantly, the poor majority of the populace have not been included and have never participated in the political, economic and social life of the ruling governments. This leads to their cynicism and suspicion of the ruling elites. Nowhere is this more clearly demonstrated than in the refusal of many poor sectors of the population to cooperate with the new Macapagal-Arroyo government and their continuing strong support for the populist Estrada. Many have argued that this is due to lack of information, lack of education, and wrong value systems of the masses. All these may have partial contributions to the phenomenon. But the constant answer one gets if you ask the Estrada supporters their view is that all governments without exception have been corrupt and the poor have never gained anything from any of the governments. This points to one important point: a democratically elected reformist government will have to win the support of the poor majority and make them feel that they are respected participants and beneficiaries of the developmental process of the country.

The need for a reformist government capturing power in a democratic context implies the hard task of building genuine political parties with clear and serious political reform platforms with party members committed to these reforms. This is an arduous task for us as a people since historical forces have made political parties in the country convenient venues for diverse politicians to compete for political positions and posts. No genuine political parties with clear interests and stands on issues have yet emerged.

Positive Factors

HISTORY PROVIDES conjunctures and opportunities for a people to irreversibly change their destinies for the better. The EDSA revolution in 1986 was one occasion that in many ways brought us forward, although unfortunately it did not change things drastically enough to improve our governance structures and development prospects. People Power 2001 should provide another such opportunity, one we can ill-afford to waste.

Today there is a strong feeling from a large section of society—the business sector, the intellectuals, the media, a sizeable portion of the youth and the middle class, and practically all organized people's and sectoral organizations—that the most important current issues are corruption and governance. Although the current political parties are still traditional and operate through political favors, lobbying, connections, and wealth, the lines are pretty clear as to which parties and political candidates cater to strong vested interests (and their attempts to escape corruption and other criminal charges), and which ones are more open to political reforms and better governance. This coalition of People Power 2, if politically astute and unified, must be able to effect the electoral victory of politicians who will be more cooperative in starting the difficult task of rebuilding political and social institutions as well as governance structures.

Another bright spot is the eagerness with which people's organizations and civil society organizations (including Left-leaning ones) are now joining the electoral processes (and party-list system) and their determination to effect changes and reforms in government and civil society. These organizations need not just be watchdogs and fight for cause-oriented issues; they can become potential partners of the state in the development process, especially in the difficult task of including the poor and disadvantaged in the political processes and economic benefits of the country. Indeed the genuine reformist political party we are envisioning to take over power in the country must be in alliance or partnership with organized sectors representing the peasants, the workers, the urban poor, the indigenous peoples, women and other sectors of civil society.

In concrete terms, political empowerment of the masses via these organizations cannot be successful without economic empowerment. The anti-poverty struggle in the current economic liberalization context must be interpreted as ensuring the capacity and ability of the poor and disadvantaged sectors (let us call these the people's sector) to effectively become productive and compete in the economic and business arena. This concretely requires them access to resources (infrastructure, skills, education, capital, market outlets, input sources) which the state can more effectively provide with the help and cooperation of the various people's and civil-society organizations.

Negative Factors

ALTHOUGH WE ARE FACED with a positive environment for change, we must be aware of the even stronger negative forces deeply entrenched in our society that will oppose moves for reforms and positive changes in governance. The most obvious forces are those vested interests that have good access to top government positions. Even the main political party of the new government includes factions and individuals who have joined the political processes for their own narrow interests. With the patronage and personalistic system still dominating, the dangers of the new dispensation falling into the same traps as its predecessors are very real. This has become very apparent with the political favors given to some government appointees, who come to their positions not because of better qualifications and abilities but because of access to the main political party and powerful forces.

These dangerous forces have, as in the post-EDSA revolution in the second half of the eighties, succeeded somewhat in instilling in the mainstream political thinking that the only flaw in our political system was the greed and evil of one man or one family who gained power, not the pervading dominance of vested interests and patronage and personalistic culture in government and civil society. This view, as we have mentioned, led previous governments to forego necessary political reforms and go back to the old ways of allowing alternating factions of the elite to take over government via elections and sham political parties without platforms. It is so much easier to get rid of a bad government than to build a genuinely good one.

The biggest enemies are not the existing vested interests but the dominant culture and values system that permeates after centuries of patronage and personalistic systems in Philippine politics and governance. One can see this in the lack of concern of the general public concerning genuine political issues in the current electoral campaign, and the fascination with personalities and celebrities. While this is largely due to the lack of community and national consciousness (over and beyond family and clans), it must be emphasized that this is also due to the frustration and cynicism with government we have discussed earlier.

Indeed rising above personal and familial interests—to interests that concern the community and the nation—requires a change in the educational and values systems which a reformist government will take decades to implement. A shortcut to deriving national interest from the populace is to make them feel that they have a stake in the government that takes over power, and that they and their families will benefit from this government. This is a miracle that the cause-oriented groups, together with reformist political parties and a little help from committed and charismatic leaders, may be able to do within our lifetime.

[1] In economic parlance, market failures occur when there arises problems in externalities, moral hazards, adverse selection, and asymmetric information.

[2] For example, in times of recession lack of confidence prevents firms from investing and households from spending, but it is precisely the joint increase in investors' and consumer spending that is needed to regain confidence and get out of recession.

[3] Hutchcroft (1997) p.231

[4] This was done in a highly charged volatile and explosive atmosphere of a "low-intensity conflict", where many Left organizations and individuals were being harassed and threatened.

[5] In fact, from the accounts of the Philippine Center for Investigative Journalism, it seems that the other competitor for the bidding of the reclaimed land in the PEA/Amari deal was allegedly "bought off".

[6] Further investigation would most likely reveal that another bank owned by a presidential friend would also be involved.

[7] This section is largely written by Grace Ong, the research associate of this project.

[8] Grand Air of course died a natural death some years later.

[9] Lucio Tan's hidden shareholdings of PAL (via Tony Boy Cojuangco) and eventual takeover of PAL should itself be a study of how key privatization of lucrative state enterprises had not been based on every transparent and accountable processes.

[10] Amando Doronila, "New Air pact Puts Strain on Estrada-Tan Relationship," *Philippine Daily Inquirer*, Oct. 2, 2000.

[11] This is not helped at all by the "old boys' club" and fraternity mentality, which absolves influential wrongdoers of any punishment or ostracism simply because they are one of the boys.

[12] Again this is what the Lee Kuan Yews, *Time, Newsweek*, and *International Herald Tribune* fail to see, so much so that they cannot distinguish genuine People Power from plain "mob rule".

[13] i.e. the weak and negative impact of governance structures in the post-liberalization administration in the eighties and nineties.

[14] The case of Russia wherein the shock treatment of market liberalization, deregulation, and privatization without the corresponding institutions and governance structures would be the most striking example.

[15] This affects not just "corrupt" policies but also controversial policies that break social cohesion, such as the recent banning of "Live Show", which effectively nullified decisions by the regulators by top officials.

[16] This allows the reformist government to change the rules of the "game", incentive structures and political practice (in short, institutions and governance structures) permanently so that succeeding governments will inherit a system of conducive and viable set of economic and political institutions.

REFERENCES

Bello, Walden (2000), "Political Science 101: The Mafia as Government in the Philippines," *Focus on the Philippines*, an electronic newsletter of Focus on the Global South.

Campos, J. Edgardo, ed. (2001), *Corruption: The Boom and Bust of East Asia*, Ateneo de Manila Press, Manila (forthcoming)

Coronel, Shiela, ed. (2000), *Betrayals of Public Trust*, Philippine Center for Investigative journalism.

Doronila, Amando, "New Air Pact Puts Strain on Estrada-Tan Relationship," *Philippine Daily Inquirer*, Oct. 2, 2000.

Hutchcroft, Paul (1996), "Corruption's Obstructions: Assessing the Impact of rents, Corruption, and Clientelism on Capitalist Development in the Philippines," A paper prepared for the Association for Asean Studies, April 11-14, 1996, Honolulu, Hawaii.

Hutchcroft, Paul (1997), "The Politics of the Privilege: Assessing the Impact of Rents, Corruption and Clientelism on the Third World Development," in Heywood, Paul, ed., *Political Corruption*, Blackwell Publishers, Oxford, U.K.

North, Douglas (1984), "Transaction Costs, Institutions, and Economic History," *Journal of Institutional and Theoretical Economics*, no. 140.

Polanyi, Karl (1957), *The Great Transformation*, Beacon Press, Boston.

Rodrik, Dani (1996), "Understanding Economic Policy Reform," *Journal of Economic Literature*, Vol. 34, no.3.

Rodrik, Dani (2000), "Development Strategies for the Next Century," presented at the conference on "Developing Economies in the 21st Century," Institute for Developing Economies, Japan External Trade Organization, Jan. 26-27, 2000, Chiba, Japan. http://orion.forumone.com/ABCDE/files.fcgi/145_rodrik-japan.pdf

Stiglitz, Joseph (2000), "Development Thinking at the Millennium," http://orion.forumone.com/ABCD/files.fcgi/211_Stiglitz.pdf

A Diary of Disenchantment

RANDOLF S. DAVID

JOSEPH EJERCITO ESTRADA became a phenomenon from the moment he ran for senator. A college dropout, a movie actor, a confessed womanizer, he was jeered by educated voters when he announced his candidacy for a national position. But he and Juan Ponce Enrile, a major figure in EDSA 1, were the only two candidates to survive a near-sweep by Cory Aquino's choices in the first post-EDSA elections of 1987.

"Erap," as he is more popularly known, seems to personify everything bizarre about Philippine politics. No one believes he has what it takes to administer the affairs of government. He is not known for any meaningful initiative in public affairs. His fans confuse him with the roles he plays in the movies. His votes always come from the lowest social strata of Philippine society. They look up to him as their champion; in their eyes he can do no wrong.

Having heard that I once helped draft some of his speeches when he was a senator, the foreign press would sometimes ask me to explain Erap to them after he became president. Professional and business organizations invited me to lecture about the new president and what his rise to power meant for the country. I kept notes and wrote my lectures about Erap, but I did not publish them. Looking back, I think I must have been vaguely aware of the danger of interpreting an elusive figure like him who had six years to falsify everything I was telling the world about him.

When his fall became imminent in November 2000, I revisited my notes to see how I read or misread the man at various points in his brief career as president of the country. I wanted to know for myself where I might have been misled, and at what point I began to see Erap in a different light. Chastened and hopefully a little wiser, I now offer these notes as a diary of disenchantment.

I suppose I was one of those wide-eyed academics from the University of the Philippines who, like the rest of the Filipino masses, were fooled by this clever *politico*. In both the literal and the theoretical sense, this experience could be summed up as one of *disenchantment*. The German sociologist Max Weber understood *disenchantment* as signifying an awakening from the spell of custom and charisma; in short, the beginning of rationality. Erap is a very friendly and charismatic person; it is difficult not to be charmed by him. Until the last moment just before he stepped down from Malacañang, members of his Cabinet, unable to free themselves from this enchantment, could not leave him. No longer president, Erap to this day continues to cast a spell on the psyche of the Filipino poor.

He had walked into the presidency with an electoral mandate that exceeded the record of all previous presidents of the republic except Ramon Magsaysay. In a field of 11 candidates, he won 39% of all the votes cast, more than twice the number of votes obtained by his closest rival, the administration's anointed candidate. With Erap, it may be said the spirit of EDSA 1986 has come to an end. For not only was Estrada not at EDSA; in fact he was in Malacañang consoling his friend and patron, Marcos, during the dictatorship's closing days. He remained a staunch Marcos sympathizer right to the very moment People Power was getting rid of the dictator. And he never apologized for this. It is thus understandable that his election to the presidency would be hailed by his enemies as a kind of restoration of the Marcoses.

Strictly speaking, Erap's victory did not signal the return of the Marcoses. The Marcoses had all already returned to the country before Erap became president. We can say however that Erap's assumption of the presidency was the *masa's* way of getting back at the post-EDSA elite for their benign neglect of the poor since 1986. Erap, to them, was the symbol of everything that was not EDSA. Unlike Cory, he was a friend of Marcos. Unlike Fidel Ramos, he was not an EDSA hero. He did not have a grand vision for the country. He was just a simple man with a simple message— *Erap para sa mahirap* (Erap for the poor).

His election affirmed the viability of Philippine democracy, but it also signaled the full return of patronage politics and crony capitalism. The educated and the middle classes rejected his candidacy, and many panicked when he got elected. The composition of his Cabinet however was very reassuring. There were hardly any politicians or businessmen in his official family. Erap loved to boast of the academics he had recruited into his Cabinet. Unlike Marcos, Erap did not threaten the oligarchy. He wanted to be accepted by the ruling class. Everybody assumed that his legendary intellectual limitations would prevent him from becoming another plunderer or dictator. The middle classes and the business community were skeptical about his managerial abilities, but they were willing to suspend their disbelief.

Erap's concern for the poor, though simplistic, seemed authentic enough. The intelligentsia saw in his special rapport with the masses a clear political mandate to carry out urgent social reforms. In their view, this grossly underestimated president, with proper guidance, might just surprise everyone.

It was against this background that I drew a sanguine picture of what the nation might expect of an Erap presidency in the next six years to a conference of medical doctors:

> **June 28, 1998.** There is no reason to doubt the genuineness of his concern for the poor, the propertyless and the marginalized in our society. As senator, he authored only two bills that became law and both of these addressed the needs of the Filipino peasantry. The first is a national irrigation act which remains unimplemented to this day, and the second is a carabao stock improvement and dispersal program that has benefited thousand of small farmers. He put all his earnings as a government official, from the time he was town mayor of San Juan to the time he became vice president, into a scholarship fund for indigent students, and year after year he raised money from his wealthy friends to replenish that fund.
>
> He plans to extend the reach of that scholarship fund now so that every year he can send some Muslim students abroad to do graduate studies so that they can become pioneers of modernization in Mindanao when they come back. [Little did anyone suspect this was supposed to be taken from *jueteng* collections.] As a movie actor and producer, he established the movie workers' welfare fund or Mowelfund to take care of the needs of the underpaid contractual workers in the movie industry—the cameramen, the drivers, the stuntmen, the extras, who earned only a small fraction of the fees of the big stars. But this certainly doesn't make him a socialist or even a social democrat. For, he does not seem to believe in the wisdom of government running business enterprises. In fact, he wants the remaining businesses of government privatized. He believes in foreign

investments, in the constructive role of the IMF, in deregulation, and in private enterprise. He does not believe in confiscating private property, not even for agrarian reform. He has vowed to continue all the economic reforms introduced by President Ramos. None of his economic advisers may be regarded a radical—they are all free-market advocates.

Like everyone else who wished him well, I believed Erap when he said that although he could be accused of many things, his name had never been associated with corruption. But controversy hounded his presidency practically from day one. When he announced he would not mind allowing Marcos to have a hero's burial, veterans of the anti-Marcos struggle protested it as an insult to the spirit of EDSA. Not having been part of the campaign against Marcos, Erap did not understand what the fuss was about. To him what was important was that Marcos had been his friend:

All in all, I think Erap is a Filipino who tries to live by the code of honor of an older generation. This code of honor revolves around old-style values like keeping one's word (*palabra de honor*), loyalty, obedience to one's parents and elders, courage, generosity, defense of the weak, and accountability for one's actions. To this day, he told me in an interview, he fears his 93-year-old mother. All his life, he said, he has been trying to be what he thought would make his father proud of him. His father was a sanitary engineer for 30 years, and he kept reminding the young Joseph that the family's greatest wealth was its clean name. None of his children should do anything to tarnish that good name.

I think that Joseph Estrada knew that he had nothing to gain from insisting that the remains of Ferdinand Marcos be buried in the *Libingan ng mga Bayani*. Like Fidel Ramos, he could have ignored the request of the Marcos family, or pleaded for more time to consider its implications, or followed the path of least resistance, and left it to Congress to debate its wisdom. But he went ahead and stuck his neck out on a matter that held for him absolutely no political value. Why?

First of all, I do not think it was, as some people viewed it, just a matter of repaying political debts. Everyone knows that Erap did not need whatever votes the Marcoses could command to ensure his victory. By the time Imelda Marcos announced her withdrawal from the presidential race, the surveys were already pronouncing an Erap victory. Moreover, unlike in 1992, Imelda's base had already dwindled considerably in the last election. Any association with her would be for Erap more a liability than an asset.

Neither could it have been blind loyalty. Erap was just a small-town mayor during the time of Marcos; he was never, according to him, a Marcos crony. He too opposed martial law, he says, and campaigned against constitutionalizing the legislative powers that Marcos had grabbed for himself in 1972. For six years he fought Marcos, and twice Marcos had him arrested.

But Erap does not deny that after Marcos talked to him and told him he was lifting martial law, their relationship became better. He might have been naive to believe him, but the support he got from Malacañang, he now recalls, was crucial to the success of his projects as mayor of San Juan. "I will always be grateful to the man," he told me in a recent interview, "for what he did for my constituents in San Juan."

I think it is quite obvious that despite the grave mistakes that Marcos committed during his presidency, Erap still finds much to admire in this man, the most reviled leader in the country's political history. "I kept quiet during the EDSA revolution," he told me in the same interview, "but I was one of those who went to see Marcos in Malacañang when everybody else seemed to have abandoned him. He was all alone. *Kawawa naman.*"

Erap remembers that he paid dearly for being seen as standing on the wrong side of EDSA in 1986. Investigators from the Cory government came to examine his assets and the accounts of his municipality and, though they could find nothing they could use to charge him, he was dismissed as mayor of San Juan. "I might not have aspired to become senator or even president someday," he now reminisces, "if not for Nene Pimentel and Cory Aquino, who unjustly removed me as mayor."

Here, I think, we have a clue to a facet of Erap's character: an almost instinctive need to side with the underdog of the moment. He sees himself as a warrior who must rise above enmity in order to provide comfort to someone who is already down. It is ironic that he himself is seen as a bully, for he seems to have a sharp aversion to any kind of bullying. Looking back, I now believe it was this image of the bully that he saw in the U.S. negotiating panel on the bases, and that strengthened his resolve to fight the American bases no matter what the costs.

We can mock this quality as a hangover from his days as a juvenile toughie in Ateneo or as a *masa* hero in many Tagalog movies. But that is the way he was molded by the contingencies of his personal life. It is also, not surprisingly, what endears him to his countless movie fans.

Perhaps it is unavoidable that people who are interested in knowing what an Erap presidency is going to be like should invariably ask what kind of person he is. Governments in our part of the world are expected to be critically defined by the personalities of their leaders, whereas western governments tend to be defined more by the program of the political party in power than by the idiosyncrasies of the president or prime minister. The reason for this is the low level of institutionalization of political life in developing societies like ours as compared to the highly bureaucratized systems of developed countries like, let us say, Germany or the U.S. Thus, while it seems senseless to ask what a Helmut Kohl government is like, it makes every sense to wonder what an Erap government or a Mahathir, or a Lee Kuan Yew government is like.

Yet, we all know that, while crucial, the personality of an incoming president is only one of many factors that determine the future of a nation. Just as important are things like: the quality of the new Cabinet and the state of the national, regional, and global economy. Furthermore, a new administration must always work within the formed routines of an existing bureaucracy, within the bounds of an existing social system, and within the constraints of an existing culture. Such things do not change and cannot be changed overnight; rather, they serve as the overall formative context within which a new regime must operate, the basic ground rules within which power must be exercised.

Only a radical revolution can change these rules, but, even then, a revolutionary government must still contend with the inertia of an inherited culture and the pragmatics of an economic crisis. The Sandinistas of Nicaragua discovered this for themselves a few years after their revolution, and ended up practically handing over power to the bourgeoisie's Violeta Chamorro.

With all the good intentions that Erap brings into the presidency—his desire to equalize opportunities for the poor, the landless peasantry, the underemployed workers, and the marginalized cultural minorities, while fostering economic growth through private enterprise—I feel confident that our nation is in safe hands as it crosses over to the next millennium.

It was clear to me from the start that Erap is a product of his culture. I knew that his instincts would incline him to one direction, but I was confident that there were enough countervailing forces to neutralize the pernicious effects of a traditional political culture. The first few months of the Erap administration saw the appointment of very credible individuals to the Cabinet and to various top positions in government. But rumors of new and old cronies hovering around the president all the time quickly began to spread. At the same time, the media had a field day reporting many instances of presidential gaffe at social functions and ambush interviews. The media did not distinguish between the big and small lapses. Erap complained that he was being made into a laughing stock. I tried to address these concerns in a sympathetic way in a talk before a small group of business, almost a year after Erap assumed the presidency:

> **March 1999.** Foremost in the minds of the business community is the wholesale return to cronyism. I argue that if we adopt a historical perspective, we will see that this pernicious practice is basically a function of the very structure of our politics, and is not particular to any president or administration, or for that matter to our culture. Cronyism is traceable to the expensiveness of our elections, the immaturity of our political parties, the enormous personal debts that a president incurs on his way to the top, and the personalistic culture that contradicts the legal-rational premises of our formal institutions.
>
> I note with alarm President Estrada's hasty repayment of political debts to his patrons. This invites suspicion that the ghost of Marcos is upon us. But I remain hopeful that countervailing forces will make it difficult, if not nearly impossible, to revive the kind of crony capitalism that the Marcos regime so classically exemplified.
>
> One such countervailing force is the presence of crucial checks in our democracy—a militant and irrepressible media, a vocal church, and a vibrant civil society, all of which will become silent only if we allow another dictatorship to be established in our country. The other is the more direct and immediate form of fiscal and political discipline that participation in a globalized economy has made possible, as we have seen from the recent events in Indonesia, Thailand, and South Korea.
>
> By his appointment of credible individuals to key economic positions, the President has shown a readiness to abide by the ethic of transparency that international investors and agencies now insist upon as a measure of creditworthiness.

It is clear that I was banking on the strength of our economic institutions and on the effectiveness of the disciplinary powers of international agencies as deterrents to corruption. I was also optimistic that the vocal media and the watchfulness of civil society would serve as a powerful antidote against cronyism and corruption. I was right about the militancy of media and civil society, but I was wrong about the integrity of our economic institutions. Media did not leave him alone and became more mocking in its criticisms. But again, I took a kinder view of the situation and thought that the media was being unduly harsh and was not giving him a chance to prove himself:

> **March 1999.** Skepticism about President Estrada's ability to lead has persisted. The media, the business community, the diplomatic corps, and indeed the whole nation, have watched and listened in bewilderment, and sometimes disbelief, each time the president pronounced his views on a variety of issues. More to express their dismay over his style than to analyze the wisdom of his positions, some media commentators have characterized him as an impulsive, tough-talking, macho movie actor, a shameless crony-coddler, an unwitting godfather to questionable contracts, a closet dictator, a boor, and an ill-mannered male chauvinist.
>
> At the base of such descriptions is the educated Filipino's discomfort with the kanto-boy kind of vulgar wit and coarse behavior that the president seems to exude when he has not been rehearsed. Erap seems to be the very opposite of political correctness. Whenever he speaks without a prepared speech, whether in English or Tagalog, he slides into a familiar grunt, a patented way of talking tough that immediately connects him with the *masa*, but which sharply alienates him from the intelligentsia and the middle classes, who expect more decorum from the highest official of the land.
>
> I sometimes wonder whether his pronouncements would sound more respectable and reassuring if they were uttered with greater deliberation and care than he has so far shown in his public appearances. I often wonder if it is largely a matter of style and projection. Or whether it is more than that. What is it that troubles us about the president?

The situation was obviously more than just a public relations problem, although the tendency of the people around him had been to treat every negative reporting as precisely nothing more than a p.r. job. But I felt then that it was too early to declare the Estrada presidency the unmitigated disaster that his most vocal critics had painted it to be. This was too cruel and premature a verdict, especially for the more than 10 million Filipinos who had voted for him. I kept a fervent hope that he would not disappoint the *masa* who trusted him so much:

March 1999. On more than one occasion, I have heard him say that the *masa* made him what he is today. The same *masa* who patronized his movies also made him mayor, senator, vice president, and president. The more the elitist press laughs at him for his lack of refinement, the more he identifies with the oppressed. In the vocabulary of his own culture, he is transparent; he detests the hypocrisy of those who imagine themselves to be morally superior to the average Filipino. He perceives himself as nobody's tool. We may not agree with such a perception, but it is how he thinks of himself.

Here is a man who is out to prove he is a much better person than what the snobbish educated classes may have imagined him to be. He wants them to realize that they have misjudged him. At the heart of such a redemptive wish is a yearning to be remembered as a quiet doer, a flawed hero with a pure heart who proved his detractors wrong. In a sense, this is a re-run on a larger scale of the parable of the prodigal son who came home to redeem himself in the eyes of his father.

Only with this thought in mind can we begin to understand some decisions of the president that pleasantly stunned even his critics, and which seem to contradict our negative impressions of him. There's the appointment of Justice Hilario Davide as chief justice of the Supreme Court, and of former Justice Cecilia Muñoz-Palma as head of the Philippine Charity and Sweepstakes Office, a milking cow that would have made an Erap supporter very happy. There's also the appointment of Harriet Demetriou to the sensitive Comelec post of head commissioner.

We have seen other examples of this kind of surprising persistence. There's, for example, the politically suicidal resolve to get rid of the pork barrel, the refusal to give up on the Philippine Airlines even when it had become almost pointless to try to revive a moribund national flag carrier, and the decision to champion the cause of the persecuted Anwar Ibrahim, former deputy minister of Malaysia.

And let us not forget the current presidential obsession with the clean-up and rehabilitation of the Pasig River. He imagines this river to be the mirror of our national self-esteem, and he aims to bring it back to its old glory, though from another point of view, there may be more pressing tasks than this.

These may all be just for show, but I think these are decisions that tell us something about the president. Unfortunately, they are dwarfed by the longer list of presidential pronouncements that seem to show the darker side of the president—for example, his misplaced extravagant praise for his friend Lucio Tan, even as the man is facing a P25-billion tax-evasion charge; or his refusal to lift a finger to stop the return of San Miguel Corporation to Danding Cojuangco even if the timing is indecent, or the ease with which he cleared two members of his Cabinet of any culpability in connection with the P3-million bribe attempt while it is still being investigated.

Well, this is the Erap of the *barkada* culture, the tough guy who knows how to repay debts and how to protect and take care of his own people so long as he knows implicitly that they have done no wrong. He will go out of his way to accommodate his friends provided they do not abuse his trust or profit too much at the expense of the people. If he can find an overlap between what is good for the nation and what is good for his friends, that, for him, would be the ideal situation. Still, he wants to draw the line: he will not accommodate a private request if it means having to sacrifice the larger interests of the country. That may be a delusion on his part, but, again, that is his own belief and perspective.

As things turned out, the more crony and personal interests he had to accommodate, the narrower his definition of graft and corruption became. So long as he thought he was not directly stealing public funds, it was all right for him to receive gifts or cuts from transactions that his office had approved. Indeed, as we now know, he did not have any qualms about using his powers to enrich his multiple families. This was information that was already fairly known in business and government circles. But no one among his closest associates had the courage to tell him it was wrong. Instead, they encouraged the view that some quarters in media were getting out of hand. Malacañang responded to these attacks by suing the

Manila Times and organizing a boycott of advertisers against the *Philippine Daily Inquirer*. This attack on the media galvanized middle-class sentiment against Estrada. On August 20, 1999, the first of many demonstrations against Erap unfolded in Makati. The key issue was the fight against Charter change, which Estrada was pushing. But in fact, the rally became an omnibus attack on media suppression, cronyism, and corruption. My assessment of the presidency at that point was contained in a situationer I wrote one week after that rally:

> **August 27, 1999.** Without meaning to slight their importance, but only to alert us to the way the president approaches these difficult issues, let me say that the August 20 issues are basically middle-class concerns. By this I mean they do not bear directly upon the situation of the vast masses of our people who are poor, the way issues like agrarian reform, employment, poverty, and high prices would. Nevertheless, they are powerful issues that can ignite massive protests; they have a potential for destabilizing the presidency.
>
> Erap's response will be to ignore the middle classes and instead to explain himself to the *masa*, while silently mounting a low-intensity war against his most strident critics. For him, the August 20 issues will not affect his popularity with the *masa*. His chosen operative framework permits him to rationalize everything in the name of lessening the poverty and the economic insecurity of the many. What puts him truly on the defensive is the charge that he has done nothing to alleviate the poverty of the *masa*.

Erap treated with ill-concealed contempt everything that was emanating from Makati. So long as he was sure the poor were happy with his administration, he could not care less what the elite thought. He also wanted to make sure that the international financial institutions were happy with his policies. This is why he was pushing for Charter changes. These proposals became a lightning rod for criticisms against his presidency, but the issues were too technical to be adequately grasped compared to the problem of cronyism:

> I believe that in the short term, the Charter change issue will die down as will the brouhaha over press freedom. What will persist through the remaining years of the Estrada administration is the charge of cronyism and the coddling of the Marcoses.

As expected, the Marcos hidden-wealth issue was overshadowed by the problems brought about by the aggressive Chinese-Filipino cronies of Erap. Most of these businessmen did not enjoy a good reputation either in the business community or in the local Chinese-Filipino community. But Erap enjoyed having them around, to the dismay of his Cabinet members who felt their presence fanned the negative perceptions about the president. These perceptions soon found their echo in the plunging approval ratings of the president. The October and December 1999 ratings caused Erap to panic. I wrote an assessment of this worsening situation:

January 18, 2000. When Erap received the latest SWS results last December, he knew they spelled more trouble. He decided to jump the gun on media by informing reporters at a Christmas gathering in Malacañang of the latest scores, which showed a further drop to 5% of his net satisfaction rating. What he did not tell the reporters was that the dissatisfaction cut across all classes this time, with the sharpest drop occurring among his vaunted constituency—the D and E classes.

The first time that Erap panicked over poll ratings was in mid-October, when the public disapproval of the fight he picked with the *Inquirer* and of the settlement on the Marcos wealth he tried to broker first registered in the surveys. His ratings had dropped from +65 to +28. His public reaction then was to dismiss the value of these ratings. But he was so troubled by the survey results that he called in a group of his closest advisers to quickly line up a few announcements that would win him some *pogi* points. For example, he named himself housing czar and created an ill-conceived Presidential Commission for Mass Housing in order to project the impression that he was doing something about his avowed pro-poor program. He hastily signed an executive order prepared by Lenny de Jesus and his cronies in the housing sector, but he apparently did not understand its whole meaning and implication. Among other things, the EO gave to one of his unaccountable advisers, Sel Yulo, full powers as co-chairperson of the commission over all line agencies of government involved with housing. In December he did the same thing by creating the Economic Coordinating Council, a superbody that diluted the authority of his own economic managers, notably the secretary of finance. Unfortunately for him, his principal housing officials, led by Karina David, and the finance team, led by Ed Espiritu, quit unexpectedly to protest the questionable role being played by unaccountable presidential advisers in the crafting of public policy.

The 5% net satisfaction rating for the last quarter of 1999 mirrored the alarming erosion of the president's popularity. To be sure, it is not the lowest score for a Philippine president. President Ramos registered a 1% net satisfaction in October 1995 as a result of the mishandling of the Flor Contemplacion case and the rice shortage that hit the country during the year. But that was more than three years after FVR's election as president. In contrast, Erap's scores underwent a steep decline after just one year of his presidency. They may well continue to slide down to below zero levels even before he reaches the midpoint of his term. When that happens, the question to ask is how he can continue to govern the country with any degree of effectiveness.

Unfortunately for Erap, the opinion polls are conducted every three months. What he won in the elections he now has to affirm every quarter. This is both good and bad for the country. It is good in the sense that apart from the media, the opinion polls help force the president to abide by the law and to respect public opinion. But it is bad in the sense that when you have a publicly doubted and deeply insecure president like Erap whose leadership stands on nothing else but popularity, the quest for quick *pogi* points becomes the primary aim of government. The situation forces the government to go for short-term responses and cosmetic changes rather than for long-term enduring institutional reforms. The few genuine reformers in government become timid overseers of bureaucracies run by inertia, until they themselves are forced to give up. Or they themselves become cynical practitioners in the art of government by photo opportunity.

Meanwhile, the same problems that have bedeviled our society, some of these over the last one hundred years—absolute poverty, the scandalous gap in wealth and opportunity, disease, the drug menace, rampant crime, insurgency, graft and corruption, urban blight, the ecological destruction of the countryside, and cultural malaise—remain untouched. Wrong leadership and bad government lie at the root of these problems. We stand helpless before them because it is far easier to adjust to wrong leaders and bad governments than it is to mount a political and moral challenge against the system they represent.

We are all familiar with the basic features of this system. It is the system that links money politics to expensive elections, that looks upon government as primarily a means to protect, consolidate, accumulate or expand private wealth. In this system, politicians are forced to spend millions to launch a campaign, as well as to buy votes, and the bulk of the money needed is supplied by political patrons and investors who expect a payback after the elections. In a recent speech before the Foreign Correspondents Association of the Philippines (Focap), Erap admitted that he had incurred huge political debts to patrons like Lucio Tan and Danding Cojuangco in his quest for the presidency. He said he would pay them back with good government. No one, of course, not even the most ignorant voter in this country, believes that.

The *masa* knows that cronyism is part of our political reality, but they are also hoping that even as he repays his patrons and earns some money for himself, Erap would do something to change their situation. This is not what they see however. What they are seeing, to their dismay, is at best a confused and mis-advised leader and at worst an incompetent and corrupt president who cannot get away from the evil clutches of his *barkada*.

By this time, the situation in Malacañang had become unwieldy, with so many advisers and consultants feeding the president all kinds of advice. As these advisers typically saw it, however, the problem was no more than perceptual. Their plan of action revolved around the idea of overriding the negative perceptions with positive ones. And the reckless solution they hit upon was to start a shooting war in Mindanao. Throughout April and May 2000, the government launched a war not only against the Abu Sayyaf hostage-takers but also against the Moro Islamic Liberation Front. The Mindanao war almost completely swept cronyism and corruption from the front pages. Even the initial calls for Erap's resignation started by the Exclamation Point Movement had to be shelved in view of the Mindanao problem. In September 2000, I wrote the following national situationer:

> **September 6, 2000.** The war in Mindanao and the Sipadan hostage crisis easily dominated national attention in the last five months. Almost overnight these two events swept the anti-Erap calls for resignation out of the front pages and TV headlines. In the face of a real war and an internationally embarrassing hostage situation involving victims from many nations, it seemed suddenly unsporting or unpatriotic to continue attacking the president. But more important, the tough stance taken by the government towards the Abu Sayyaf in Basilan and the MILF in Central Mindanao tapped into deep-seated

Filipino Christian prejudices and gave the administration the break it had been longing for. The overrunning of the MILF camps and the hoisting of the Philippine flag in every captured Islamic stronghold became, as it were, a replay of the Crusades in the Filipino public's imagination. As expected, Erap's net approval ratings for the second quarter rose by six points, confirming in his mind the essential correctness of his strategy in Mindanao.

Mindanao so dominated the news during this period that hardly anyone noticed the two well-documented report of the Philippine Center for Investigative Journalism that came out at around the same time that the military offensive in the south began:

> **September 6, 2000.** The one issue that has dogged the Erap presidency relentlessly is the issue of corruption and cronyism. To the foreign media and investors, it is this, more than the handling of the Mindanao situation, which makes them deeply skeptical of the present leadership. Lucio Tan and Danding Cojuangco are the two most important friends of the president, to whom he cannot say no. It is not an accident that they were his biggest campaign financiers, for they are the ones who also stood to gain most from an Erap victory. Danding got San Miguel without much trouble; now he awaits a favorable resolution of the long-standing case over the coco levy funds. Lucio got PAL, then PNB, and now he will walk free without having to pay a single centavo of his P25-billion tax liabilities. I have said before that Erap is a creature of *utang na loob*; he will not hesitate to go out of his way to personally intercede to make *areglo* for his friends. He did it for the small fry like BW's Dante Tan. He will do it again and again for Danding and Lucio Tan.
>
> Not to be outdone in the frenetic race to accumulate while they are in power are the various families and relatives of the president. The two reports of the Philippine Center for Investigative Journalism (PCIJ), detailing the various Erap households that have bought choice real estate in plush subdivisions in Metro Manila and the businesses of the companies associated with children or the mistresses, show only the tip of the iceberg.

The issue of presidential corruption re-occupied the center stage as soon as the situation in Mindanao settled down. The tale of the mistresses and the mansions built for them became the talk of the town. But Malacañang brushed all this aside. The furor was expected to die down, but did not. An unlikely whistle-blower turned up in the person of Ilocos Sur Gov. Luis 'Chavit' Singson, one of the closest friends of Erap's. I noted:

October 16, 2000. While, for now, Erap's popularity may have received a boost from the military victory over the MILF, corruption and cronyism will nevertheless continue to hound him for the remainder of his term. The reason for this is the man's recklessness and almost spiteful attitude toward his political opponents. He seems convinced that the corruption and cronyism he is accused of are an integral part of our political system. Therefore, in his view, these charges would never stick.

I thought that the chances were low that someone would emerge who could provide the crucial information. Erap is feared by his friends and enemies because of his capacity to hit back by exploiting one's vulnerabilities. A catalyst was needed who would bring energy back to the flagging state in which the anti-Erap movements have found themselves. Luis 'Chavit' Singson was farthest from my mind as that possible crucial catalyst.

The man is a known die-hard inner circle *kumpadre*, a member of the regular presidential mahjong quorum, the primus inter pares of the palace gofers, the quintessential Erap loyalist. The sort of buddy who would die for his friend, who understood the unspoken rules of the underworld subculture, where loyalty more than anything else was paramount.

Such a man would betray his patron only under the most extreme condition. For example, if his own life has been threatened. Erap says he has learned at least one lesson in the past week—that he was wrong about his choice of some friends, in obvious reference to Chavit. We can be certain that that is exactly how Chavit feels about him too. His own boss humiliated him, dumped him in favor of a young cocky Chinese-Filipino chum, and treated him as if his own loyalty meant nothing. But the final straw was that his erstwhile friends even tried to draw Chavit into a gunfight by staging a police apprehension, in the hope maybe of finishing him off.

From the day of Chavit Singson's first explosive press conference, things moved very fast. The senate Blue Ribbon Committee initiated an investigation of the charges aired by Singson. But appearing stunned, Malacañang could not mount a coherent response to the fast-developing crisis of the presidency. I wrote:

> **October 23, 2000.** It took Malacañang exactly one week before the president's men could respond with any coherence to this devastating threat on Erap's presidency. That period of inaction was very costly. All that Erap could mouth was that his conscience was clear, and that he never benefited from *jueteng* money. Such blanket denial was no match against the very detailed narration of events provided by Chavit Singson. The result of this has been the massive erosion of the president's credibility. Damage control was all that the presidential brother-in-law Raul de Guzman had in mind when he sought the counsel of colleagues from academe. For a while Malacañang found comfort in the quick survey done by Pulse Asia, showing 53% of the 395 respondents surveyed still supporting Erap against the *jueteng* charges. But the other side of those figures showed an equally disturbing picture. A significant number of Filipinos approaching 50% of the population no longer trusted the president.
>
> As a diversionary tactic meant to recover some lost moral ground for the president, a decision was made not only to crack down on *jueteng*, but also to cancel jai alai, online bingo, and casino online which had flourished under Erap. He also announced a plan to privatize Pagcor, the government's gambling agency. The proposal backfired. Newspaper editorials and comments laughed at the announcement as another attempt by Erap to enrich his cronies by handing over to them the government's foothold in the highly profitable gambling industry.
>
> The following days saw the president's men mounting a counteroffensive on two fronts. First, at the House of Representatives, where Erap rabid supporter Congressman Danilo Suarez circulated for signatures a declaration of unconditional support for the president. On the day the impeachment case was filed by 42 representatives, Suarez gifted the president with a list of 145 congressmen manifesting their confidence in his leadership. The following day, these signatories followed a line of congressmen to the palace with only one purpose—to secure the quick release of the pork barrel allocations for their districts.
>
> On the second front, the secretary for housing, Lenny de Jesus, and the head of the National Anti-Poverty Commission (NAPC), Donna Gasgonia, organized high-profile sorties for Erap to depressed

squatter communities in Metro Manila. In three days, he went to five locations' distributing certificates awarding homelots to settlers who have taken over government lands over the years. These certificates have no legal value; the process of legalizing the homelot awards can well extend beyond the term of Erap. In short, the president is distributing illusions once again, buying loyalties with extravagant promises of land.

As he speaks from makeshift stages in these communities, Erap skillfully deploys the class-conflict-laden language of his early movie scripts, denouncing the "*insulares* and *peninsulares* of Makati" who, he says, have opposed his presidency from day one. He ends his speeches by reiterating his decision not to resign so that he could continue serving the poor, who were after all, he says, the ones responsible for putting him there. Not content with these populist tactics, Erap has used television quite extensively to denounce his enemies, who he says are trying to destroy him, singling out former presidents Ramos and Aquino. He is hurting and he is dangerously desperate.

Indeed Erap's credibility had been irreparably damaged by this time. The call for his immediate resignation resounded throughout the country. Public pressure was focused upon the members of his Cabinet. If they all resigned, the ensuing isolation of Erap could hasten his resignation. It wasn't to be. But the pressure had built up so powerfully it found its mark in Congress, and yielded a dramatic impeachment resolution at the Lower House. In November 2000, I thought the situation had become untenable, especially on the economic front. From a speech I gave, I excerpt the following:

November 15, 2000. The peso's fall has continued, breaking one psychological barrier after another. When it hit 50 and beyond, everyone became convinced that the greatest pressure for resignation was coming from the fear of an economic collapse. The steep decline in the value of the peso mirrors the erosion of any remaining confidence in the Erap administration. The palace was so gripped by panic that Erap's spin doctors brought in the American strategist who had helped him in 1998. The wily Ernie Maceda, our ambassador to Washington and a veteran in political manipulation, was also asked to map out a plan of action to ensure the survival of Erap.

But it was the unified call for resignation emanating from the business community that has caused the strongest tremors. This was followed by the mass resignation of the senior economic advisers, which seemed so stunning and so sudden that Malacañang at first denied knowing about it.

Finally, Mar Roxas's departure from the Cabinet signaled what everyone thought was the beginning of the much-awaited desertions of Cabinet members. Roxas's resignation however found echoes not in the Cabinet, where they were most awaited, but in the ranks of the ruling party, the LAMP.

At that point, the momentum that had built up during the last two weeks of October seemed to fizzle out. Erap kept in close contact with his Cabinet; Maceda was tasked to ensure that the president had the minimum number of votes in the senate that would block an impeachment. The senate Blue Ribbon committee suspended its hearings on the *jueteng* charges for two weeks, thus preventing an early interrogation of Edward Serapio, Erap's personal lawyer. And the SWS, with remarkable timing, released the results of an October 30 survey purporting to show that 44% of the people did not believe that Erap should resign. Malacañang seized upon this survey as if it were a lifesaver thrown to a drowning man.

I think we are fast approaching the midpoint of this extended process. Erap has dug in; I don't see him resigning within the next six weeks or before the end of the year. I think there was a real chance that he would have resigned during those crucial days following All Saints Day, if only his Cabinet had been bold enough to leave him.

In any case, the resign movement has gone far enough, and the *jueteng* revelations have been validated enough by other witnesses, that no one who has followed these events closely in the last few weeks could possibly think that Erap would survive this crisis. Definitely he will not be able to finish his term. The question is no longer whether he will go, but when.

My quick answer to this question is: before the May 2001 elections. I think the resign movement and the impeachment case will be drawing strength from one another in the coming weeks. We have seen how the resign movement in the streets drove an incredible number of congressmen to the side of the impeachers. That same strategy will have to be applied on the senate. While impeachment is very much a partisan exercise, there is every reason to think that the fear of alienating public support may force the re-electionists among the senators to be more circumspect in deciding how to vote on the case. But on the other hand, it may well be that money does speak louder than honor, and therefore it may be foolish for us to expect that we can find 15 incorruptible and brave senators who are willing to unseat a president.

In other words, there is a strong possibility that a minority vote in the senate may acquit Erap. All he needs are the votes of eight senators. With the recent reorganization of the senate, following the removal of Franklin Drilon as senate president, the chances of those eight senators voting to exculpate Erap have become very real.

But here's the irony. Erap may get off the hook by a minority vote, but at the end of the impeachment proceedings, he will have had no shred of credibility left. The decision to acquit him will thus provoke further protests. He will not be able to govern. If he does not resign in the face of massive protests and amid a collapsing economy, he will likely be ousted by other means.

The impeachment trial at the senate took off on a very dramatic note, with the revelation of the Jose Velarde check capping the opening statement of prosecutor Joker Arroyo. That set the tone for the rest of the trial. Suddenly, *jueteng* bribes were no longer the main issue. The main issue became the hidden wealth of the president. No one knew what kind of evidence was available. Each trial day brought out one more piece to a puzzle whose pattern was becoming clearer and clearer. I wrote about the preparations that were being made toward a post-acquittal scenario:

> **January 8, 2001.** I think we can now safely assume that under no circumstances will Joseph Estrada resign as president. The ongoing Cabinet revamp, marked by the installation of a technocratic proxy government led by newly designated Executive Secretary Edgardo Angara, represents his final desperate attempt to save his administration and to give it a legitimacy it could not hope to achieve with the likes of Ernie Maceda.
>
> It appears that our least preferred scenario—acquittal—may actually be the most plausible at this point. In previous analyses, I held out the possibility that in the event of an acquittal, public outrage may be so strong as to force Estrada to step down anyway. I also considered the possibility of a military intervention.
>
> I believe that Estrada has crossed the threshold—he is not interested in an acquittal as a form of moral vindication, or as an occasion

to step down gracefully. An acquittal for him would be a license to continue stealing and lying till the end of his term, and a reason to retaliate, if he can, against all his perceived political enemies. In short, I do not see Estrada ever resigning, especially not after an acquittal.

We are thus left with only three possibilities: (1) Conviction by the senate, (2) acquittal and (3) ouster by a popular uprising/cum military coup. Of the three scenarios, ouster is probably the most open-ended, the one full of surprises but also pregnant with danger. Its timetable will begin the moment the verdict of acquittal is handed down, but its timeline will be short. If Estrada is not removed by the end of March at the latest, the election fever will negate its urgency.

What frightens me about the ouster option is that by whatever means it is executed, it cannot be played out without the active cooperation of the military. We cannot assume that the military will remain a unified entity. We cannot discount the existence of elements within the institution that may be thinking of installing a junta to fill in the power vacuum in the event of widespread public disorder. Only a strong credible and professional leadership in the military—with a strong constitutional orientation—can avert the fragmentation of the army into warring forces. I am not sure if Gen. Angelo Reyes has that kind of clout. The role of civil society in ensuring that the military continuously adheres to its constitutional role cannot, of course, be overstated.

Estrada may force the issue of military loyalty if he declares a state of emergency and bans all public demonstrations. We cannot predict how the military and the police will respond to this order. I think much depends on the perceived legitimacy of the impeachment verdict.

We are actually in a bind here. We want to reform our institutions and promote a public culture appropriate to the globalized world and the new century in which our nation must participate. But we do not have the luxury of starting from scratch. We have to build from what we have, taking care not to destroy what is already in place no matter if our existing institutions are being abused by the buccaneers of a bygone age.

Up to that point, all indications pointed to the likelihood of a protracted struggle extending to the May elections. No one anticipated the rapidity with which the government would eventually collapse. The suppression of the second envelope containing vital bank documents pertaining to the Jose Velarde account triggered a quick succession of events that led to the downfall of Estrada on January 20. I wrote a postscript to my January 8 notes immediately after the assumption of the presidency by Gloria Macapagal-Arroyo.

January 22, 2001. Contrary to our worst fears, the resolution of the political crisis has come sooner than expected. It has also been decisive and non-violent. In short, the best of all possible scenarios has unfolded.

I am referring to the unceremonious ouster of President Joseph Estrada on January 20, 2001, after four days of popular demonstrations that culminated in what is now known as People Power 2.

How does one explain this swift almost surgical resolution of a multifaceted social crisis? To do so, we only need to review the key events of the past week.

With the installation of former Senate President Edgardo Angara to the position of executive secretary, the Estrada administration started to enact the basic elements of a post-acquittal script. Its basic aims were to assure the public of the Erap presidency's renewed capacity to govern, while ensuring the acquittal of Estrada in the impeachment case.

The impeachment trial itself managed to acquire a level of legitimacy in the public perception largely because of the fairness and even-handedness with which the presiding officer, Supreme Court Chief Justice Hilario Davide, ruled on legal and procedural issues during the trial. But as important, the trial gained much-needed credibility because the impeachment court permitted the presentation of evidence and testimony that was very damaging to the president. This gave courage to many vital witnesses who would otherwise have been intimidated from testifying or submitting crucial documentary evidence against the president.

Despite the open partiality of many senator-judges (which is allowed by law because of the political nature of an impeachment process), the public nevertheless looked upon the senate impeachment tribunal as the last constitutional guarantor of justice and truth. Failure by the senate to discharge this constitutional duty would push the country to the brink of an extra-legal resolution, whose consequences could be very costly.

Unfortunately for the president, the series of damaging testimonies by key witnesses—for example, SVP Clarissa Ocampo of

Equitable-PCIBank, former Finance Secretary Edgardo Espiritu, former Clark Development Authority Chief Rufo Colayco, former PSE President Jose Luis 'Nonoy' Yulo, and former SEC Chairman Perfecto Yasay Jr.—wounded the presidency so much that its trust ratings fell drastically day by day.

So we had a situation where the president was sure to be acquitted because he controlled the votes of at least 11 senator-judges. But at the same time, while he was on trial, he had to suffer the devastating negative publicity unleashed by the evidence and testimonies of the witnesses against him. He was confident of the senate vote, but he was distressed that he was fast losing the public trust. His allies were therefore in a hurry to finish the trial and end the presentation of adverse evidence, so that by mid-February the inevitable vote of acquittal could be handed down.

The dilemma of the president's lawyers was whether to allow all the evidence to be presented without questioning any of it just to speed up the process, or whether to block the presentation of damaging evidence for as long as they could in order to protect what remains of the president's mangled image. I think they have now realized on hindsight that they should have allowed the trial to proceed unhampered, since at the end of it all they had the numbers anyway. But, as we have seen, the president's men committed the biggest blunder of their lives. They miscalculated the public's capacity for outrage.

The penalty for this error became apparent on Tuesday evening, January 16, 2001. After a long discussion and debate on whether a second envelope sent by the Equitable-PCI Bank, purportedly containing the records of the mother account of the so-called Jose Velarde accounts, should be opened in court and its contents revealed, the presiding officer, Chief Justice Davide, was about to rule on the question. But, to everyone's dismay, he was preempted by a motion by Sen. Francisco Tatad, a known Estrada ally. Tatad called for a vote. Enrile seconded. The result was the ignominious 11-10 vote in favor of suppressing the evidence on the ground that it was irrelevant to the case at hand. The nominal voting allowed the public a preview of who among the senators would likely vote for Estrada's acquittal. This senseless "victory" of the Estrada side caused Sen. Tessie Oreta, a close personal friend of the president, to break into a dance. But to their horror, it also triggered the dramatic resignation of Senate President Nene Pimentel and, worst of all, the spontaneous indignation rallies that exploded on Tuesday evening and all through the succeeding days of that fateful week in January.

To this day, I don't think Estrada's forces knew exactly what hit them. They had misread the public pulse, and they had arrogantly mocked the strength of the citizens movement in the streets. From there on, the struggle for good government shifted from the senate to the streets once again.

From 20,000 outraged protesters who trooped to the EDSA shrine at midnight of January 16, Tuesday, the crowd grew to 100,000 the following day. By January 18, Thursday, half a million angry citizens calling for Estrada's ouster filled the vicinity of the shrine, spilling into the nearby shopping malls. By January 19, Friday, there were already more than a million people at the EDSA shrine, and they were determined not to leave until Estrada stepped down. After the commanders of the major services of the Armed Forces and the police announced before the crowd on Friday that they were withdrawing their support from Estrada, preparations were quickly mounted for a final march to Malacañang palace, the following day January 20.

On Mendiola, the street leading to the palace, a pro-Erap crowd of about 500, brought in by his political allies from various parts of the city's depressed communities as well as from nearby provinces, continued their vigil. They said they had come to protect the president. It was a menacing group; many of them were armed with stones and sharp sticks. The march to Mendiola could quickly lead to a bloody confrontation if the situation went out of hand. Jaime Cardinal Sin called on the EDSA shrine groups to abort their march to Mendiola. But the decision had already been made by the civil society organizations. They argued that it was necessary to force Estrada to flee the seat of the presidency and to put a final closure to the people's victory.

The historic march of citizens proceeded as scheduled. The police feared a bloody showdown. By the time the Mendiola marchers reached their destination, the pro-Erap group dwindled to no more than 200. Most of them later said they could not leave because the money promised them for their transportation back to their communities had not been paid. There were brief clashes, but they were not serious. In the end, Estrada had to flee with his family. It was 2:30 in the afternoon, January 20, 2001. He was forced out of the presidency by People Power. He issued a brief statement saying he was leaving the Palace in order to avert violence, but he refused to sign a formal letter of resignation. On the same day, at 12:30 noon, Gloria Macapagal-Arroyo was sworn in by Chief Justice Hilario Davide Jr. as the 14th president of the Republic.

On the day of his ouster, Estrada went home to his private residence in San Juan, Metro Manila, possibly the only head of state in the world to be removed by a bloodless popular uprising and allowed to go home. Today, January 22, 2001, there are rumors that Estrada's lawyers are planning to contest the legality of Macapagal-Arroyo's assumption of the presidency. There are also talks that Estrada forces might re-group, and with some backing from a segment of the military and the police they may attempt to re-take Malacañang. This dual presidency scenario is nothing new. We had it briefly in 1986, after Marcos announced to the world that he did not formally relinquish power, and that in fact he was "kidnapped" by the Americans. Rallies by Marcos loyalists continued too for some months, but eventually reality caught up with them.

What could happen here? It is possible that Estrada's men could create some trouble for the new administration, and they may use crowds to accomplish this. I think, however, that the objective is not so much to recapture power but to establish a negotiating position. There is a growing public clamor to press criminal charges for economic plunder against Estrada and his cronies using as evidence the various documents and testimonies given at the impeachment trial. The penalty for economic plunder is death. If he does not flee to another country, Estrada may well find himself behind bars before the year is over. I believe the purpose of these threatening moves by Estrada forces is to compel the new government to come to a compromise settlement. It would be a mistake, however, for President Macapagal-Arroyo to enter into such deals with Estrada because public outrage remains fresh.

Finally, let us turn to the legal and political questions here. Estrada lawyers like Rene Saguisag question the legality of Macapagal-Arroyo's takeover. This is a strange objection in the face of an undeniable political reality. Saguisag may as well file sedition charges against everyone who came to the EDSA shrine. People Power supersedes the Constitution—this is the political reality. If the people wanted to dissolve not just the Estrada administration but also the Constitution and along with it the whole government, it was within its power to do so. No law could have stopped it. But by an act of will, the people pulled back the revolutionary process and placed it on a constitutional track in order to allow the designated constitutional successor to ascend to the presidency. The resulting product is what I would call a "Constitutional Civil Society Revolt". A sitting president has been removed from office by the direct popular action of citizens—in that sense it is an uprising. The uprising has received the open and explicit support of the armed forces and the police, and, as well, the blessings of the entire Supreme Court. It is a creative mixture of the political and the legal—one more case for the political theory books.

As I write this, the Supreme Court, by a vote of 13-0, has just affirmed the constitutionality of Gloria Macapagal-Arroyo's presidency, thereby rejecting Erap's claim that he is a president-on-leave. This lays to rest the issue of legality that troubled the Macapagal-Arroyo presidency on its first month.

But there are problems ahead of a long-term nature. Two of these are poverty and corruption. They should be at the top of the new president's agenda. Macapagal-Arroyo is well positioned to begin the process of renewal in our political life. She is the first Philippine president to ascend to the highest office of the land without having to incur any political debts to the usual sources of campaign contributions. It will be recalled that Estrada became a captive of the tradeoffs resulting from the financing of expensive elections. Macapagal-Arroyo governs with a clean slate. She only needs to be sensitive to the voice of the people that put her where she is today. That situation opens up an entirely different dynamics between government and civil society. It is a wonderful time to reinvent our nation and its institutions. We can only hope we don't squander it a second time.

Yet it cannot be denied that for all his crimes, Erap continues to have a place in the hearts of many Filipinos. The poor will continue to cling to Erap as the leader who was unjustly kicked out by the rich. They will not accept that they had made a mistake in making him president. As far as they are concerned, he was not given enough time to prove himself as a president of the poor. Erap may no longer be president, but the disenchantment that is needed to free the *masa* from the spell of his charisma will not occur overnight.

March 3, 2001

Epilogue

THE SUDDEN RISE in the approval ratings and public acceptance of President Gloria Macapagal-Arroyo a month after she was installed to the presidency by People Power 2 was demoralizing to the former president and his followers. The events leading to Erap's ouster had been very swift; his supporters were simply too stunned to react. Meanwhile, the electoral fever had begun to spread across the whole nation. Nothing energizes the country more than preparing for elections. Unless the events of the past few months could be woven into electoral issues, the tragic fate of the former president seemed on its way to being sealed. After the Supreme Court affirmed the validity of Macapagal-Arroyo's succession to the presidency, nothing else could stop the filing by the Ombudsman of the corruption cases against the former president.

Erap seized upon the electoral campaign as a platform from which to rebuild his tattered constituency. Seeing that the Supreme Court had effectively closed his legal options, he found himself moving back into the political arena if only to make the point that he should not be treated as a spent political force. Now he was no longer fighting to get the presidency back; he was fighting to stay out of jail.

As in 1998, when he ran for president, he launched a renewed campaign to consolidate his support in the heart of the country's urban slums. In these well-attended campaign sorties, he wove a narrative of elite conspiracy and revenge that, he said, was aimed at unseating him from the moment he became president. He spoke of a collusion between the established church and the Makati business community that successfully pressured the military and the police to switch sides at the last moment. Never was such rhetoric heard before outside of Leftist circles. Media charged that he was dangerously fomenting a class war.

The wild reception he received during these slum visits lifted his morale. The speeches he gave were liberally spiced with lines from his movie scripts. He painted himself as the proverbial hero who took all the blows until he was down and presumed dead, only to come back with blazing fists. His audience loved the images of oppression and final redemption that he drew. They saw in his fall a reflection of their own misfortunes in a society run by the rich. They would not abandon their hero; they would fight with him.

The senatorial candidates that Erap endorsed saw that the same socially marginalized electorate who made him president could make them win in the May elections. Thus did their party, the Puwersa ng Masa, hit on the campaign slogan *"Walang Iwanan!"*, a toast to the virtue of fierce loyalty that binds friends to one another.

For as long as the mobilization of the underclasses remained within the parameters of the electoral campaign, the inflammatory speeches that Erap delivered before his supporters bothered no one. The new government saw the May elections as a step toward the full normalization of the political situation following the succession of Macapagal-Arroyo to the presidency on January 20. It was a prospect that was just too good to believe.

The Ombudsman had begun a process that was being carried forward by its own momentum. The haste with which it filed the corruption cases, only to withdraw and replace them with a single non-bailable case of economic plunder, sent the message that the government was determined to put Erap in jail before the elections. That message was not lost on Erap's supporters. What they saw was a man flat on his back, and the elite bent on sending him to jail. Erap played the role of the defenseless hero to the letter. He did not resist arrest; he maintained an enigmatic silence. He meekly went through the rituals of degradation to which all criminal suspects are subjected upon arrest. He was fingerprinted like a common criminal. A mug shot of the former president showed him stoically looking at the police camera, completely stripped of his dignity. That photograph found its way to all the newspapers and television stations. On hindsight, one could say it was the equivalent of Sen. Tessie Oreta breaking into a mocking jig during the impeachment trial. That image launched so-called "EDSA 3" and its companion, the May Day Mendiola siege.

The government completely mishandled Estrada's arrest. Instead of allowing him to voluntarily give himself up to the Sandiganbayan Court, the police insisted on serving him the warrant of arrest at his residence. More than a thousand policemen accompanied the arresting team in a massive show of force. The vehicle that carried the disgraced president was flanked on all sides by a phalanx of policemen. Television cameras recorded what looked like a funeral cortege on its way to the cemetery. Face to face with this theater of humiliation, Erap's supporters exploded in fury and could think of nothing else at that moment but to vent their anger and resentment in that very site of People Power 2—the EDSA shrine.

Denied round-the-clock coverage by mainstream media, the participants of "EDSA 3" boiled in absolute resentment over this mark of final exclusion from the affairs of society. They took the absence of extensive coverage as a sign that media regarded their rally as politically insignificant.

Erap's political allies and candidates saw in this outburst of fervor an opportunity to further polarize the electorate along class lines in the hope of capturing the support of the more numerous lower classes. Everyone who addressed the crowd thus found it obligatory to harp on the class theme, no matter how incongruous it was for a Juan Ponce Enrile, a Dong Puno, or a Jamby Madrigal to speak as if they had known the face of poverty all their lives.

Whether they realized it or not, the politicians who inflamed latent class resentments over four nights of relentless demagoguery were creating a mob that would take on a life of its own. The "EDSA 3" crowd attained its peak of possibly close to a million people on the night of April 29. Members of the Iglesia ni Cristo and El Shaddai, whose leaders counted themselves as Estrada's abiding political allies, contributed the necessary density to the already restive crowd. Metro Manila mayors and governors of neighboring provinces aligned with the Puwersa ng Masa transported their followers to the site every night. The crowd swelled especially during mealtimes, when packed meals were distributed from delivery vans.

Unlike EDSA 2, this was a crowd spoiling for a fight. Night after night, their leaders prodded them to express their pain before the imagined ruling class that had overthrown their president. The targets of their fury were identified for them: Gloria Macapagal-Arroyo, Cardinal Sin, former presidents Fidel V. Ramos and Cory Aquino, the millionaires of Makati, and the two giant TV networks that would not honor their "Poor People Power" by giving it the coverage they thought it deserved. The goal was to surround their homes or offices and then to charge into the presidential palace.

What began as a rally demanding justice for Erap quickly metamorphosed into an uprising demanding the resignation of the government. The divergent calls mirrored the complex motives that brought the crowd's participants together. Many came to manifest their sympathies for the fallen president. Some were paid for their participation. Many others thought they were participating in a *miting de avance*. Only a few had become aware that they were to be the civilian component of a well-planned coup.

The night of Sunday, April 29, was supposed to have been the moment of the big discharge. But the politicians who funded and managed the affair were split on the question of what to do with the crowd. One group wanted to march to Malacañang, the other insisted on staying put at the EDSA shrine. The split proved costly; before the leaders realized it, the crowd had started to dwindle. The following day, the government sent its emissaries to the leaders of the Iglesia ni Cristo and El Shaddai to warn them of the political adventure that was being cooked up by some members of the opposition, in which their members could become unwitting victims. With the withdrawal of the religious groups, the density of the crowd, the source of its strength and morale, significantly diminished. The restless thousands that remained sent a small test contingent to Makati to bring their message of anger right to the door of the elite. But they looked puny rather than menacing on Ayala Ave., and elicited from the office-bound morning commuters not fear but an amused gaze.

Malacañang capitalized on this momentary setback to announce that the planned coup against the government had been shelved. President Macapagal-Arroyo went on TV to say she wished they had gone ahead with their sinister power grab so she could crush them. She was referring to the politicians who were trying to break the unity of the military in order to form a military-civilian junta. But the remaining demonstrators at the EDSA shrine heard it as an arrogant dare. The crowd had dwindled to less than one-third its size by April 30, and was determined to discharge its remaining energy. At that point, no one would have been able to stop it from marching.

About a thousand civil society warriors, veterans of EDSA 1 and 2, were on their second night of vigil in Mendiola. Upon hearing that the "EDSA 3" forces had begun their march to Mendiola, young priests and nuns and students instinctively locked arms and took a position in front of the police. Fortunately, sensible leaders prevailed on them to move back. San Beda College opened its gates and allowed them to seek refuge inside the school even if no one expected the marchers to get that close to the palace.

Security around the palace was surprisingly thin. Blocking forces of the police had meant to stop the marchers at various points to prevent them from reaching the critical Sta. Mesa Bridge, the main approach to Malacañang from the back. But the marchers, numbering about forty thousand, just rammed through the police barricades. They penetrated Mendiola without much difficulty, some of them wildly banging on the closed gates of San Beda to scare and flush out the partisans of People Power 2 whom they knew had sought sanctuary inside.

Fighting the police and the military with stones, sticks, and molotov and pillbox bombs, the rampaging mob attempted several times to break down the front gate of the palace. Emboldened by the police's staunch refusal to fire at them, the rioters, now leaderless, engaged the police in a street battle that lasted more than ten hours. When they were finally dispersed, they formed small hunting packs that would vent their collective frustration on any symbol of authority or property they could lay their hands on—traffic lights and signs, media vehicles, a Red Cross ambulance, fire trucks, stores, etc. The last time something like this happened was the night the Marcoses left Malacañang in 1986, when for one brief moment, there were no guards at the palace.

This was no longer People Power as Filipinos had known it. The public could not identify with the violence, fury, and resentment that propelled "EDSA 3." This was the dark side of People Power. This was the mob power that the Western media had imagined People Power 2 to be. Its explosion on Mendiola on May 1 drove the difference between the unruly mob and the disciplined ranks of People Power more sharply than ever.

EDSA 1 and EDSA 2 were driven by righteous indignation, not by resentment. In these gatherings, outrage was always tempered by cheerfulness. The anger of the speeches was always balanced by the sense of hope embodied in the songs and in the religious rituals. In contrast, self-pity and resentfulness drove "EDSA 3." Its participants could not see beyond their fury. Yet for the first time, the poor were brought to a realization of the power that was potentially in their hands. Unlike at EDSA 1 and EDSA 2, they saw for themselves how they could shake up society in ways they have never before imagined.

It is most unfortunate, however, that the violence of "EDSA 3" should be associated with the underprivileged classes of Philippine society. Regardless of its class composition, any crowd has the potential of being transformed into a mob if subjected to the same rabble-rousing and inflammatory speeches that the EDSA shrine demonstrators went through.

In the final analysis what spelled the crucial difference between the first two EDSAs and their dark cousin was the quality of the leadership. There were many leaders at EDSA 1 and 2—no unbridgeable gap separated them from the rank and file. In contrast, "EDSA 3" was a gathering of followers who had nothing in common with those who directed and exploited their anger. True to form, these leaders were nowhere to be found when the marchers hit Malacañang.

Clearly, the poor must produce their own leaders if they are to become an enduring and constructive political force in our nation's life. They must create their own symbols, rid themselves of the weight of their bitterness, turn their backs on the patrons who promised them redemption but robbed them of their will to self-reliance, organize themselves, and fight for their children rather than for the politicians who habitually use them. Until then, they will remain raw material for the ambitions of cynical politicians and media icons, or warm bodies for military power grabs disguised as people power.

The self-organization of the poor will however not happen without basic changes in our existing social order. Worse than poverty, the marginalization of the Filipino poor has meant their exclusion from the world of meaningful and dignified employment. The nation must find productive use for their labor. We can only do this if we resolutely invest in the development of our people. Education, health and housing are the key areas of critical intervention. We cannot expect the market to access these for those without regular incomes. The government has no choice but to jumpstart the whole process. Only then can social renewal truly begin.

June 1, 2001

The ERAP Economy

CAYETANO W. PADERANGA JR., CRISTINE ATIENZA,
FERDINAND CO, and FLORA BELLE VILLARANTE[1]

IN MAY 1998, Joseph Ejercito Estrada was elected president of the Philippines. Among the ten serious candidates, he received nearly 40% of the popular vote. The next highest number of votes was a mere 14% of the total. While there was uncertainty resulting from the recent Asian crisis and the presidential elections, the belief was that President Estrada would be able to convert his electoral triumph into a surge in economic confidence and rapid growth. Instead, on January 20, 2001, he had to leave Malacañang palace after the military and police forces, together with a substantial portion of the Cabinet, withdrew their support. This had resulted from hugely sustained protest rallies at the EDSA shrine. The ensuing political turmoil created uncertainty and economic disorder.

The immediate trigger for this political explosion seems to be revelations of illegal activity at the highest levels of government. This combination of political doubts and economic insecurity may have ultimately spelled the fall of President Estrada. This paper, however, examines economic developments in the last two and one-half years and their role in the background dissatisfaction leading to the commotion.

Economic Performance

THE CONDITIONS right after the Asian financial crisis showed the Philippines to have been the least hit among the neighbors. Its exports had continued to grow in the period leading to the crisis—and would grow at an even faster rate after the ensuing currency adjustments—while the other countries had started to experience negative growth, at the same time that their imports were ballooning. The Philippines also had, finally, a few years of fiscal surplus to show, which signaled two things: convincing indications that it could control its fiscal deficit and, with that promise, a reduction in inflationary expectations.

Unfortunately, a series of political mishaps doused expectations. For example, even before Joseph Estrada took office, the controversy arising from his proposal to bury the dictator Ferdinand Marcos as a hero at the Libingan ng mga Bayani shook up middle-class confidence. Other embarrassing, if probably minor, incidents followed, but some raised governance issues that caused business and professional sectors to worry and take a longer time waiting and seeing. As a result, the investment and production recovery expected from the new government, given its large electoral mandate and the perceived strong economic fundamentals, did not materialize. Instead of the surge in economic activity that usually goes with a new administration, the Estrada administration could only manage modest increases in spite of fairly aggressive fiscal spending for pump-priming. The extremely fickle weather phenomenon El Niño, which wrought particular havoc on agriculture, may have been largely to blame. The mood, in any case, was one of disappointment.

Here are tables of comparative growths among Philippine administrations and among selected countries in the Association of Southeast Asian Nations (Asean).

Table 1. Philippine growth rates (1986 - 2000)

Year	Real Gross Domestic Product	Real Gross National Product	Population	Per Capita Real GDP	Per Capita Real GNP
1986 - 1990	4.7	5.4	2.4	2.3	3.0
1991 - 1995	2.2	2.9	2.7	0.5	0.2
1996 - 2000	3.5	4.1	2.2	1.3	1.9
1986 - 2000	3.5	4.1	2.4	1.0	1.7

Source: National Statistical Coordination Board

Table 2. Growth Rates of Real Gross Domestic Product in Asean (1986-2000)

Year	Philippines	Indonesia	Malaysia	Thailand	Singapore
1986 - 1990	4.7	6.3	6.9	10.4	8.2
1991 - 1995	2.2	7.8	8.7	8.6	8.6
1996 - 2000	3.5	1.7	4.9	0.5	6.3
1986 - 2000	3.5	5.2	6.8	6.5	7.7

Sources: National Statistical Coordination Board and Asian Development Bank

During1986-2000, the Philippine economy came under three presidents: Corazon Aquino (1986:Q1-1992:Q2), Fidel Ramos (1992:Q3 - 1998:Q2) and Joseph Estrada (1998:Q3: 2000:Q4). The highest GDP growth rate that the Aquino administration reached was 6.8% (1988) and the lowest was -0.6% (1991). The range for Ramos was between 5.8% (1996) and -0.6% (1998). The Estrada economy, however, did manage to grow moderately – 3.3% in 1999 and 3.9% in 2000 (although slackening in the last quarter). If the growth momentum had not been disrupted by controversies in 2000, the economy might have performed better. Figure 1 plots it:

Figure 1

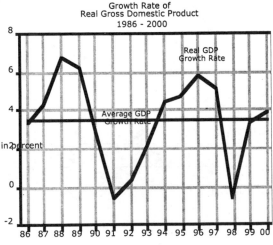

Source: National Statistical Coordination Board

In 1997, when the peso depreciated significantly, there occurred an unambiguous shift in the industrial. Because a compensating rise in the price level did not negate the depreciation, the composition of viable industries probably changed substantially. This arcane observation has real world equivalents: as some old industries stagnate, new ones acquire potentials for fast growth; some firms suffer, others gain at least in promise. However, the speed of stagnation may exceed the rate at which new firms are nurtured, leading to a decline in overall growth, even if temporary.

Figure 2 shows the shift toward the service sector that occurred in the last three years. From 43.4% of GDP in 1997, the share of the service sector went up to 45.7% in 2000, while that of the industry sector went down from 35.9% to 34.4%. The share of agriculture also declined.

Figure 2

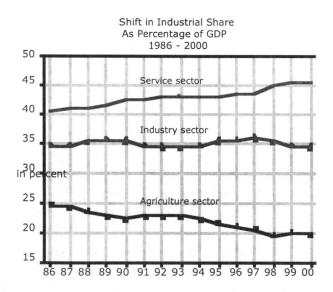

Source: National Statistical Coordination Board

The sectoral distribution of jobs also confirms this (Figure 3). Employment in agriculture went down from 45.7% of the total labor force in 1993 to 38.0% in 2000, while that in the service sector rose from 38.7% to 46.2%. The industry sector was consistent, absorbing around 16%.

Figure 3

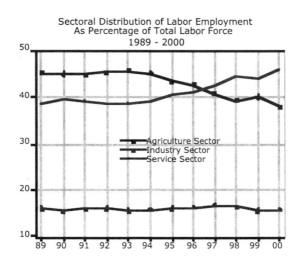

Sectoral Distribution of Labor Employment
As Percentage of Total Labor Force
1989 - 2000

Source: National Statistics Office

From 1986 to 2000, service remained the fastest growing sector, with an average growth rate of 4.3%, followed by industry (3.4 %) and agriculture (2.1%). However, in the last two years of Estrada, agriculture (4.7%) grew faster than industry (2.3%). This is attributed to the 6.0% growth in agriculture in 1999, a mere a rebound really from the negative 6.4% in 1998. Unfortunately, the moderate positive growth of agriculture and industry in 2000 has not generated enough jobs to keep up with the growing labor force in these sectors.

Table 3. Growth rates of the National Income Accounts – by industry
(1986 – 2000)

Year	Agriculture	Industry	Service	GDP
1986 – 1990	2.7	5.0	5.7	4.7
1991 – 1995	1.5	2.2	2.6	2.2
1996 – 2000	2.0	2.9	4.8	3.5
1986 – 2000	2.1	3.4	4.3	3.5

Source: National Statistical Coordination Board

Table 4. Contribution to GDP growth – by industry (1986 – 2000)

Year	Agriculture	Industry	Service	GDP
1986 – 1990	0.7	1.7	2.3	4.7
1991 – 1995	0.3	0.8	1.1	2.2
1996 – 2000	0.4	1.0	2.1	3.5
1986 – 2000	0.5	1.2	1.8	3.5

Source: National Statistical Coordination Board

It is also worth noting that, while imports remained the fastest growing component during 1986-2000, they posted a growth rate of negative 0.2% during the Estrada administration.

Table 5. Growth rates of National Income Accounts – by expenditure share
(1986 – 2000)

Year	Private Consumption	Government Consumption	Capital Formation	Exports	Imports	GDP
1986 – 1990	4.8	5.6	16.1	9.8	16.7	4.7
1991 – 1995	3.2	2.9	2.0	9.7	9.9	2.2
1996 – 2000	3.8	2.5	1.5	6.3	3.0	3.5
1986 – 2000	4.0	3.7	6.6	8.6	9.9	3.5

Source: National Statistical Coordination Board

Meanwhile, personal consumption expenditure continued to account for the largest share of GNP on the demand side (more than 70%). The high share of private consumption leaves the economy with less resource for domestic investment, thus reducing the prospect for economic growth.

Table 6. Percentage share to Gross National Product –
National Income Accounts by expenditure share (1986 – 2000)

Year	Private Consumption	Government Consumption	Capital Formation	Exports	Imports
1986 – 1990	74.8	7.8	19.8	29.8	32.0
1991 – 1995	76.3	7.8	21.8	36.1	43.7
1996 – 2000	74.5	7.6	21.9	43.5	53.1
1986 – 2000	75.2	7.7	21.1	36.4	43.0

Source: National Statistical Coordination Board

Since investments lead to capital accumulation, lower investment means less improvement on a key factor to economic growth and development—infrastructure. Figure 5 verifies this alarming picture of declining investment share since 1998.

Figure 4

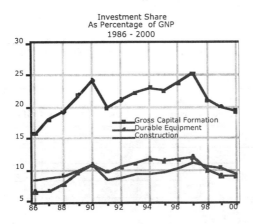

Source: National Statistical Coordination Board

One possible reason for this declining investment share is the declining share in domestic saving (Figure 5)—in good times, the current account deficit (foreign savings) increases. This indicates a relatively weaker domestic saving capacity. Lack of savings leaves the country more exposed to shocks and disturbance. As a nation, the Philippines has one of the lowest domestic savings rate in the region.

Figure 5

Source: National Statistical Coordination Board

The Fiscal Sector

AN IMPORTANT HIGHLIGHT of the Estrada administration is how lack of confidence primarily blunted its effort to pump-prime the economy. It left the new government with a very weak fiscal position as shown in the large national deficit, poor revenue collection, slow accumulation of savings, poor budgetary priorities, and the public debt overhang.

A major threat to the sustainability of the fiscal sector is the ballooning budget deficit, which can be traced to the large revenue shortfall relative to the rapid implementation of projects. After successfully turning up surpluses in 1994 to 1997, total deficit soared to P50 billion in 1998, P111.7 billion in 1999, and P132.5 billion in 2000. Hence, the Estrada government, which was characterized by three consecutive years of rising deficit financing, ended with a more vulnerable fiscal system than it had had when it began.

The government's inability to improve tax collection—in fact, a deterioration—in the last two years has led to the disappearance of the primarily surplus, resulting in an unsustainable public debt level and large public sector deficit. This basic inadequacy also has contributed to the low saving rate. This weakness extends to (and perhaps, is also caused by) the "distorted" public expenditure pattern—a disproportionately large share to personnel services (70%) and much less to maintenance and operating expenses (MOOE, 2%) and capital expenditure (10%).

The poor revenue collection is illustrated by the stagnation of tax buoyancy, which implies that, contrary to what the literature suggests, increases in economic activity lead to much lower percentage increases in tax revenue. One possible explanation is the weak revenue collection mechanism during the Estrada rule, which allowed huge leaks. The amplitude of tax laws, not to mention additional administrative measures, did not help. There is a growing consensus among policymakers and tax researchers that losses due to tax evasion of personal income taxes are extremely large. In 1999 tax buoyancy for taxes on net income and profits was depressed to 0.01 from a range of 1.5-1.7 in earlier years, beginning in 1994.

Another reason for the failure of the Philippine economy to sustain growth is its inability to accumulate savings to finance public investments. Low public-sector savings have been neutralizing high private-sector savings.

Meanwhile, government spending for economic services is continuously being cut. Allocation for infrastructure was down to 8.54% in 1998 from over 20% in 1980. The share for agriculture was particularly poor— 4.7% in 1998 and 5.7% in 1999. Given the government's lopsided priorities, in which spending for general services is maintained at a little more than 18% while that for economic services is shrinking—there's simply no way growth can be sustained.

Lastly, the Estrada administration ended with a large stock of outstanding debt, adding pressure on the long-term fiscal position of the government. Total public-sector debt escalated to P3.7 trillion in 1999 from a mere P957.2 billion in 1989, by then already twelve times the 1980 level of P77.0 billion.

The Financial Sector

THE FINANCIAL SYSTEM underwent a series of reforms in the late eighties and early nineties in response to the financial crisis of the mid-eighties. Foremost among these reforms are the lifting of the moratorium on the entry of new banks; the relaxation of restrictions on bank branching; the deregulation of the foreign-exchange market; the creation of an independent central bank; the lifting of restrictions on foreign exchange transactions; and the redefinition of the prudential limits on foreign-exchange position of banks. These reforms greatly improved the state of the financial system. The number of financial institutions also increased from 7,846 in 1990 to 18,353 in 1998[2], and with that, so did deposits and loans.

In 1997 the Philippines was hit by the Asian financial crisis. While the Philippine case showed some of the symptoms that led to the collapse of the banking systems of other affected countries, it did not come to that. To begin with, unlike Thailand and Indonesia, for instance, the Philippines was not plagued by systemic banking crisis. Strong capital bases limited bank closures to a few. The sector's total resources even managed to grow by P9.3 billion in 1998 and its total network of banks (head offices and branches) went up by 6.47%.

Figure 6

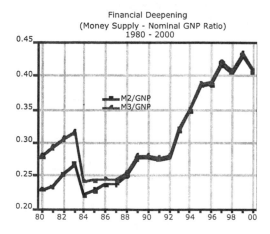

Source: Bangko Sentral ng Pilipinas

The Estrada administration entered when the economy was trying to recover from the crisis. However, governance issues as well as scandals, some involving the president directly, sent the financial sector into another tailspin. Figure 7 shows how the political crisis of Estrada's time was reflected in the stock and exchange rate markets.

Figure 7

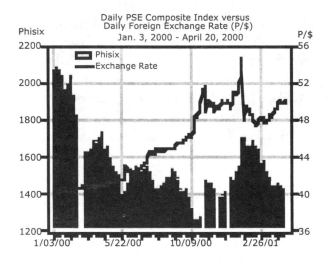

Source: Bangko Sentral ng Pilipinas

Figure 8

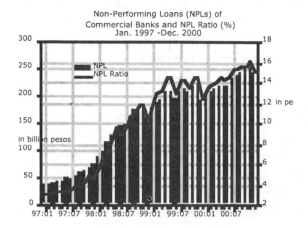

Source: Bangko Sentral ng Pilipinas

Figure 9

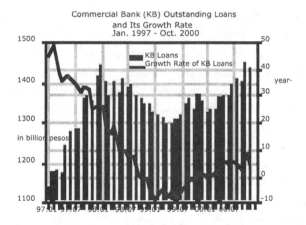

Source: Bangko Sentral ng Pilipinas

Further, a slowdown in credit was observed as nonperforming loans continued to increase. Figure 8 shows that commercial banks' nonperforming loans as a percent of total loans went up from below 5% before the crisis to double-digit percentages from 1998.[3] This ratio is critical because it indicates the quality of portfolio loan, hence the quality of bank assets (i.e., the higher the nonperforming loans, the lower the ratio of earning assets to total assets). Financial institutions were unwilling to lend despite the positive economic performance in 1999 and 2000. Businesses were complaining of tight credit. Figure 9 shows that total outstanding loans of commercial banks never returned to pre-crisis levels, worrying policymakers and analysts about the prospects of recovery. With the government pump-priming efforts sputtering and with the lack of financing coming from the private sector, the economy found little room for expansion.

The External Sector

ALTHOUGH THE Estrada administration posted trade surpluses, a reversal from the deficits that persisted in previous administrations, the export sector was afforded no sustainable development. This was more an effect of imports declining because of the peso depreciation, which in turn had the effect of reduced domestic absorptive capacity. Another issue left unaddressed by the Estrada government was the country's overdependence on the electronics sector, which accounts for around 65% of Philippine exports and therefore a delicate item. It was also during Estrada's term that dependence on foreign capital flows had to be drastically cut, thus tightening the source of financing for most businesses.

Just before the 1997 financial crisis broke out, in President Ramos's time, Philippine exports may have been the fastest growing in Asean (in fact, a few countries in the region had started to see negative balances in trade), but the balance of trade remained negative—and widening yet. But then, again, large capital inflows attracted by the liberalization of the capital markets made up for it. The gross international reserves were increasing steadily, bolstering the perception of a stable exchange rate.

Table 7. Balance of Payments, 1992 – 1999 (in million US dollars)

Items	1992	1993	1994	1995	1996	1997	1998	1999
Current Acct.	-858	-3,016	-2,950	-3,297	-3,953	-4351	1546	7239
Merchandise Trade	-1,675	-3,715	-3,886	-4,179	-4,542	-5431	1111	6753
Services	3,020	2,507	3,964	4,765	6,800	5696	1139	2458
Transfers	817	699	936	882	589	1080	435	486
Capital & Fin'l Acct.	1,850	2,820	4,547	3,393	11,075	6593	478	-1007
Overall BOP Position	1,492	-166	1,802	631	4,107	-3363	1359	3839

Source: Bangko Sentral ng Pilipinas

Capital inflows soon slowed as investor confidence deteriorated with the Asian crisis. In fact the financial panic led to massive capital outflows. With declining bank credit and tight monetary policy in the financial sector and the dwindling confidence in the Estrada government, reduced domestic demand and higher exchange rate pulled imports down. Hence, the overall current account position became positive during Estrada's time.

The Labor Sector

PERHAPS, MORE THAN any other economic undercurrent, the unemployment situation appears to be the main explanation for the collapse of the Estrada administration. One of its main failures appears on hindsight to be its inability to generate employment from the economy's growth.

On top of the rising labor force, the Philippine labor market is now faced with slow growth in employment even as output continues to expand, hence, a state of "jobless growth" or an "output-employment lag", The more glaring indication of this divergence is the persistence of double-digit unemployment rates for four consecutive quarters.

Figure 10

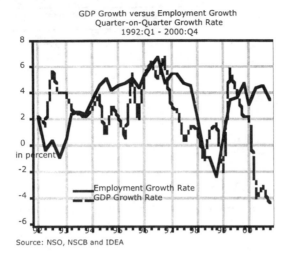

GDP Growth versus Employment Growth
Quarter-on-Quarter Growth Rate
1992:Q1 - 2000:Q4

Source: NSO, NSCB and IDEA

Source: National Statistics Office

The output-employment paradox, which suggests economic growth without improvement in social welfare, is contrary to the lay understanding that an economic upswing would augur well for industries and in turn for employment. In short, higher employment rate or lower unemployment rate is generally associated with higher aggregate output.

When the economy recovered in 1987-1989, employment picked up and the unemployment rate tapered. This positive relationship between output and employment was also observed during the administration of Fidel Ramos. However, the "jobless growth" phenomenon started to set in during the presidency of Estrada, blunting its anti-poverty thrust. From the third quarter of 1998 until the last quarter of 2000, just before his ouster in January 2001, average GDP growth was 2.6 %, but this growth failed to provide employment to the rising labor force. Employment only slightly increased, by 0.4%. In fact, for 2000, GDP posted a 3.9% growth while employment dipped by 1.9%. In the second quarter the phenomenon was marked: In spite of a 4.5 percent GDP growth, employment posted an almost proportionate decline (4%). In the succeeding quarters, employment continued to stagnate even as the domestic economy managed to grow.

Figure 11

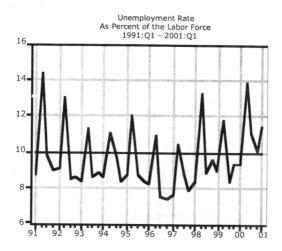

Unemployment Rate
As Percent of the Labor Force
1991:Q1 - 2001:Q1

Source: National Statistics Office

    This output-employment paradox is also illustrated by the double-digit unemployment rates, which persisted for four consecutive quarters—a phenomenon peculiar to Estrada's term. Historically, unemployment would breach the double-digit mark in the second quarter, as fresh graduates enter the labor force. The following quarters would then see unemployment rates reverting to single digit. However, since the 13.9% unemployment rate was posted in the second quarter of 2000, the highest in nine years, it remained within the double-digit range. In the third and fourth quarters of 2000, unemployment rate stood at 11.1% and 10.1%, respectively, the highest and only double-digit third- and fourth-quarter figures since 1991. In the January 2001 survey, the unemployment rate deteriorated again to 11.4%.

Figure 12

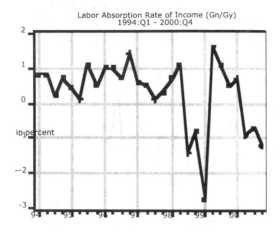

Source: National Statistics Office

Employment growth highly depends on the labor absorption rate of income—i.e., the faster the labor absorption rate of income, the higher the employment growth. During the Estrada administration, the labor absorption rate of income deteriorated across all subsectors and in the economy as a whole. The labor absorption rate for the entire domestic economy dropped to a meager 0.2%—that is, a one percent increase in GDP was accompanied by a 0.2 percent increase in employment—from 0.8% during the Ramos years. Both agriculture and industry sectors turned up negative labor absorption rates (-0.1 percent and -1.9 percent, respectively) during the period. Only services managed to post a positive labor absorption rate (0.8%), although lower than the 1.2% during the Ramos years. Note that the year 2000 held the record for the worst labor absorption rates (-0.5%) in the nineties.

For 2000, the positive output growth of the agriculture and industry sectors apparently did not lead to new jobs, as indicated by their negative absorption rates (–2.2% and –0.4%, respectively). Agriculture posted a 3.4% output growth but employment dropped by nearly 8%. Likewise, the negative employment growth in the industry sector did not match the 3.6% increase in output. Only the services sector was able to take additional workers—at a rate of 0.5%. In the fourth quarter of 2000, negative absorption rates were true for all the sectors.

Figure 13

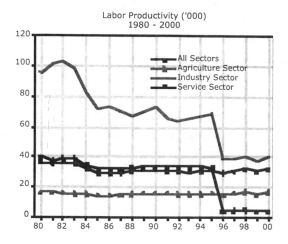

Labor Productivity ('000)
1980 - 2000

- All Sectors
- Agriculture Sector
- Industry Sector
- Service Sector

Source: National Statistics Office

Another underlying issue left unaddressed by the Estrada government was the productivity slowdown in most sectors, hence, the incapacity to absorb more labor in either the short or the long run. With declining productivity and competitiveness of labor, hopes of accelerated labor absorption, pinned on high productivity, will have to be scrapped.

Conclusion

THIS EXAMINATION of economic events during and right before the Estrada administration shows how freer information flow and the increasing sophistication of the Philippine public and institutions have affected the public consensus building and decision making. One way to grasp this change is to compare the fates of Joseph Estrada's and Ferdinand Marcos's presidencies. With Marcos, the economy had to go into a deep recession in the mid-eighties before a triggering event led to his ouster. With Estrada, the mere threat of an economic decline was enough to convince the people and critical institutions to fire him.

Luck probably also plays some role. The triggering events could have been absent. But those convinced by waves of history would argue that other triggering events would have appeared. What is significant is how institutions have evolved in 15 years to induce institutions to move faster.

Several broad economic changes occurred during Estrada's watch, although some of these were extensions of those initiated in the previous administration. For example, contrary to the frequent observation that no structural change has occurred, we find that an unambiguous shift toward the service sector occurred in the last three years. We also note that the relative price ratios have changed in favor of the services sector in the last 15 years. Exports have grown faster in the last ten years, ending with the series of current accounts surpluses in the last three years—unprecedented in the post-World War II period. We note that the export sector has been the main growth source on the demand side during the Estrada period. The attempt to pump-prime the economy was not sustainable, in the end leaving us with a huge debt sure to limit our immediate growth prospects. Finally, strains left from the Asian financial crisis and lingering doubts about the government left the financial sector unable to support the economic expansion expected at the start of the Estrada administration.

This review also highlights the political and economic importance of employment generation. Jobless growth during the Estrada administration takes on added importance in the context of the succeeding events. Possibly the phenomenon induced an underlying angst that needed only a triggering event for it to boil over. This is a lesson that the Macapagal-Arroyo administration may want to look into as it seeks to maintain public acceptability and political legitimacy.

Finally, the importance of governance in the context of globalization and market reaction seems magnified. With the freer information flow and the consequent availability of local and international norms, the presence of early indicators through market reactions and confidence measurements, and the overall change in public sentiment, an administration can no longer afford major lapses in public acceptability based on quality of governance. Philippine institutions may have changed toward demanding more public transparency and accountability. Administrations now have to account for themselves more often and with increasing openness.

ENDNOTES

[1] Institute for Development and Econometric Analysis, University of the Philippines School of Economics, Diliman, Quezon City.

[2] This was largely due to the increase in non-banks, which jumped from 3,849 in 1990 to 10,706 in 1998. Banks, meanwhile, increased from 3,637 in 1990 to 7,647 in 1998.

[3] The increase in the ratio of nonperforming loans to total loans is attributed to three factors: 1) the decline in corporate performance; 2) the redefinition of nonperforming loans; and 3) the decline in absolute loans.

Mindanao
The Making of the Crisis

FERMIN D. ADRIANO

WHILE THE "JUETENG-GATE" SCANDAL and the subsequent impeachment trial that took place in the last quarter of 2000 triggered the eventual demise of the Estrada administration, it was the heightened armed conflict, combined with the hostage drama, in Mindanao that revealed the incompetence of the Estrada government most clearly. It was in Mindanao that the most serious challenge to the ability of President Estrada to govern was raised. In April 2000, a full-scale armed confrontation broke out between the Armed Forces of the Philippines (AFP) and the Moro Islamic Liberation Front (MILF). Shortly thereafter, another Muslim rebel faction, the Abu Sayyaf, took Filipino hostages from Basilan and foreign ones from the neighboring island of Sipadan, Malaysia and brought them to the jungle of Sulu. The latter in particular caught the attention of the international media because a number of the hostages came from Western countries.

Against the MILF, the Estrada government pursued an "all-out war", which culminated in the capture of the rebel's main camp, Camp Abubakar. With the Abu Sayyaf, on the other hand, the government tried to negotiate the release of the hostages by paying huge amounts of ransom. Failing to free all the hostages, it also resorted to a full-scale attack, which fortuitously enabled the hostages to escape amid the confusion. In both instances, the government's incompetence was clearly exposed.

An assessment report (2000) by a United Nations Development Program (UNDP) expert[1] on conflict management predicted that the "worst-case scenario" was for the government troopers to overrun Camp Abubakar because the rebel troops would splinter into several groups, making it difficult for the military to track them down and to gather intelligence work on the plans of the MILF rebels. His warning was proven right by the turn of events. After the military's invasion of Camp Abubakar, the MILF partisans broke into several guerrilla units, spread around Maguindanao and neighboring provinces to wage a protracted guerrilla warfare against the government on several fronts. Besides surprise attacks on government positions, they also engaged in terroristic bombing, bringing the war to the prime urban areas of Mindanao. Investors and tourists were scared away, jobs were lost, and productivity plunged for the island economy.

Meanwhile, the mishandling of the hostage situation led to several changes in the composition of the negotiating team, disrupting the talks for several months, and eventually, to charges that members of the negotiating team skimmed commissions off the ransom money. Whether the accusation was true or not, the international reputation of the Estrada administration was severely tarnished.

But why, despite these negative results, did the Estrada government persist with its all-out-war policy in Mindanao?

For the Sake of Rating

THE OBVIOUS RESPONSE is that President Estrada felt that he was gaining tremendously in popularity, which various public opinion poll surveys indeed showed. Never mind that it was a war that imperiled Mindanao's prospect for development, or a war that could not be won militarily. For as long as he was raking in "*pogi* points", President Estrada was unmindful of war's socio-economic consequences on the people of Mindanao.

Unfortunately for Mindanao, the debilitating armed conflict could have not come at a worse time. The island economy was still suffering from the economic and social havoc wrought by the 1997 Asian financial crisis and the 1998 El Niño drought phenomenon. The year before the war erupted, investments in Mindanao were still below the pre-crisis levels (Table 1); domestic trade for most regions was on a declining trend (Table 2); construction was down (Table 3); and tourism, while picking up, barely filled half the hotel rooms (Table 4).

Table 1. Private Investments in Mindanao, 1998-1999 (P million)

Region	Investments				Growth Rate (%)
	1999	%	1998	%	
9	5,198.8	9.3	20,482.7	24.3	-74.6
10	13,515.0	24.2	7,891.9	9.4	71.2
11	27,201.1	48.8	44,845.4	53.3	-39.3
12	2,452.3	4.4	6,529.4	7.8	-62.4
CARAGA	7,064.8	12.7	4,254.4	5.1	66.1
ARMM	353.2	0.6	200.0	0.2	76.6
Total Mindanao	55,785.2	100.1	84,203.8	100.0	-33.7

Source of Basic Data: National Statistics Office (NSO)

Table 2. Domestic trade for Mindanao, 1998-1999 (quantity in '000 tons; value in P million)

Region	Coastwise trade						Air trade					
	Quantity			Value			Quantity			Value		
	1998	1999	GR %	1998	1999	GR %	1998	1999	GR%	1998	1999	GR%
9	n.d.	n.d.		n.d.	n.d.		n.d.	n.d.		n.d.	n.d.	
10	1,879	2,033	8.2	21,058	21,335	1.31	2,417	592	-75.5	171,016	22,453	-86.9
11	2,468	1,653	-33.0	33,032	22,646	-31.4	11,060	4,076	36.7	2,923,582	497,135	-83.0
12	2,141	1,511	-29.4	14,771	11,010	-25.5	-	-	-	-	-	-
CARAGA	1,145	1,199	4.7	13,587	13,912	2.4	449	196	-56.3	23,072	10,803	-53.2
ARMM	220	79	-64.1	3,646	1,250	-65.7	143	412	-248.8	10,577	1,724	-83.7

n.d. – no data
Source: National Statistics Office (NSO)

Table 3. Private Building Construction Indicators for Mindanao, 1st-3rd Quarter of 1998 and 1999 (total in number of buildings; floor area in '000 square meters; value in P million)

Mindanao	Total Construction						Non-residential Construction					
	Total		Floor Area		Value		Total		Floor Area		Value	
	1998	1999	1998	1999	1998	1999	1998	1999	1998	1999	1998	1999
Region 9	1,453	2,257	140.1	195.5	565.9	708.5	180	278	48.0	80.2	252.0	302.9
Region 10	4,434	3,988	406.0	311.5	1,773	1,369	421	346	149.5	118	785.9	505.0
Region 11	5,496	4,838	472.8	406.6	1,936	1,621	459	491	174.0	159	759.8	602.3
Region 12	1,252	1,237	149.7	111.4	612.4	434.3	154	77	66.4	21.0	327.8	116.8
CARAGA	-	795		63.1		226.3		67		15.4		52.1
ARMM	20	193	1.9	28.4	9.8	123.2	8	42	1.5	17.5	5.3	72.9
Mindanao	12,655	13,308	1,170	1,116	4,898	4,482	1,222	1,301	439.5	411	2,131	1,652
% of Phils.	15.3	21.3	13.7	13.0	7.1	9.2	15.3	19.5	8.2	11.6	5.8	7.6

Source: National Statistics Office (NSO)

Table 4. Tourism in Region 11, 1998-1999

Indicators	1998	1999	Growth Rate (%)
No. of tourist arrivals	439,796	586,051	33.2
Foreigners	41,464	67,926	63.8
Filipinos	398,332	518,125	30.1
Total receipts (PB)	4.8	6.5	35.4
Purpose of visit			
Commercial		261,051	44.5
Pleasure		92,400	15.8
Convention/Conference		119,200	20.3
Visit friends/relatives		67,700	11.5
Others		45,700	7.8
Hotel occupancy rate (%)	47.6	49.8	4.7

Source: Department of Tourism Region 11, 1999

The Asian financial turmoil and the long drought spell had worsened the poverty situation in Mindanao. A recent study of the Asian Development Bank (2000) revealed that among the six regions in the country with the highest poverty incidence, four were in Mindanao, i.e., ARMM (56% of total population), Caraga (55.4%), Western Mindanao (52.4%), and Central Mindanao (49.9%) (Table 5). The poor in Mindanao are among the poorest in the country. Worth noting is that the heart of the armed conflict in Mindanao was in the ARMM and Western Mindanao provinces, where Muslims as a socio-cultural group dominate and where poverty incidence is highest. These regions have the lowest per capita income, and most of its inhabitants have no access to essential services like safe water, electricity and health care.

Table 5. Poverty incidence, by region, 1998

Region	Percentage of Poor	
	Value	Rank
Ilocos Region	38.7	4
Cagayan Valley	39.0	5
Central Luzon	21.0	2
Southern Luzon	25.0	3
Bicol Region	54.1	14
Western Visayas	43.7	7
Central Visayas	50.2	12
Eastern Visayas	49.8	10
Western Mindanao	52.4	13
Northern Mindanao	47.6	9
Southern Mindanao	44.4	8
Central Mindanao	49.9	11
NCR	11.3	1
CAR	39.5	6
ARMM	56.7	16
CARAGA	55.4	15
Philippines	36.7	

Source: Asian Development Bank (2000). Poverty and Well-being in the Philippines with a Focus on Mindanao

Too High a Price

WHILE THE ESTRADA GOVERNMENT claimed victory over the Muslim rebels, it was silent on the huge costs of that victory. The enormous human, physical and economic costs of the "all-out war" policy would have indeed made the "victory" a Pyrrhic one. Collier (1998), an expert on the economics of conflict, noted that a year of non-stop conflict stagnates growth and results in as much as a 2.2% annual reduction in the GDP per capita because of the combined effects of production losses and diminishing capital stocks. Other studies inferred that it is the poor, the vulnerable, and the marginalized groups who bear the brunt of these losses as they have the least accumulated assets and reserves for coping with the conflict. Mindanao is no exception.

The war has claimed the lives of at least 810 soldiers, unaccounted rebel Muslim casualties, and 47 innocent civilians. Add to these the more than 2,156 soldiers and 139 civilians wounded, and 90 soldiers missing during the five-month military offensive starting April 2000. Roughly 8% of the population in the affected provinces and cities, or close to 158,000 families, had been driven from their homes, and most of them (72%) came from the provinces of Maguindanao, Lanao del Sur and North Cotabato (Table 6). About 22,000 displaced families were housed in crowded evacuation centers where 15-18 families (average family size is 7-9 members) were cramped in a 7x8 classroom or 4-5 families in a 3x3 cubicle.

More importantly, the civil strife was taking its toll on Mindanao's future generation, the island's human capital for the new millennium. Education was seriously set back by lack of classrooms, books and supplies at the evacuation centers. The other unquantifiable, but no less serious, repercussion of the war is the heightened ethnic tension and hatred that it has sown among the ethnically diverse people of Mindanao. It would take years to repair the socio-psychological trauma for the victims, knowing that majority of the Christians supported the all-out war policy of the government against the Muslims.

The damage to physical facilities was estimated to be more than half a billion pesos (Table 7). Specifically, 6,550 shelters were totally wrecked and another 2,343 units partially, most of them (45%) in Maguindanao. The government will have to disburse around P131 million for the reconstruction of these dwellings. The damage to roads and bridges amounted to P195 million and to water facilities P13.5 million.

Table 6. Number of affected families/persons, September 2000.

Region	Province/City	Affected Population		Total Population	% of Total Population
		Family	Person		
IX		**5,008**	**22,962**	**3,208,352**	**0.72**
	Basilan	3,822	17,352	137,454	12.62
	Zamboanga del Norte	991	4,901	770,697	0.64
	Zamboanga del Sur	43	263	571,804	0.05
	Zamboanga	152	446	1,728,397	0.03
XI		**9,838**	**46,984**	**4,072,523**	**19.61**
	Compostela Valley	571	2,676	55,030	4.86
	Davao Oriental	2,698	14,227	413,472	3.44
	General Santos City	248	837	327,173	0.26
	Sarangani Province	1,759	8,827	367,006	2.41
	South Cotabato	4,091	18,650	219,093	8.51
	Davao City	193	739	1,006,840	0.07
	Davao del Sur	278	1,028	1,683,909	0.06
XII		**77,082**	**403,337**	**1,572,267**	**31.04**
	Iligan City	641	3,631	273,004	1.33
	Lanao del Norte	43,210	225,384	440,783	51.13
	North Cotabato	25,714	131,034	336,293	38.96
	Sultan Kudarat	7,517	43,288	522,187	8.29
ARMM		**65,539**	**354,406**	**1,797,185**	**19.72**
	Maguindanao	42,477	238,625	662,180	36.04
	Lanao del Sur	8,344	44,069	571,804	7.71
	Sulu	14, 718	71,712	563,201	12.73
	Grand Total	**157,467**	**827,689**	**10,650,327**	**7.7**

Source: MCC Technical Committee Secretariat (2000). Strategic Action Plan for the Immediate Relief and Short-Term Rehabilitation of the Conflict-Affected Areas in Mindanao

Table 7. Total cost of damages, December 2000

Sector	Cost of Damages
1. Shelter	P 142,760,000.00
2. Agriculture	124,761,572.00
3. Roads and Bridges	195,275,000.00
4. Water Supply Facilities	13,500,000.00
5. Distribution Lines of Electric Cooperatives	18,080,472.21
6. Facilities of the National Power Corporation	2,603,222.00
7. Health Facilities	16,175,000.00
8. Educational Facilities	18,933,693.00
9. Government Facilities	3,887,585.80
10. Other Infrastructure Facilities	20,350,800.00
TOTAL	P 556,327,345.01

Source: MCC Technical Committee Secretariat (2000). Strategic Action Plan for the Immediate Relief and Short-Term Rehabilitation of the Conflict-Affected Areas in Mindanao

Economically, Mindanao represents around 37% of the country's agriculture and supplies 44% of the country's food requirements. Given the contraction of the total area devoted to corn, cassava and rice production due to the conflict in Central Mindanao, where some of the most fertile lands are located, it is no surprise that as early as December last year the government was already announcing a plan to import around 500,000 metric tons of rice and as much corn.

The fisheries in Mindanao were badly affected too. Commercial and municipal fishing contracted by as much as 22% and 24%, respectively. Many fishermen missed work for fear of being caught in the crossfire or mistaken as enemy.

Naturally, construction, tourism (worth noting was the closure of the landmark Davao Insular hotel) and also services suffered. In fact, even projects funded by international donor agencies had to be halted because of the inability of project teams to visit the island and monitor the implementation, an indispensable prerequisite of donor agencies. Massive job losses were the result, as reflected in the very high open unemployment rate—more than 8% in Mindanao.

The military costs of the war ranged from a low of P2 billion to a high of P5 billion.[2] The exact figures cannot be determined, although at the height of the armed conflict against the MILF it was in the vicinity of P3 million a day. If one adds the costs of a similar campaign in the Sulu and Basilan islands, which was more costly because logistics had to be brought in by ships and planes, the amount was probably more than double.

Relief and rehabilitation work alone, by the estimates of the Mindanao Coordinating Council Technical Secretariat Committee report (2000), would come up to P1.1 billion. The government already had spent P815 million as of September 2000. If one factors in the costs of the reconstruction work, which will require more resources, the inevitable conclusion is that the country is paying an exorbitant price for the Estrada war against the Muslims. What is absurd is that the government is spending twice for this war—first for destroying Muslim camp communities and infrastructure and then, for rebuilding what the military destroyed. The money cost of the conflict is so huge that, had it been channeled to real development efforts, it would have improved the lives of the poorest of the poor and could have affirmed the previous government's pro-poor agenda.

The Making of the Crisis

THE MINDANAO WAR sharply demonstrated the lack of historical appreciation of the Muslim issue and the nature of ethnic war by the Estrada administration. It thought that it could annihilate the rebels in just one bold
stroke. The government forces thought the MILF would engage them in a
positional warfare particularly in defense of their main camp, Camp
Abubakar, wherein the superior force would emerge as the decisive victor.
To their surprise, the Muslim rebels withdrew into small guerilla bands
with their arms intact, hitting military and civilian targets at their whim.
The military thought it could finish the enemy in a few months only to
find out that ethnic wars like this one could last for generations as has been
the experience in Bosnia-Hezergovina, Sri Lanka and Ethiopia, to cite only
a few cases. The Estrada government believed that it could contain the war
within Mindanao only to discover that the rebels could bring it not only to
the key cities of Mindanao but, worse, to Metro Manila. The result was
the contraction of the economy due to a decline in investments, both local
and foreign.

Recently, the Macapagal-Arroyo government has announced that the
budgetary deficit is more than P200 billion—not P130 billion, as the
previous administration has estimated. Financing the Mindanao war was
undoubtedly one of the major factors.[3] And if the war in Mindanao continues (and will likely so because the Muslim rebels have resorted to the
protracted guerrilla type of struggle), the financial burden of the war will
prove too heavy to an already battered economy. The bombings in Metro
Manila and key cities in Mindanao alarmed not only inhabitants but scared
off potential investors. It is becoming crystal clear that, without an end to
the Mindanao conflict, the crisis of the economy and polity cannot be
solved. Mindanao first demonstrated the ineptness of the Estrada administration to respond to a crisis. From its "all-out-war" policy, to the
bungling of the hostage negotiation, and to the creation of a futile organization called the "Mindanao Coordinating Council" whose membership
was dominated by Metro Manila based officials, many Mindanaoans
believed then that the administration did not know what it was doing.
Consequently, calls for his resignation also reverberated across the island,
echoing those in Luzon and the Visayas.

Restoring Normalcy

IT IS BY NOW EVIDENT that an integral component of restoring political and economic normalcy in the country is attaining peace and alleviating poverty and ethnic conflict in Mindanao. Gains in the popularity of the administration are far outweighed by the socio-economic, political, and human costs of waging the war. To the credit of the Macapagal-Arroyo government, it recognizes that the conflict on the island poses the biggest security problem to the government. The task at hand is to ensure that the peace negotiations take place. A cease-fire should immediately be secured even before any political settlement (through negotiations) of the conflict can be achieved. It will allow economic activities, such as rehabilitation and reconstruction, to proceed more smoothly as peace workers' lives will not be imperiled. In turn, the rehabilitation and reconstruction will positively contribute to building trust and confidence between the combatants and the affected communities, making peace more achievable.

There has been so much analysis and thinking already rendered in addressing Mindanao's peace and development concerns.[4] The problem of the previous administration was that it showed little appreciation of what had been done in the past and chose to re-invent the wheel by giving its own interpretation of the problem through the prism of a Metro Manila bias. The result was nothing short of a disaster, whose fruits the country is now reaping. It is therefore incumbent upon the Macapagal-Arroyo government to heed the collective wisdom and experiences of the past, and dialogue with the people of Mindanao, who best know what is good for their island. Riding the crest of People Power 2, which brought the new administration to power, this task would not pose a serious problem. The more daunting challenge is undoing the harm that had been done by the Estrada administration not only to the Mindanao political economy but, more importantly, to the people of Mindanao as a result of its ethnic war against the Muslims.

ENDNOTES

[1]Oquist, Paul (2000). *"Multi-donor support to peace and development in Mindanao – Phase 4 preparation"*, unpublished report (UNDP).

[2]During the initial month of the armed conflict, the military was requesting for a supplementary budget of P1.4 billion from Congress to finance the war effort. The full military costs of the war, however, have not been divulged to the public by the previous administration.

[3]Already, economists are assessing that it will take the country around three to five years to be able to attain a balance budget because of the fiscal irresponsibility of the Estrada administration.

[4]**Refer** for instance to APRAAP (1995). Mindanao 2000 Development Framework Plan. (Usaid).; Adriano L and F. Adriano (2000). *Is there hope for Mindanao's development?"* unpublished paper read at the Kusog Mindanaw's Peace Summit held in Marco Polo, Davao City, May 26-27, 2000; and Adriano, et.al. (2000), *The First 100 days agenda for Mindanao",* unpublished paper submitted to the Macapagal-Arroyo transition team. In terms of the BIMP-EAGA economic cooperation, the best resource material is the Asian Development Bank (1996). East Asean Growth Area- BIMP, (ADB).

REFERENCES

Adriano L. and F. Adriano, 2000. *"Is there hope for Mindanao's development?",* unpublished paper read at the Kusog Mindanaw's Peace Summit held in Marco Polo, Davao City, May 26-27.

Adriano, et al., 2000. *"The First 100 days agenda for Mindanao",* unpublished paper submitted to the Macapagal-Arroyo transition team.

Adriano, F, L. Adriano, et.al., 2001. *Mindanao's Agenda for Development.* To be published.

Agricultural Policy Research and Advocacy Assistance Program, 1995. Mindanao 2000 Development Framework Plan. (Usaid).

Asian Development Bank, 2000. *"Poverty and Well-being in the Philippines with a focus on Mindanao",* unpublished report.

Asian Development Bank, 1996. East Asean Growth Area-BIMP. (ADB: Manila).

Bureau of Agricultural Statistics, Department of Agriculture. Various issues.

Collier, Paul, 1998. *"On the Economic Consequences of Civil War"*, Oxford: Centre for the Study of African Economies. Mimeo copy.

Garilao & Associates. 2000. *"Peace and Development Initiatives in Mindanao"*, Philippine Business for Social Progress (PBSP).

MCC Technical Committee Secretariat, 2000. *"Strategic Action Plan for the Immediate Relief and Short-Term Rehabilitation of the Conflict-Affected Areas in Mindanao"*. Unpublished report.

National Statistics Office, 1999. Statistical Yearbook. NEDA-NSO.

Oquist, Paul. 2000. *"Multi-donor support to peace and development in Mindanao— Phase 4 preparation"*, unpublished report. UNDP.

Philippine Business for Social Progress (PBSP)

Surviving Erap

KARINA CONSTANTINO-DAVID

MOST OF THE INFORMED SECTORS of Philippine society dreaded the prospect of having a known womanizer, a whiskey-guzzling actor and a college drop-out at the helm of government. But Joseph Ejercito Estrada's victory in the 1998 presidential elections was a foregone conclusion. His rise to power was perceived as a testimony to the immaturity of the masses who would tend to vote on the basis of popularity, rather than competence.

For the poor, in any case, Erap represented hope. After decades of elite democracy, here at last was the man they had been waiting for—someone who had portrayed their lives on film, who had promised a government centered on the poor, and who, like them, had inhabited the margins of an unequal society. With a vengeance, they voted for Erap.

Apart from the masses, there were others from business, academe, and the Left who sincerely believed that Erap could lead a reform-oriented government. I was not one of them. I had known Erap since he was a senator; I did not trust the underworld characters who constantly surrounded him. Yet I ended up in his Cabinet.

Immediately after the elections, some leaders of my NGO community, which had been working with the urban poor, met to discuss the prospects of the sector under an Erap presidency. Foremost among our concerns was the team that Erap would appoint to the Housing and Urban Development Coordinating Council (HUDCC) and its allied agencies. We realized, as other sectors perhaps also did, that we knew very little about the networks of people now in power.

On May 20, 1998, much to my surprise, I was asked to go to Erap's home on Polk St., Greenhills, San Juan purportedly to give him a briefing on the urban poor. Armed with the latest studies of urban poor NGOs, I convinced myself that this was an excellent opportunity to try to influence the policy directions of the new government.

The Unexpected Offer
to Join the Erap Cabinet

POLK STREET was swarming with people—old friends, campaign financiers, volunteers savoring the first taste of power, and aspirants to the thousands of appointive positions waiting to be filled. After the usual exchange of pleasantries, I started to summarize the demands of the urban poor. But after two minutes, Erap said, "*Mayron 'yung* H... D... U....*" "Ah, *yung* HUDCC *po,*" I said. "*Yon, ikaw na 'yon.*" My immediate reaction was to refuse and to offer to head a committee that would recommend a blueprint for the housing sector. But Erap was insistent. It was important, he said, for his pro-poor program to immediately have a face. He said he knew that the housing sector was dirty, and that that was why he wanted someone incorruptible. He added that since he intended to devote his energies to agriculture, he needed someone he could trust who could be in charge of the urban side. He said he would give me a free hand—and full support. He also assured me that he would not allow business or political interests to intervene in this sector. He said that it was the poor who elected him, and that he wanted to repay them with good government.

I told him that I was leaving for Canada in two days but that I would think about it. His last words were "*Basta* off limits *ang* housing *hanggang bumalik ka, pero talagang kailangan kita dyan.*"

There were hurried but quiet consultations with family and friends. While in Canada, I learned that Erap, in an ambush interview, had been asked about his anti-poverty advisers and he had mentioned my name. The media first assumed that this was an appointment to the National Anti-Poverty Commission but later got it right. I was being appointed chairperson of the Housing and Urban Development Coordinating Council (HUDCC). I still had not fully decided whether to accept the appointment by the time I returned. But the other appointments to the Erap Cabinet that had been announced gave me reason to hope—these were very professional people with whom I could work.

A series of consultations especially with the NGO community took place. The consensus was that after decades of advocacy work for and with the urban poor, no one among us should turn down an opportunity to institute changes from a position of power. I accepted the challenge knowing that this was going to be yet another brief episode in a life spent mostly with non-government organizations. Moreover, I was conscious that I could always walk out of the position, if necessary, without feeling a great personal loss.

Together with what was basically a lean NGO-oriented team, I pored over transition reports and identified people for various staff positions. Together, we drew the outlines of a plan for housing. On June 20 I met with Erap to update him, give him the names of people I was recommending to the various housing positions, and obtain his assurance that I would indeed have a free hand in running the housing sector. He readily agreed to all my proposals.

Signs of Things to Come: The First Six Months

IN THE VAN that was to take us to Barasoain church for the June 30 inauguration, I learned that Erap had decided to appoint Angelo Leynes as general manager of the National Housing Authority (NHA). In the afternoon, during the oath-taking of the incoming Cabinet, Erap told me that he had found someone to help me with NHA. All I could say was "*Pag-usapan po natin*". The next day, Erap had signed the appointment papers and was ready to swear in people to sub-Cabinet positions. I tried to dissuade him but he said almost apologetically, "*Alam mo naman na walang hinihingi si Guing. Ito lang, kaya hindi ko mapahindian*". "Guing", of course, was Guia Gomez, also known as wife No. 2. I wondered whether this was an indication of how the government was to be run—no consultations with Cabinet members, favors granted to friends and relations, and a complete reversal of agreements made barely a week before. In the housing sector, appointments as a mode of repayment for past favors was to be repeated in the case of two commissioners of the Housing and Land Use Regulatory Board (HLURB), the recommendees of then Speaker Manny Villar and Ombudsman Aniano Desierto were appointed without my knowledge.

Three weeks later, a number of newspapers carried a photo of the oath-taking of Jose Luis 'Sel' Yulo, alleged owner of the so-called "Boracay" mansion, as presidential consultant on socialized housing. I met with Yulo a few days later. He told me that his instructions from the president were to attend all board meetings, to be the personal representative of

Malacañang and to report to the president weekly. Before leaving, he asked for office space and a staff. I was aghast. I told him that I would personally speak to the president. I immediately wrote a confidential memo to the president stating my displeasure, and on the same day I went to Malacañang. Erap dismissed my fears by saying "*Wala yon*, he just wants to help." He assured me that Yulo would not interfere and that his designation was nothing more than an honorific.

I only realized later on that the same situation was occurring in other departments. A rash of appointments of friends and relatives as presidential advisers, consultants, or assistants, very often duplicating the responsibilities of Cabinet members, was taking place. Many of these appointees frequently flaunted their positions and actually interfered with policies and programs. Such appointments were clearly a misuse of presidential prerogative, the early signs of an informal and personalistic approach to official power.

Compounding these troublesome signs, Erap began to exhibit what I could only describe at the time as improper or ethically questionable behavior. I was summoned to Malacañang "to attend a presentation of Dante Tan". I had no inkling who this person was. I sat through a presentation of Tan's housing initiative called *Bahay para sa Kinabukasan*, Inc. The plan was to build 50 medium-rises in Taytay. The first of these buildings was presented as a gift on the president's birthday. After the presentation, I told Erap, not knowing his relation to Tan, that it would be best to course such offers through HUDCC so they could be properly assessed. I advised him that only when such projects had been properly screened and pronounced ready for implementation should the president's presence be required. Erap gave me a reassuring smile. In April of the following year, Erap celebrated his birthday and proceeded to inaugurate the first building in Taytay. After that, he asked me to make arrangements for the financing of the succeeding 49 buildings. I responded that Tan had not bothered to go through normal channels and that there was no ready budget. I also mentioned that the cost of the units was beyond the cut-off for socialized housing. No funds had been allotted to this project during my term, although after I resigned my job, a few more buildings were constructed, using funds apparently released to the municipality of San Juan from the President's Social Fund.

Erap knew that I was not the sort of person who would knowingly participate in transactions that were less than above-board. I found out later that, either because he did not know the structure of decision-making in the housing sector or he assumed that most board members of corporate agencies took their functions lightly, he had directly asked Angelo Leynes, NHA general manager, to facilitate certain transactions.

One of these pertained to the government purchase of two parcels of land totaling almost nine hectares in Kalookan from Annalou Nunag and Platinum Sales International Corp. When the matter was brought up to the board of the NHA, I objected because the asking price was way above the market value. Sometime later, Erap himself asked me whether we had already bought the Asistio property. I told him that I was still negotiating. On at least two other occasions, Erap followed up saying that the Asistios needed the money badly. There was no question that the land was indeed appropriate for socialized housing, but the initial price was steep. Without being influenced by extraneous factors, the price was later reduced to way below the appraised value, which meant savings of nearly P50 million for the government. But the point was not lost on me—the president would not hesitate to intercede for his close friends even to the point of calling up his own Cabinet officials.

There was another piece of property, totaling about 13.5 hectares at P370 million, in San Jose del Monte, Bulacan. This was owned by a Ruben Reyes and it was also overpriced. Erap had apparently already discussed this with NHA's Leynes who in turn relayed the conversation to me. During an NHA board meeting Erap himself called Leynes, who, from snatches I overheard, explained that the rest of the board were not inclined to approve the transaction. Erap then asked to speak to me, and he proceeded to explain that the owner was a good friend of his and that it was his wish to see the sale completed. Since all transactions above P50 million needed presidential approval and a memorandum order had been released by Malacañang stipulating that no purchases that were more than 10% above zonal valuation should be approved, the NHA board sent the papers to Malacañang. By the time I resigned, the sale had not been consummated.

Factionalism within the Cabinet, meanwhile, had arisen. Right during the first Cabinet meeting after the inauguration, in fact, a memorandum detailing the flow of papers to Malacañang was distributed. It was obvious that a turf war was already being waged between the Office of the Executive Secretary, under Ronnie Zamora, and the Presidential Management Staff, under Lenny de Jesus. Instead of clearly subdividing and delineating functions, the memo actually left the Cabinet with two or three options for official communication, thereby encouraging us to course papers through the channel of our choice. This was to be a constant irritant and cause for inefficiency and confusion.

Erap involved himself too much in micro-management and showed an impatience for policy discussions. He would get excited by projects, but not by programs. In certain moments of inspired decisiveness, he preferred to tap his reservoir of common sense, rather than to rely on serious studies. He would demand instant results, forgetting that there were processes and procedures that could not be dispensed with. Because of the president's extremely short attention span for policy issues, the weekly Cabinet meetings not only became less frequent they also degenerated into updates and reporting sessions. Members of the Cabinet could have profited from collective discussions of directions and plans.

Facing the Challenges of Reforming the Housing and Urban Development Sector

BUT THERE WAS much work to be done. The irritants and frustrations of the first semester were minor given the magnitude of the tasks. The housing and urban development sector received a boost from Erap's public pronouncements. As secretary of finance, Ed Espiritu was unstinting in his support and was constantly surprising us with his innovative approaches to housing finance.

A rapid review of the past programs of government revealed that of the total funds expended only 19% went to socialized housing. In addition, the housing finance policies were unsustainable, resulting in a recurrent boom-bust cycle. And yet government shouldered most of the risks compared to the private sector. The major source of mortgage funds, computed at below market rates, came from the three pension funds—SSS, GSIS and HDMF. The net effect, especially because of miserable collection efficiency, was devastating to the millions of ordinary Filipinos who owned these pension funds. In addition, subsidies and targeting mechanisms were inefficient; there was poor coordination among the key shelter agencies and tedious procedures and huge transaction costs (including inefficiencies and corruption), among others.

Our response was to draft a viable and sustainable program summarized through the following vision:

In 2004, we envisage the shelter and urban development sector to have a functional National Urban Development and Housing Framework, a viable market-oriented housing finance system with sufficient sources of long-term mortgage finance, on-budget subsidies and an improved targeting mechanism focused on the bottom 30%, ensuring that women and female-headed households are not marginalized, a rationalized shelter agencies' operation, a redefined relation between the national and local governments and greater LGU ownership in urban management and shelter delivery, parity with other critical social or economic sectors as a priority of government, and an internal institution which can enable the preceding and sustain it beyond the year 2004.

This meant that shelter security must be within a broader national urban policy framework that recognized shelter as both a component of social policy as well as an instrument for economic growth. Crucial in this regard was the localization and decentralization of urban and shelter policy, an emphasis on ecological balance in relation to the brown environment and reforms in resettlement policies and processes. The cornerstones of the latter lay in stakeholder participation and genuine consultations with the poor, expanding innovative schemes like the Community Mortgage Program and cooperative housing, an insistence on voluntary rather than forcible relocation, and revising the pricing system to ensure affordability.

On the internal organizational level, initiatives were taken to create a cohesive working team within the sector, energize the bureaucracy, reduce inefficiency and corruption, and rationalize operations of the key shelter agencies. On the external front, the thrust was to build effective linkages especially with the social, economic and infrastructure sectors of the national government and to strengthen working relations with LGUs.

But the most controversial of the policy shifts we initiated related to housing finance. This required that while at least 80% of public resources would be channeled to the needs of the poor, major reforms in the housing finance system be introduced. Mortgage funds would no longer be sourced from the pension funds through a single lending system. Instead, bonds, securitization, guarantees, and incentives to ensure the participation of the banks and therefore multiple lending windows would be used as alternatives. The critical components of these reforms lay in making a clear distinction between housing subsidy and housing finance. Since the poor could obviously not afford the terms of the market, a Housing

Assistance Fund (HAF) would have been in place by the year 2000. The HAF would have given direct subsidies to qualified socialized households borrowing from the mortgage market. At the same time, strengthening the primary mortgage market, catalyzing a private-sector-managed secondary market and out-sourcing of collection servicing would complete the housing finance reforms.

Reactions to Reforms

GOVERNMENT IS NECESSARILY a balancing act between competing legitimate interests. Change is always threatening especially to those who currently benefit from any system. But I did not expect the virulence and self-righteousness that some groups exhibited in an effort to derail the reforms. Three main stakeholders—the private sector, the bureaucracy, and the NGOs and people's organizations (POs)—are worth mentioning.

From the day my appointment to the HUDCC was made public, I was besieged by messages and invitations from various groups and individuals. Those whose paths I had crossed suddenly re-emerged. Others, notably the private sector, contacted my relatives and friends, but, knowing me, they refused to lift a finger. Within the first two months in office, I had made the rounds of practically all the organizations that had a stake in housing. We had inherited a sector in disarray and an industry that had languished in the doldrums. There were lively discussions. Except for the Chamber of Real Estate and Builders Association (Creba), the other organizations engaged us in open dialogue, vocal with their recommendations yet ready to cooperate in crafting a new program. Creba, on the other hand, while talking to me, also arranged for a courtesy call on Erap through Jose Luis "Sel" Yulo, to whom they presented their program to build hundreds of thousands of houses.

The Creba officers were very insistent on their housing program, and while other organizations actively participated in various consultations, such as on the Medium Term Philippine Development Plan for Shelter (MTPDP-S), Creba did not. We studied its proposals and incorporated some of these into the new program. But two major components of the Creba program depended on the continued use of pension funds for low-cost and socialized housing and what was essentially a revival of the unified home lending program. When Creba realized we were not going to swallow their program hook, line and sinker, they went to war. They came out with a full-page ad in the major dailies asking Erap to replace his housing team. They conspired with Yulo, with one of their top officers becoming his consultant, resulting in a confidential paper attacking my person. The paper also claimed that it was done in consultation with the heads of NHA, HIGC and HLURB.

With the first Creba salvo, Erap called me to say that I should not mind these attacks and just go on with my work. Sometime later, in a public gathering, he even alluded to Creba by asking whether any of their members were present and saying that he did not want to have anything to do with them. But the advertisement war escalated. Creba claimed we did not have a program, which of course was not true. When we responded with the new program, they criticized it and compared it to theirs, conveniently caricaturing the government side while cleverly disguising or omitting crucial facts. For example, they claimed they could build houses without government having to spend a single centavo. If this were so, why did they need to bother with government financing policy? The truth is that they wanted government to mandate the pension funds of the SSS, GSIS and Pag-Ibig for housing finance at concessional rates and with little risk to developers.

An uneasy truce was called when Erap asked me and six other Cabinet members to face the various private-sector organizations with government taking a unified stance. This was necessary because, apart from Yulo, there seemed at least one other Cabinet secretary toeing the Creba line. A lot of time and energy was wasted on the entire exercise. And yet, even much later, as we tried to put the finishing touches on the program, Creba, in alliance with their champion, Sel Yulo, stubbornly refused to participate, preferring to work on their agenda behind the scenes. In June 1999 Erap formally launched the MTPDP-S, which, together with the year 2000 budget, would have been in full operation in a few months. But of course, this was not to be.

The battle inside the bureaucracy involved only skirmishes, but, it was fought on the terrain for guerrilla warfare. Because the housing agency does not operate like the usual line agency, HUDCC, as the highest policy making body, oversees the sector through corporate structures that have functioned largely as independent fiefdoms. While the housing bureaucracy generally acceded to the reforms and actively participated in the discussions that led to the plans, it was undeniable that there were some housing officials who felt, at the very least, uncomfortable with the new program. There might have been a grudging respect for the reforms we were trying to put in place, but, at the same time, resistance was mounted when there was any hint of incursions into anyone's turf both in policy as well as in operations. Actually, the various shelter agencies were not used to an interventionist HUDCC chairperson. But there were no frontal clashes. Instead, there were attempts to create patronage linkages with other Cabinet members, legislators, and Erap cronies. When they disagreed with some decisions, they would delay implementation, hoping the matter would be forgotten or they would find ways of not bringing issues up to the board, which was the HUDCC chairperson's only real access to these corporate entities. By and large, however, the bureaucracy had some excellent people and was not a major obstacle to change.

It was, ironically, with the NGOs and POs that I had my biggest heartaches. This was the sector I had come from. A resolve to meet regularly did not materialize. There were two basic sources of tension: the micro nature of their demands coupled with a lack of appreciation of policy, and the judgmental, even self-righteous, reactions to decisions that they did not completely agree with. The micro demands were exhausting because the NGOs and POs treated each case separately without much appreciation of the demands of policy-based rather than ad hoc decisions. They seemed more comfortable dealing with promises rather than being told the facts. Perhaps because I came from the NGO world, their expectations were higher. Although they had greater access to me, both of us could not seem to adjust to our new roles and many misunderstandings arose. Although there was only one instance when battle lines were drawn, and placards were raised and red paint thrown at my house, it was a painful experience to be isolated from the community with which I identified myself. But while this is altogether another story I refer to it here because it was a major factor in the buildup of frustrations and the eventual ease with which I decided to resign on October 15,1999.

The Point of No Return:
The Last Nine Months

I HAVE OFTEN SAID that a major turning point of the Erap administration came with the transfer of his residence to Malacañang in 1999. On Polk Street, he had been at least forced to keep some semblance of official hours and maintain a clear separation between public and private space. Erap moved into the presidential residence (PR), a guesthouse within the palace grounds and just across from the main palace structure. Like most traditional politicians, Erap started to hold court mainly in the living/dining room of the PR. Because the PR served essentially as his private quarters, a more relaxed air of informality came in swiftly. The immediate impact was a further deterioration of professionalism that took its toll first on simple matters like attending to formal engagements on time. During the Luneta celebration of the National Anti-Poverty Commission, I was at the PR for a meeting at 10 a.m. This went on until lunchtime and although Erap was supposed to be at the event at 1 p.m., despite repeated reminders, he continued with the small talk and ultimately left more than an hour later.

The PR also effectively shielded Erap from the public eye. Because Erap is a naturally gregarious person, enjoying the company of his friends, he often found himself refusing to attend scheduled formal functions. During one Galing Pook Awards, Erap was supposed to be the main speaker at the palace. He had called for a meeting of some of the members of the Pasig River Rehabilitation Commission at 10 a.m. I arrived half an hour early and was told to go to the main palace to wait, since Erap had not yet come down from his bedroom. Heroes Hall was filled with local government officials, ambassadors and academics, all waiting for Erap to begin the program. At slightly past 10, I was told to go to the PR. Erap had just come down and I thought I would have to wait for him to finish the scheduled program. But he decided he was not going to appear at the Galing Pook Awards. Instead of crossing the road to give his speech and come back to the PR for our meeting, he decided to ask Ronnie Zamora, who was not available, and then Jerry Barican, to substitute for him.

The informality of the PR also meant that Cabinet members never knew how long they needed to stay there. Precious executive time was wasted. Cronies and classmates, gofers, business partners and relatives, could come and go as they pleased. They were constantly around, mingling the public with the private, blurring the dividing line between issues of state and personal concerns. Since Cabinet members had line functions to attend to, these people had greater access to Erap. In fact, some of Erap's orders came straight from the suggestions of these informal groups. One example had to do with the group called New San Jose Builders. I recall that in 1998 Erap had warned me against three groups as cronies of Ramos—New San Jose Builders, RII Builders and Filinvest. While I was identifying potential resettlement sites for the Pasig River, Erap himself mentioned a project in Rodriguez, Rizal of the New San Jose Builders. I had already inspected the site—it was one among a number being considered. NHA ultimately acquired the subdivision called New San Jose Plains, later to be called Kasiglahan Village I. The main liaison to Erap of this group was Tony Evangelista, a former classmate. Sometime later, I learned that they had started to discuss plans about Erap City, an ambitious project that would develop a new town with tens of thousands of socialized and low-cost housing. But I was purposely excluded from these meetings, in the same way that I was kept in the dark about the plans for PNP and military housing.

It was also at the PR where the luxury of Erap's lifestyle became more and more pronounced. The fiesta atmosphere created by abundant food and drinks available at all hours, the gifts he received and gave out, mocked his avowed pro-poor policy. In the informality of the PR, Erap let his guard down. Sexism, lack of discipline, pettiness, the cavalier way in which he treated the bureaucracy, the lack of a concrete grasp of what anti-poverty meant, his narrow definition of corruption, the absence of any semblance of system, the lack of respect for institutions, and more—all this became immediately apparent.

By October 1999, Erap's popularity ratings had plunged, a series of scandals had seriously marred the government's credibility, and a year of playing government by ear had taken its toll. Cabinet meetings were irregular and infrequent and factionalism within the Cabinet was out in the open. For those of us who refused to belong to any faction, life was not easier. We were met with suspicion by all and caught in the crossfire of the warring camps. While coordination across departments was severely limited to individual initiatives, Cabinet members had at best spotty information about national thrusts. A case in point was the Concord. As late as September 1999, the Cabinet had to demand that we go through a workshop regarding these plans as we were being asked to push the Concord without so much as a discussion. But a culture of acquiescence had already set in. Due to the factionalism, the lack of a regular venue for debate and the obvious dislike of Erap for lengthy discussions, we could not function as a collegial body. Thus, the Cabinet became nothing more than a loose friendship group of individuals who could enjoy partying with their boss who had little understanding of the requirements of the presidency. This was not governance. Many of us in the Cabinet desperately tried to run our departments as best we could but professional work was becoming more and more impossible.

The Only Way to Go: Resignation

IN AUGUST OF 1999, while attending one of the oath-taking ceremonies in Malacañang, I was surprised to see Sel Yulo taking his oath as presidential adviser on socialized housing. The housing front had been relatively quiet for a few months and we were at the tail end of completing the new program for a big start in the year 2000. While this was a sign that something was brewing, I let it pass. It was budget defense time, and we were in the final stages of the World Bank Housing Finance Technical Assistance program. We were starting the resettlement of the Pasig River informal settlers, and were midway into the streamlining of the NHMFC and a host of other pressing concerns. In September I joined Erap on a four-day trip to Mindanao with no warning that anything was afoot. Shortly afterward, Erap left for an extended trip to New Zealand, Brazil, Argentina, and the United States. I saw him a number of times at the PR after his return, and everything seemed normal.

But on Sunday, October 10, I received a call from one of his secretaries asking me to be at the PR the next day at 10 a.m. for a meeting. There was no agenda, but I did not find this unusual. The meeting was attended by Hernandez of HIGC, Leynes of NHA, Yulo, Jacinto Ng Sr., developer and long-time friend of Erap. Later we were joined by PMS head Lenny de Jesus and Budget Secretary Ben Diokno. Erap started the meeting by saying *"Bumababa ang ratings ko, kailangan may ipakita tayo sa housing."* He then proceeded to go through the staff complement of each of the shelter agencies remarking that there were too many employees. We spoke briefly about the obstacles we faced. There was talk about Yulo overseeing the low-cost and economic housing projects. The conclusion was that I should work with PMS to come out with an executive order to streamline the housing sector. Secretary Diokno agreed saying *"Basta si* Karina *pa rin ang bastonera ng buong* sector."* Erap also wanted to inaugurate the resettlement site for the Pasig River settlers in Montalban and to have an aerial view of the proposed Erap City. He then asked his secretary to call Tony Evangelista.

As I was about to leave, I wondered why the rest of the group was still hanging around. At the guard house, waiting for my car, I received a call from an officer of the Philippine National Bank. He informed me that Zorayda Amelia Alonzo, president and CEO of the Home Development Mutual Fund (HDMF) better known as Pag-Ibig, had been replaced by Ramon Palma Gil, brother of the PNB president, and that he was calling to set a courtesy call with me for Palma Gil. As I was walking back to the PR to check out the news, Evangelista arrived.

I found the people I had been with in the earlier meeting huddled inside the office of Lenny de Jesus. Since the PMS took charge of the paper work for all appointments, I asked her about the new appointment to HDMF. She confirmed the news saying that Erap had seen Alonzo on TV with former President Ramos and wanted her replaced. She further said that it was Congressman Luis 'Baby' Asistio who recommended Palma Gil. I had not been consulted. Alonzo, after 13 competent years in the service, was not even given the courtesy of being informed before she was replaced. Erap and company had again run roughshod over the bureaucracy. I left the PR in disgust.

Again, as I was walking out, a secretary ran after me saying that Erap was looking for me. There was merienda on the table, and the people in the De Jesus office were still there, obviously conspiring. Seeing me back, they slowly left. Erap was trying to be extra nice. I protested about the Alonzo case but he mumbled something to this effect: *"Tao pala siya ni* Ramos *bakit di ako kukuha ng tao ko?"* He also told me not to pay much attention to Yulo because he just wanted to help. I excused myself as soon as I could, went back to the office to try to sort out what was happening. Without my knowledge, the PMS and Yulo were already drafting an executive order on housing.

At lunchtime of October 13, Yulo called me to say he was faxing me an order from Erap. I took one look at the order, and I started to write my resignation letter. The executive order created the Presidential Commission on Mass Housing with Erap himself as chairman and Yulo co-chairman, duplicating the functions of HUDCC and putting all the housing agencies under it. I called PMS, outlined my objections, said I was resigning, and was asked by De Jesus to wait for a return call from Erap. Three hours later, Erap had not called. Instead, it was Juliet Javellana of the *Philippine Daily Inquirer* who called asking for a comment on the press statement of Erap on housing. He had announced the creation of the PCMH adding that he was impatient with the slow pace of housing. I had no knowledge of this press statement. The *Inquirer* had to fax it to me!

I called Malacañang once again, and this time Erap came to the phone. He sheepishly said, in response to a barrage of strong words from me, "*Siguro* typographical error *lang yon*. We will correct it. *Pag-usapan natin*; lunch *ka bukas dito*." I met with my immediate staff and the officials who had come into government with me and we decided to lay down clear conditions under which we would be willing to stay.

On October 14, I met with Erap. He had revised the order making the HUDCC head co-chair of the newly-formed Presidential Commission for Mass Housing. He insisted that he had full trust and confidence in me and that I was still in charge of policy and would stay in the Cabinet. But it was obvious from the conversation that he either did not understand what was happening or he had debts to repay and deals to make. My last words to Erap were, "Mr. President, you will get my letter of resignation tomorrow." I shook his hand, turned my back, and walked out.

In that one incident, Erap confirmed all my worst doubts. I had trusted too much. There was no shred of professionalism and decency in his government. Here was a president who did not have any capacity to govern and did not care. Here was an administration where Cabinet members were routinely denied the courtesy of trust and where cronies and relatives treated the state as their own private playground. Here was a government that had squandered all the goodwill and hope that the masses had placed in it. At that moment, I became convinced beyond any doubt that this was an administration I could no longer be part of, and that this was a president who would only bring the entire nation down.

The Road to Impeachment and Ouster Was Short and Bumpy

RAUL J. PALABRICA

WHEN CONGRESSMEN HEHERSON ALVAREZ and Ernesto Herrera and 15 leaders of non-government organizations filed on October 12, 2000, a verified complaint for impeachment against President Joseph Ejercito Estrada, very few gave them a chance of succeeding. The political allies of Estrada were in control of both Houses of Congress. Franklin Drilon had been elected senate president under a power-sharing arrangement Estrada had brokered with the majority senators. In the House of Representatives, Speaker Manuel Villar Jr. owed his position to the political coalition that supported Estrada and had the numbers to stop any move to unseat him.

Besides, history was on Estrada's side. Since the impeachment process became part of the country's political system in 1935, no president had been impeached, much less convicted. The House of Representatives, from where impeachment complaints ordinarily emanate, always rallied behind whoever was in power whenever his or her term of office was threatened to be cut short.

Aware of the serious implications of impeachment, the framers of the 1935, 1973, and 1987 Constitutions spelled out the causes and rules for the removal of a president. Under the 1935 Constitution, the president can be removed from office on impeachment for, and conviction of, culpable violation of the Constitution, treason, bribery, or other high crimes. These voting requirements made it difficult to unseat a president: the House of Representatives needed a vote of two-thirds of all its members to impeach, and the senate, as the impeachment court, needed a vote of three-fourths to convict.

The 1973 Constitution added "graft and corruption" to the 1935 list and, since it provided for a one-chamber Congress, the Batasang Pambansa (or National Assembly), gave it the power to initiate, try, and judge. To initiate impeachment, a vote of one-fifth of its members was needed, and to convict, a vote of at least two-thirds.

Under the 1987 Constitution, a president may be impeached or removed for culpable violation of the Constitution, treason, bribery, graft and corruption, and other high crimes, or betrayal of the public trust. It is this Constitution that now applies, and, compared with the two previous ones, it makes the impeachment process a lot easier. It has returned the two-House legislature and requires a vote of one-third of the members of the House of Representatives to impeach and a vote of two-thirds for the senate to convict.

Failed Attempts

ELPIDIO QUIRINO (1948-1953) was the first president to undergo the impeachment process. He was charged with culpable violation of the 1935 Constitution, in particular, with removing civil service officials without justifiable cause and exercising certain powers that the Supreme Court had already ruled as no longer in effect. The majority of the congressmen, who belonged to Quirino's party, voted down the impeachment complaint.

Every president after Quirino—Carlos Garcia, Diosdado Macapagal, Ferdinand Marcos, Corazon Aquino, Fidel Ramos, and Joseph Estrada—became the subject of impeachment complaints, but only Estrada actually has been impeached.

Initially, only two congressmen signed the complaint when it was filed on October 12, 2000. By the time the complaint was endorsed to the House Committee on Justice for evaluation, the number of signatories had risen to 38, or 35 votes short of the number needed to convert the complaint to Articles of Impeachment and send it to the senate for trial.

By November 6, 2000, after Speaker Manuel Villar Jr. and his political allies left the pro-Estrada coalition, 77 congressmen, four over the magic number, had endorsed the complaint. The Articles of Impeachment eventually reached the senate with 105 signatures, or almost 50% of the entire House membership. The vote was a stinging rebuff—the first time in Philippine history that a sitting president lost control over a legislative chamber. The transmittal of the Articles of Impeachment to the senate by Villar was a masterstroke that underscored the ineptness of Estada's political lieutenants in the House.

Villar was aware that his defection would lead to his own ouster as speaker and that, if he were replaced inopportunely, the impeachment complaint could be stalled indefinitely with the justice committee or the House itself.

On that fateful day, Villar personally led the opening prayers for the day's session, then proceeded to read the report of the judiciary committee on the complaint. Invoking the constitutional provision that, with a House vote of one-third, the president became effectively impeached, he ordered the transmittal of the complaint, now converted to Articles of Impeachment, to the senate for trial.

Although caught flat-footed, Estrada's remaining allies managed to elect a new speaker. For still unexplained reasons, however, they did not make any effort to reconsider or set aside Villar's action even if they could have done so legally. Even the senators were surprised. Aquilino Pimentel Jr., himself elected senate president on the same day that Villar was ousted as Speaker, had not expected the events to move that fast. Within two days of receiving the Articles of Impeachment, the senate took a look at the rules of procedure used by the United States senate for the trial of President Bill Clinton and, except for minor adjustments, adopted them as its own.

Lack of Control

WHAT HAPPENED? Where did Estrada go wrong? How could he have lost control of a situation effecting his own presidency? Why did he fail to use his influence over the congressmen? Several reasons have been offered to explain the "posture of independence" taken by many congressmen on the impeachment issue.

It was six months before a congressional election, a time when re-electionists especially needed their pork barrel, over which Malacañang presides. Therefore, it must have taken a truly strong motivation not to please the president, let alone go against him.

The fact is Joseph Estrada lost his moral influence and authority over the congressmen when Ilocos Sur Gov. Luis Singson presented strong evidence of his involvement in an illegal numbers game (*jueteng*) and in an unlawful diversion of public funds. By allegedly taking a cut in collections from *jueteng*, the poor man's game and source of quick redemption, and in excise taxes meant to alleviate the living conditions of the impoverished tobacco farmers, the president was seen as a rich man stealing from the poor. The additional allegation that he had did it to sustain his and his mistresses' lavish lifestyles tended to add insult to injury. In the eyes of the congressmen, Estrada was a king reduced to a petty thief, deserving to be stripped of crown and robe in public.

The surveys conducted during the investigation of Singson's accusations by the senate Blue Ribbon committee showed the steady erosion of public support for the former president, a point not lost on the congressmen. Political sense told them that continued support for Estrada might be perceived by their constituents as toleration or approval and could therefore damage their public career—they could go down with him. Loyalty to the President Estrada, in other words, had to give way to the realities of political survival.

Incompetent Advisers

ANOTHER THEORY points to Estrada's lack of understanding of how congressmen think. Having served as town mayor for too long, as a senator as vice-president for only one term, and never as a congressman, he was disadvantaged by an outlook either too narrow or too general to be any help in dealing with congressmen. He had not experienced their fears and concerns and therefore had no sense of their expectations, did not know what motivates them to take which side on national and local issues, indeed had only a vague idea of their collective and individual weaknesses and strengths.

Neither were Estrada's advisers of much help. Though once an effective congressional leader himself, Executive Secretary Ronaldo Zamora hardly played a role in maintaining good legislative-executive relations. He was a virtual non-entity in Malacañang, a mere fixture in the official power structure, definitely not the "Little President" that his position suggests. He was appointed to the job by Estrada only out of a sense of gratitude to his brother Manuel, the banker, a friend of long standing.

Luis Asistio Jr., although a congressman (for Kalookan City) himself, did not possess the political acumen and charisma that can marshal support for Estrada. Colleagues in fact regarded Asistio as a political weakling, in spite of his closeness to Estrada, a friend of 40 years.

Jaime Policarpio, the president's legislative liaison, had been ineffective from the beginning. Not having served in any elective position before, he not only did not belong to the "old boy" network but was regarded with contempt by congressmen, a mere messenger or baggage boy of Malacañang. He was seldom invited to congressional caucuses and had to rely on second-hand information.

It did not come as a surprise therefore that, when the impeachment complaint started to snowball and draw endorsements, Malacañang was caught flat-footed. It did not know whom to talk to in Congress or how to prevent the president's own impeachment.

In fact, it did not even take one serious step to stop Villar's defection.

Yet Estrada himself appeared confident. Acting on the advice of then Ambassador to the United States Ernesto Maceda that the furor over impeachment complaint would fizzle out in two weeks, Estrada ignored whatever signs of eroding legislative support he sensed.

And why not? The polls showed he continued to enjoy widespread grassroots support. Huge crowds greeted wherever he went. The May 2001 elections were coming, and he expected the congressmen to line up for their pork barrel.

His cordon sanitaire assured him that the political turmoil was limited to Metro Manila and that he remained the darling of the poor and rural masses. Except for the resignation of two secretaries (social welfare and development and trade and industry), his official family, the Cabinet, rallied around him.

He believed his own propaganda that only the rich Makati businessmen, Jaime Cardinal Sin and former Presidents Fidel Ramos and Corazon Aquino wanted him removed. In fact the forces against him were large, powerful, and active, campaigning quietly with congressmen for the impeachment vote. And before Estrada could move, Villar had banged the gavel sounding impeachment. The case was in the senate's hands.

Impeachment Trial

AT THE TRIAL, the prosecutors suffered from opening-day jitters. They missed their cues. Their demeanor was affected by the presence of television cameras. They were conscious of how audiences in their homes and offices would find them. The entire trial was televised live.

They fumbled in the presentation of their first witness, Roberto

Lastimoso, former national police chief. Out of practice, they had to be reminded by the presiding officer, Chief Justice Hilario Davide Jr., of the proper way to qualify a witness. The defense lawyers, on the other hand, were cool and composed. After the opening statements, they sat back and waited for the prosecution to begin the presentation of evidence.

Initially, the contending lawyers argued about the interpretation of the Articles of Impeachment, the marking of documents, the number of copies to be reproduced, and other procedural matters. It was only on the third day that the lawyers, senator-judges, and other participants finally got settled in the business of determining whether the respondent is guilty or not.

Except for Singson, the witnesses presented by the prosecution did not show enthusiasm; some of them even expressed fear for their lives, not altogether misplaced. The person on trial, after all, was the most powerful in all the land. He controlled the resources of the government. Men and machine moved at his command. And his vindictive streak was common knowledge.

Of the 35 witnesses presented by the prosecution during the 24-day trial, five were working in the government at the time—Anton Prieto was presidential assistant for Bicol affairs; Singson himself was provincial governor; Emily Padua worked at Philippine Amusement and Gaming Corporation; Gwen Samontina at Social Security System; Eleanor Madrid at Land Transportation Office; and Ferdinand Sales at Securities and Exchange Commission. Four others had previously held high positions in the government or government-controlled corporations—Roberto Lastimoso had been chief of the national police; Rufo Colayco, president of Clark Development Corporation; Perfecto Yasay Jr., chairman of the Securities and Exchange Commission; and Edgardo Espiritu, secretary of finance. The others came from private sector, with Equitable PCI Bank providing the greatest number—nine witnesses. Key officials of the Philippine Stock Exchange and Land Bank and two broadcast reporters also testified.

The presentation of evidence on Article IV (culpable violation of the Constitution) was overtaken by events. Congressman Wigberto Tañada, the lead prosecutor for the article, did not get the opportunity to show that Estrada illegally appointed his relatives to government positions and ordered the release of smuggled luxury vehicles from the Bureau of Customs.

Turning Point

FROM THE HODGEPODGE of evidence presented by the prosecution, only the testimonies of Singson, Clarissa Ocampo (senior vice-president of Equitable PCI Bank), Yasay, Ruben Almadro (erstwhile head of the Compliance and Surveillance Group of the Philippine Stock Exchange), Jose Luis Yulo (former president of the Philippine Stock Exchange), and Espiritu were directly material and relevant to the impeachment charges.

Singson's own testimony was a virtual repeat of the statements he had made to the senate Blue Ribbon Committee and the media. With regard to Article I (bribery), he stated that he collected money from various *jueteng* operators and delivered them to Estrada every 15th and 30th day of the month. He kept a ledger of his collections and the remittances he made to the former president, including the expenses he incurred upon the president's instructions.

For Article II (graft and corruption), Singson narrated the circumstances surrounding the delivery to Estrada of his P130-million kickback from excise taxes intended for Ilocos Sur. He showed the money trail: from the Land Bank branch in Malacañang to the Vigan branch to the Greenhills branch, where three people closely identified with Charlie 'Atong' Ang, a close associate of Estrada's, eventually withdrew the money.

Of this P130 million, P70 million was supposedly given to Estrada, P20 million to his First Lady, Dr. Luisa Ejercito, P15 million to his son Jinggoy, mayor of San Juan, and P25 million to Ang.

Except for a few inconsequential corrections, Singson's testimony survived the cross-examination of defense lawyer Estelito Mendoza. His admission that he turned against Estrada because the *jueteng* operation in his province was awarded to his political enemy reinforced the suspicion that personal, rather than patriotic, reasons were behind Singson's accusations.

With no other witness to corroborate Singson's testimony, doubts were created in the public's mind about the ability of the prosecution to prove the bribery charges. It was the word of Singson against that of Estrada.

Until Clarissa Ocampo entered the picture.

Smoking Gun

OCAMPO TESTIFIED that it was in her very presence that Estrada signed the fictitious name "Jose Velarde" on an Investment Management Agreement covering P500 million.

If she did not provide the "smoking gun", her testimony definitely was the turning point of the trial. Hers was an eyewitness account (she sat at her elbow, she said, as he signed) to Estrada's huge, presumably ill-gotten, and therefore hidden, wealth. She established a clear link between Estrada and the bank account that supplied the money used to finance the construction of the "Boracay" mansion for one of his mistresses.

The substance of Ocampo's testimony was bad enough. The timing of her testimony—the night before the country went on a long break—made it worse.

During the holidays, when families and friends gathered and enjoyed the luxury of time and conversation, Ocampo's testimony was the talk of the town. With the defense unable to cross-examine her, her damning statements acquired gospel-truth ring.

To make matters worse still, the defense lawyers refused to cross-examine her when the trial resumed, citing technicality as justification. That gave the impression that Estrada's lawyers knew Ocampo had told the truth and that there was no way they could impugn her testimony.

The stock of the prosecution rose.

Cover-Up

ARTICLE III (betrayal of the public trust) was the subject of the testimonies of Almadro, Yulo, and Yasay. Their testimonies on the attempts of Estrada to influence the results of the investigation of Dante Tan, a close friend and majority owner of BW Resources Corp., for stock manipulation and violation of the securities laws presented the image of a president willing to let the country's stock market collapse to protect a friend. Projecting the image of clean and straight-talking professionals, Almadro and Yulo came across as credible and trustworthy, like Ocampo.

Yasay corroborated their testimonies, reinforcing the picture of a president who did not hesitate to cajole, browbeat, intimidate, and threaten a government official—the chairman of the Securities and Exchange Commission himself—for a friend. And when Estrada's first finance secretary,

Edgardo Espiritu, took the witness stand, his testimony rounded off everything. It may have been short on hard evidence, but it was long on emotional impact.

Espiritu had been one of Estrada's most trusted men, if not his most trusted man. They had worked closely since 1992, when the presidency was six years yet into Estrada's future. Espiritu had helped raise campaign funds for him.

Espiritu's testimony that he heard Estrada talk about his profits, and eventually losses, in the trading of BW resources stocks in the stock market, without showing any concern about its legality or propriety and the damage it could do to the stock market and the general economy bolstered the testimonies of Almadro, Yulo, and Yasay.

The public saw on television the emotional distress Espiritu went through as he testified. His voice shook. He bit his lips and paused to keep himself from breaking down. Unlike Singson, he had no axe to grind. Neither was he under any obligation to testify against him. He could have stayed away, safe in his home in the United States, but he chose to return and testify, at great risk to himself and his family. That sacrifice was not lost on the audience.

Second Envelope

BEFORE THE ORDINARY COURTS of justice, the testimonies of Singson, Ocampo, Almadro, Yulo, Yasay, and Espiritu would have been sufficient to convict Estrada for any of the first three offenses—bribery, graft and corruption, betrayal of public trust. Indeed, the public had become so outraged one little push would have set it off to take matters in its own hands. But it wanted the constitutional process to take its course. But then, again, it had its limits, and it soon came to that.

What 35 witnesses and 24 trial days failed to accomplish, one envelope did in five days. The refusal of 11 senators to open the envelope that purportedly contained information about Estrada's P3.3-billion bank deposit broke the dam of resentment and frustration that had built up since Day One of the impeachment trial. The constitutional process could no longer be trusted. Neither could the senators be relied upon to protect the people's interests against an abusive president.

So, the people took to the streets and gave sovereignty a new dimension.

Civil Society, the Churches, and the Ouster of Erap

JOHN J. CARROLL, S.J.

Introduction

ONLY CREATION is an absolute beginning; everything else has a history. Hence it is important to note that, long before recent developments, both the Catholic church, as represented by Jaime Cardinal Sin, and elements of civil society, as represented for example by the National Peace Conference (NPC), had been critical of President Joseph Estrada.

The cardinal's antipathy focused on the bad moral example which he felt the president gave to the youth as well as on his style of governance. The NPC, founded in 1990 for the purpose of bringing civil-society pressure on the government and the rebel groups to resolve their differences peacefully, had by 1992 taken up the sectoral issues of indigenous peoples, farmers, urban poor and others—issues which it felt were an obstacle to peace. It had been actively involved in formulating the Social Reform Agenda (SRA) of President Ramos, but was disappointed by the seeming failure of his administration to follow through, and even more so by the seemingly cavalier treatment accorded by the Estrada administration to both the SRA and the NPC.

There were personal, although not formal, links between the NPC and the Catholic church, primarily through the Society of Jesus. The executive secretary of the NPC has been Teresita 'Ging' Quintos Deles, who has also been the executive secretary of the Gaston Z. Ortigas Peace Institute, based on the Ateneo de Manila campus. The chairperson of the NPC is Bishop Francisco Claver, S.J., bishop of Bontoc-Ligawe.

Likewise there were informal links between some church-people and the military. The Philippine Democratic Socialist Party (PDSP), of which Fr. Romeo J. Intengan, provincial superior of the Society of Jesus in the

Philippines, is a key animator and adviser, had given seminars on democratic socialism at the National Defense College and the General Staff School as well as in some police and military camps. Father Intengan had kept up the contacts made in that way. Moreover, the police deputy director, Gen. Leandro 'Larry' Mendoza had for many months been meeting with the PDSP and groundworking within the police itself for any eventuality.

What follows here is a chronology of events leading to the fall of Estrada, focused on the roles played by the church and civil society, followed in turn by some analysis and reflection.

Building Up

FROM LATE 1999 to mid 2000. The National Peace Conference held consultations across the social sectors—basic sectors, business, church, academe—looking toward a call for the president's resignation. They found no readiness for such a movement: the basic sectors still hoped to get some benefits from the regime; business was still confident in the fundamentals; the church (the Manila archdiocese) was "studying the situation". There was distrust of Vice President Gloria Macapagal-Arroyo across the sectors. The NPC decided to focus on elections, concrete issues, the wrongdoings of officials. Meanwhile, the Mindanao war began to unite civil society and business in opposition.

Thus in August of 2000 a group allied with the NPC, Konsensyang Pilipino (KP), of which Teresa 'Tess' Baltazar was a key animator, organized a seminar on impeachment where Sen. Teofisto 'Tito' Guingona and Fr. Joaquin Bernas, S.J., spoke. Afterwards and with the support of Concerned Women of the Philippines (Evelyn Kilayko), Gomburza (Father Robert Reyes), they discussed filing a complaint for impeachment. The president's unexplained wealth as revealed in the Philippine Center for Investigative Journalism (PCIJ) reports and the Mindanao war were to be the key issues. Senator Guingona helped, lawyers drew up the complaint. Father Bernas: "It is something that has to be done, but it probably won't work." Business: "Someone has to do it, but we can't."

In the last week of September Ging Deles and others decided to file the complaint, through "a pure soul"—Tess Baltazar. Some congresspersons were ready to endorse it. Tess met with Congressman Michael 'Mike' Defensor. But then some interested congresspersons began to have doubts, wanted to see a constituency, more "warm bodies", for impeachment. The filing was delayed.

Meanwhile, Gov. Luis 'Chavit' Singson had had his falling out with the president, and approached former Congressman Jose 'Peping' Cojuangco for assistance. In late September or early October, Singson was brought to Cardinal Sin by Fr. Robert Reyes and a Benedictine sister, who were mediating for Peping Cojuangco and Pastor 'Boy' Saycon. The cardinal was initially cool, then became more interested especially when a Major Roque Verzoza phoned from Ilocos Sur claiming that they were being threatened by armed men.

On October 9, Monday, Chavit Singson gave his press conference on the palace's involvement in *jueteng*, following Senator Guingona's privilege speech. This created storms in both Houses of Congress—a Blue Ribbon committee investigation got under way in the senate—and in the country; as the facts came out, many cause-oriented and political groups, not only those church-linked but also those on the Left such as Bayan and Sanlakas, strongly urged resignation.

On October 11 Cardinal Sin consulted the priests' Council of the Archdiocese of Manila. He then asked Fr. Robert Reyes, Msgr. Jose Clemente F. Ignacio, and Msgr. Socrates Villegas to draft a resolution, read it and signed it in the name of the council. The statement asserted that the president had "lost the moral ascendancy to govern" and out of *delicadeza* should resign. Soon other bishops and Catholic groups and those on the Left as well as the Right-wing Rebolusyonaryong Alayansang Makabansa (RAM) were echoing the call.

Also on October 11, Paul Dominguez called a meeting with Deles, Dan Songco, Corazon 'Dinky' Juliano-Soliman of CO-Multiversity, and Domey Javier. The initiative again came from the Council on Philippine Affairs (Copa) group, of which Peping Cojuangco was the financier. They met again on October 14. A meeting of convenors followed in the following week and from it emerged the Kongreso ng Mamamayang Pilipino II (Kompil II).

On October 13 Archbishop Orlando B. Quevedo, O.M.I., of the Catholic Bishops' Conference of the Philippines issued a statement pointing to the "moral disarray" surrounding the presidency as a consequence of the jueteng scandal, expressed confidence in the truth of the statements of Governor Singson, and urged that the crisis be resolved by resolute action "including presidential resignation if need be". The statement was milder than that of Cardinal Sin—there was need to achieve a consensus among the bishops, not all of whom favored a strong stand.

At the same time the Associations of Major Religious Superiors of Men and Women in the Philippines, i.e. superiors of Catholic religious congregations of priests, sisters, and brothers, issued a statement calling for the "highest officials in our country to step down"—the phrase was seen as including Vice President Macapagal-Arroyo. Fr. Romeo Intengan asked Jesuit scholastics to begin mobilizing, and *"Simbahang Lingkod ng Bayan"* (SLB), made up of seminarians and religious, began distributing statements and documentation calling for resignation or impeachment, by email.

At the same time, Bro. Mike Velarde, leader of the Catholic lay charismatic group El Shaddai and spiritual advisor to the president, called for calm and sobriety and asked that the constitutional processes be allowed to take their course.

In the following month, Leftist groups such as Bayan and Sanlakas, Promotion of Church People's Response (PCPR) and Kairos joined in mass actions. Fathers Jose 'Joe' Dizon and Juvenal 'Ben' Moraleda reappeared on the national scene. Some religious sisters, ideologically uninformed, joined both the marches of Bayan (Reaffirmist) and those of Sanlakas (Rejectionist).

On October 18 the impeachment complaint was finally filed in the House of Representatives, in the names of three congresspersons (Heherson 'Sonny' Alvarez, Mike Defensor, and Ernesto 'Boy' Herrera), Fr. Robert Reyes of Gomburza, Tess Baltazar of KP, and members or representatives of 22 other groups including Bayan, KMU, TUCP, Pandayan, Kairos, and the Muslim Association of the Philippines. Forty-two congresspersons endorsed the complaint, but the process was clearly led by civil society. The NPC put out a paid advertisement in the newspapers with a signature form attached, and for one week its fax machine went non-stop.

On October 29 Kompil was formally launched at the Ateneo de Manila with a crowd estimated by the organizers at 2,000-2,500. More than 200 groups were represented, including Code-NGO, NPC, Labor Solidarity (FFW, TUCP, APL), and political groups (Sanlakas through Dare, Akbayan, Pandayan, Bisig, FDC). village associations, Women's Action Group, Couples for Christ, the church through Fr. Robert Reyes, Maitet Pascual for Pare, Nikki Perlas for environmental groups, youth groups of Bisig and student council organizations. Funding came from individuals and organizations, the business sector and village associations such as Forbes, Ayala, Urdaneta. Decision-making was dominated by 10-15 groups (political blocs, POs, NGOs, labor, the Makati Business Club).

At the rally Vice President Macapagal-Arroyo stated that Kompil would be the civil society component of her campaign, and that she would listen to it. For its part, Kompil made it clear that it would coordinate with her and with the United Opposition but would not take orders from them. Kompil, Bayan, and Copa, together with the United Opposition, formed the Multi-Sectoral Opposition.

On October 30, 12 business associations led by the Makati Business Club formally asked the president to resign. And on November 3, Friday, Speaker Manuel 'Manny' Villar left the administration party, taking with him more than 40 members of the ruling majority, bringing the number of congresspersons willing to support impeachment above the "magic number" of 73.

On November 4 the Archdiocese of Manila organized a rally at the EDSA shrine with a crowd estimated at 130,000. Cardinal Sin and former President Aquino spoke powerfully, asking for the president's resignation and endorsing Vice President Macapagal-Arroyo as his successor. Governor Singson and Speaker Villar were present and received thunderous applause; former Speaker Jose de Venecia also appeared on the podium, to the distress of some.

On November 6 the House Committee on Justice voted to impeach the president. Rallies and demonstrations around the country increased in intensity, perhaps the largest of these was the "3rd National Day of Prayer and Fasting" on November 11, organized by the administration with the help of various religious groups, which drew an estimated 800,000 to 1,000,000 people, including many El Shaddai members. It was seen as an expression of support for the president. During this period Bro. Mike Velarde was attempting to mediate between President Estrada and Vice President Macapagal-Arroyo. Velarde was, however, criticized by Archbishop Orlando Quevedo, O.M.I., president of the Catholic Bishops' Conference of the Philippines (CBCP). His continued support of the president despite the CBCP's position that the president had lost the moral authority to govern suggested that "political partisanship might be overruling socio-moral principles," the CBCP said.

On the opposing side, the organizational and communications network of the Catholic Archdiocese of Manila and other dioceses, Catholic religious groups coordinated by SBL, Catholic and non-Catholic schools and universities, the NGO networks, labor and peasant groups and political blocs did the mobilizing.

Newspapers and radio and TV stations on both sides, together with email and text messages, kept the issues before the public. It was noted that many of the tabloids and the A.M. radio commentators strongly supported the president and it was claimed that they were being paid to support him, from a special government fund. On the other hand, many casual observers noted that the unorganized poor, the *masa*, still identified with the president and supported him. The priest of an urban poor parish in Metro Manila, a parish which is deeply involved in programs for the poor, told the writer about this time that his people were divided. He said in effect: "There are the *barangay* officials who are pro-Estrada because they are paid, and they can mobilize quite a following; then there is Sanlakas, which can see no good in anything the government does. I don't think the parish should take sides; we focus on our savings and livelihood and housing programs."

On November 13 Speaker Villar caught the President's supporters off-guard by ruling that there were already enough congresspersons' signatures on the Articles of Impeachment, and sending them without further debate to the senate. Before the session the NPC had organized a ritual of blessing-missioning in front of Congress, in which the congresspersons supporting impeachment participated, and peach-colored ribbons were distributed.

On November 14 a massive "Welgang bayan" throughout the country brought together business, labor, the religious sector, the basic sectors, those on the left and those on the right in demanding the President's resignation or impeachment. Cardinal Sin supported it, as did Crispin Beltran of KMU, also Bayan and Sanlakas.

In the following weeks leading up to the actual trial, rallies both for Estrada and against Estrada intensified throughout the nation, climaxing in a week-long series of anti-Estrada rallies and a "People Power" lunch hosted on November 29 in Makati by the moneyed classes for farmers and others who had traveled from the provinces to voice their anti-Estrada sentiments.

By the end of November, as things heated up, Brother Mike came under strong attack from some bishops and the priests' Council of the Archdiocese of Manila. He had refused to cut his ties with the president, whether out of concern for the president's spiritual welfare or to return personal or institutional favors he from him. At the most, he was willing to advise Estrada to resign after a period of six months to a year, during which time he would share power with Macapagal-Arroyo.

On the other hand it was being said that Brother Mike should either support the official position of the bishops or leave the church. When a group of Filipinos in London prepared a statement calling for resignation, some El Shaddai members wished to wait for word from Brother Mike; others just went ahead and signed it. Fearing, it seems, a split among his followers, Brother Mike wrote to the Archdiocese of Manila assuring the cardinal that he was still faithful to the church. On the issue of President Estrada, he became ostensibly neutral: Shortly afterward he left for abroad, to accompany his wife, said to be in need of medical treatment.

The Trial

ON NOVEMBER 20 the trial officially began, but the first two weeks were taken up by procedural matters. Rallies continued. On December 7, the first witness for the prosecution was heard. On the same day, to provide another of the imaginative "gimmicks" which sustain a movement, but also to convince watchful military and police authorities that there was massive popular support for their cause, civil society organized the "Jericho March". The inspiration was taken from the Biblical account of the Jews marching around the walls of Jericho and then blowing a horn at which the walls collapsed. It began with a Mass in Malate church, followed by a march to the senate in which the Vice President Macapagal-Arroyo, former President Corazon Aquino, and other key figures participated. Participants came from the Catholic schools, fewer than expected from the parishes, and many from civil society, including Kompil and the KMU. El Shaddai leaders appeared at the church, but did not march.

It was noted that lay civil society played a larger role in the Jericho March than it had at the November 4 rally for which the leadership had come primarily from the church. But the numbers were disappointing: one account estimated 25,000 and another 70,000. This was a setback; the military was watching and was said to be asking for 1,000,000 warm bodies as proof that there was a critical mass behind the move for resignation or ouster of the president.

As the testimony of witnesses began, the prosecutors in a meeting asked for support from civil society; the private prosecutors kept civil society informed on developments. The latter kept up a watch outside the senate, and a scoreboard for the last two weeks; it also had people inside with logbooks recording what went on. More importantly perhaps, the proceedings were carried live by radio and TV and rebroadcast in the evenings. Although there was much humdrum procedural discussion and noting of evidence, there were also moments of high drama shared by the whole nation—most notably perhaps the testimony of Equitable-PCI Bank executive Clarissa G. Ocampo that she had personally seen President Estrada sign a trust document as "Jose Velarde."

Throughout the trial, the country remained deeply divided, but more and more people became convinced that as President Estrada had amassed vast sums which could in no way be explained by his legitimate income and were not included in his income tax reports. It seemed, moreover, that he had used his influence to promote and protect friends of questionable reputations.

At the same time there was the strong prospect of an acquittal based on the technicality that the evidence submitted did not relate to the specific charges in the Articles of Impeachment. This prospect was strengthened by the perceived sympathies of enough of the senator-judges to block a conviction. By early January Tito Guingona was predicting a showdown at the trial, over admission of evidence.

The End Game

ON JANUARY 14, 2001, Kompil had a big meeting on the Ateneo campus; there was talk of civil disobedience after an anticipated acquittal. There is speculation that this may have panicked the defense into calling for the vote of January 16.

In the evening of January 15, while addressing the Loyola House of Studies community, Father Intengan received a coded text message from Tito Guingona: "Go," and it meant to prepare mass mobilizations. Tito had word that on the following day the defense would move to block the opening of the second envelope from Equitable-PCI Bank, and to exclude the testimony of key witnesses such as Clarissa Ocampo.

On January 16 Senators Francisco Tatad and Juan Ponce Enrile moved to preempt the decision of Chief Justice Hilario Davide and called for a vote on the opening of the second envelope. As is well known, the vote was

11 to 10 against opening it, and this effectively terminated the trial. With the nation watching on TV, Senate President Aquilino Pimentel resigned his post, the prosecutors walked out, defense lawyer Raul Daza engaged in a heated debate with Sen. Raul Roco and the chief justice declared the trial suspended until such time as the House would appoint new prosecutors.

If the defense move was, as some have suggested, an attempt to test the popular reaction in preparation for an acquittal—since it had the necessary senate votes—it got more than it had bargained for. Metro Manila exploded in anger and frustration as people streamed onto the streets, honking automobile horns, blowing whistles and banging pots and pans. Spontaneously they began assembling at the EDSA shrine, and at 11:30 Cardinal Sin went on the air inviting others there. Former Defense Secretary Renato de Villa, aide to Vice President Macapagal-Arroyo, met some of the opposition leaders there. It was decided to wait 48 hours to see whether the reaction would last, and if it did, to move.

On January 17, the crowds at the shrine increased, crowds made up in large part of university students whose classes had been called off. There was Mass, but also speeches of protest, outrage, and ridicule. Wearing black became a sign of protest. That evening Father Intengan met with Col. Carlos Holganza (military aide of Vice President Macapagal-Arroyo), Col. Victor Corpus (classmate of AFP chief of staff, Gen. Angelo Reyes, in Harvard) and Police Supt. Rodolfo Mendoza, who represented anti-Estrada elements in the PNP. Fr. Intengan proposed a 10-day buildup of protest leading to a general strike on January 25-26, for which the Philippine Democratic Socialist Party would mobilize and business groups to paralyze transportation on land, sea, and air. Others thought 10 days too long, but Fr. Intengan insisted that the general strike must be carefully prepared.

On the morning of January 18, Cardinal Sin was consulted about the strike plan and a withdrawal of support for the president by the AFP and PNP as a response to People Power. He reacted negatively to the prospect of strong military involvement. The crowds at EDSA continued to increase, as well as protest actions in the provinces. The church was now only one player in a much enlarged game.

Before 8:00 a.m. on January 19 the word was passed that the cardinal disapproved of a strong military move. But word also came that the president was about to relieve Gen. Angelo Reyes as chief of staff and to name Gen. Jose Calimlim in his place. General Reyes decided to move, and Father Intengan hurriedly contacted PNP Deputy Director General

Leandro 'Larry' Mendoza, who with his men cornered and neutralized his director general, Gen. Panfilo Lacson, forcing him to withdraw support from President Estrada. Meanwhile, word had gone out for a full mobilization of church and civil society at the EDSA shrine for the afternoon. There, about 4:00 p.m. General Reyes appeared and announced the AFP's withdrawal of support from the president. Representatives of the National Police and the Navy as well as Defense Secretary Orlando Mercado confirmed this, and the party began. But the game was not yet over.

Saturday, January 20, was a day of tension, centering both on the EDSA shrine and on the presidential palace and the nearby streets. Inside Malacañang, negotiations had gone on throughout the night, between President Estrada's people and those of Vice President Macapagal-Arroyo. The former expressed his willingness to resign but insisting on a five-day grace period and other conditions; the latter demanded an immediate resignation to avoid the danger of mob action and violence. The discussion was short-circuited by the decision of the Supreme Court to recognize Macapagal-Arroyo as president and for her oath-taking at the shrine. Meanwhile, and against the expressed wishes of Cardinal Sin, who was concerned to avoid violence and the kind of mob action which had followed the departure of President Marcos in 1986, thousands began marching to the palace. The marchers included civil society groups which hitherto had been following the lead of the Cardinal but now decided to make their own decision. As the crowds approached and some brief skirmishes with pro-Estrada groups broke out, Estrada left the palace.

Analysis: The Roles of the Church

FROM THE FOREGOING account it is evident that the Roman Catholic Archdiocese of Manila, and Jaime Cardinal Sin in particular, played a major role in the events leading up to the accession of President Macapagal-Arroyo—rightfully the Cardinal is seen in photographs of the oath-taking, standing close to the president. It has been noted also that the Catholic Bishops' Conference of the Philippines through its president, Archbishop Orlando B. Quevedo, O.M.I., supported the call for the president's resignation "if need be" and criticized Bro. Mike Velarde for seeming to let political partisanship overrule moral principles.

Yet it would not be accurate to say that the Philippine Catholic church or its hierarchy as a whole played such an active role. It is estimated that not more than 30 out of more than 100 bishops were actively involved in the movement and "you could count on your fingers the places where the church was strongly involved". Many noted with some distress the refusal of the highly respected Ricardo Cardinal Vidal of Cebu to speak out firmly on the issue. And the bishops' National Secretariat for Social Action, Justice, and Peace was relatively inactive, apparently in deference to the hesitations of many of the bishops.

The facts, of both intense involvement and relative non-involvement, are a challenge to reflection on the roles of the Catholic church in Philippine society. And such a reflection cannot ignore the fact that in the Philippines, unlike the situation in many other countries, the church is both a major social force and a cultural or moral force. It is a social force in the sense that it possesses a network of communication (parishes, schools and universities, radio stations, lay organizations) with scores of thousands of personnel, reaching down to the smallest barrio chapel in the most remote province. A network, it is said, which only Coca Cola distributors can rival!

And the church is a cultural or moral force in the sense that it has a message to communicate not only about the person's relationship to God but also about that person's relationships to other people—on the economic and political as well as the interpersonal and family levels. Thus it naturally assumes the role of a moral center, speaking to its people and through them to the society as a whole on moral issues affecting them.

In this the Catholic church differs from some Evangelical Protestant and "born-again" churches, and also from El Shaddai, which tend to focus on a strict code of personal and interpersonal morality but rarely touch on the morality of economic and political life, or what is called "structures of sin". Thus by default these churches can easily be seen as pro-establishment.

Does this mean that the church does all of the thinking for its people, and they only follow? Not so, particularly in complex economic and political issues which typically involve not only moral principles but facts which are not always clear and concrete judgments on what is practical or impractical, on the trade-offs implied in various options etc. The Philippine bishops followed this line of thinking, it seems, in their post-election statement following the snap election of 1986 (*Pulso*, Vol. I, No. 4, pp. 336-39). In effect the bishops told the people: "After hearing reports from all over the country, it is our considered judgment that the election has failed. If so, it gives no moral mandate for the administration to remain in power. We ask you, our people, now to consult your own experience and see whether you agree that the election failed. If you do, then let us meet together, pray together, think together about how we can oblige the government, peacefully, to undo the wrong that it has done."

The bishops in that statement were speaking as a moral center within, not above, the Christian community. Yet, as we know, events did not wait for the meeting, praying and thinking of which they spoke. The military revolt broke out, and in that critical moment Cardinal Sin called the people to the streets. He did so not simply because he was a cardinal but because at the time he alone had the resources (e.g. Radio Veritas) and the confidence of the people; they responded not because he was cardinal but because through the years of martial law he had spoken out on their behalf and they had come to trust him, and most of all because at that moment he was voicing their anger and frustration at a stolen election.

Something similar has occurred in recent months. Faced by Singson's revelations, following the BW scandal and the PCIJ reports, and the apathy of many citizens toward his sermons on public morality, Cardinal Sin felt that the massive evil at the heart of Philippine society had to be challenged directly and forceably; that the church as a major institution and moral center could not stand aside or remain on the level of moral principles alone while the nation was in crisis. He should therefore use the social and moral capital in his hands by taking a specific stand—for a presidential resignation. It is widely recognized that, without his active involvement and that of former President Aquino, the movement would hardly have gotten off the ground.

But what of separation of church and state? It has been pointed out many times that this phrase forbids only the "establishment" of a church as "the" official church of the nation. Prohibitions on church people engaging in politics come more from the side of the church and its canon law, which forbids their running for public office except with special permission, than from the Constitution. Given the reluctance of the church to see its priests and bishops directly involved in political matters, it is quite imaginable that a lower Vatican official expressed to the Philippine ambassador to the Holy See some concern about what was going on here. Such concern had been expressed more directly at the time of the 1986 snap election, but the Philippine bishops had asserted their right to make their own decisions on local matters.

But can we now expect the church to dictate to the government on routine matters of government? Not at all. The two situations which we have discussed, EDSA 1 and EDSA 2, were both exceptional and unfortunate. It is to be hoped that nothing like them will happen again. And in the meantime we may abide by the principle that the faith should guide or inform our political views, but cannot determine them. For in the words of Pope Paul VI "the same Christian faith can lead to different commitments." ("*Octogesima Adveniens*", no. 50).

Here the writer admits that he felt uncomfortable with the statements of some, in the heat of controversy, to the effect that Mike Velarde should either support the official position of the bishops or leave the church. This has been explained as a matter of discipline, i.e. that a member of the church should not publicly disagree with church authority. It should not be taken as suggesting that the church would like to impose a political position on its members as the Iglesia ni Kristo attempts to do.

Moreover, it has been shown on various occasions that the Filipino Catholic faithful, while welcoming the intervention of the church in crisis situations, wish to think for themselves in more routine matters. And in fact many, especially of the poorer classes, bitterly resented the church's opposition to Estrada, with whom they identified and who they firmly believed was "on their side". There is a gap in understanding between the social classes just as wide as or wider than, the economic gap, and this is not something that the church should ignore or forget in the euphoria of "victory."

Analysis: The Civil Society

CIVIL SOCIETY is a term with a long history and many meanings. For our purposes it will include all of the organized groups which participated in the events which we have been discussing other than the government, the military, and—since this has already been discussed—the church. We speak then of the groups which made up Kompil and the NPC, Bayan, Code-NGO, the business associations, trade unions and peasant associations and village associations, the POs and NGOs—terms which overlap in many ways. These organized groups were the backbone of the protest, and anyone who realizes the effort expended by their leaders will scoff at the idea that EDSA 2 represents "mob rule"—for a mob is by definition unorganized and unthinking.

It was these groups which provided the warm bodies looked for by the military; and it was their leaders—experienced organizers—who thought up the ritual of missioning and the senate watch and peach-colored ribbons, noise barrages and marches and the entertainment at the EDSA shrine which kept up the momentum. They also made excellent use of email and text messaging to spread the word and coordinate with each other. They thought of other things as well, such as *simbang gabi* Masses in front of the senate, after which Muslims who were observing the Ramadan fast would share breakfast before sunrise with the Catholics; to their disappointment, this was not allowed by the church authorities.

A key organizer of the civil society participation noted that it was difficult to win "big name" support until Cardinal Sin and former President Aquino came out publicly. With their support and the Singson revelations, things began to snowball and eventually lay civil society became a full partner with the church and even moved on its own. One observer said that the rally of November 4 was managed entirely by the church, on December 7 lay civil society took the lead, and for the "four days in January" the lead was definitely with the lay groups. Another noted that thousands marched to Mendiola on January 20 contrary to the wishes of the cardinal, and argued that this march had a decisive effect on President Estrada's decision to leave the palace. However one may weigh things, it seems clear that lay civil society became less dependent on the church as time went on.

Noteworthy also, however, is that at the end game civil society both lay and religious provided the warm bodies and legitimation, while the key decisions were made by politicians and military men. This can be seen as in line with civil society's claim that it seeks influence rather than power. But it also raises the question whether the politicians who have gained power are concerned simply to get the nation's economic and political system back onto the same old tracks. If so, if there is to be no real structural change, then the yawning gap which events have revealed between the social classes will even be wider, and we shall face more trouble, and likely more violent trouble, down the road.

The Road Ahead

FIFTEEN YEARS AGO, in the euphoria following EDSA 1, there was an attempt to keep together the groups which had supported President Aquino, in a coalition called "Cory Aquino People Power". The hope was that they would "nudge" her in the direction in which many thought she wished to be nudged, i.e. toward social reform and structural change. They might eventually form a new political party, truly based on the organized masses and espousing their interests, challenging the elitist politics which had ruled the country for almost a century.

That was not to be: President Aquino preferred to remain "above politics"; the upper- and middle-class groups went back to their businesses and jobs and families; the NGOs and POs went their own ways in pursuit of their own sectoral interests; a progressive Constitution was adopted, but the old elite reasserted itself in the 1987 election; the land reform bill was emasculated; the military forced the president to dismiss her "Leftist" advisors; and, despite a few victories for the poor, the gap between the classes grew wider.

Will the same dreary history repeat itself after EDSA 2? Surely the old politicians and the old politics are still around. But civil society is vastly stronger and more experienced now than in 1986. President Macapagal-Arroyo is reaching out to it, and has appointed two outstanding civil society leaders—Dinky Soliman and Ging Deles—to her Cabinet. More significantly perhaps—since we have seen progressives in the Cabinet before and have seen them frustrated—elements of the Left, the Center and the Right have learned in recent months to work together for limited objectives, and perhaps even to trust each other. If they can "hang in there," and maintain their unity in diversity, debate and negotiate their values and visions, with the church perhaps as an animating force working to infuse a new political culture of truth and justice and broad social concern, then perhaps we may begin to see light at the end of the tunnel—which this time will not be the train bearing down on us!

Some may see this as an impossible dream. But it is worth recalling the unpredicted and seemingly unpredictable events which, together with much sweat and tears, turned the impossible dream of ousting Erap into a reality. One recalls, for example, the Chavit Singson expose. Who could have predicted then the agile footwork of Speaker Villar which got the "foredoomed" and "quixotic" Bill of Impeachment through the House, and again the blunder of the pro-Estrada senators in calling for a vote on opening the second envelope. We no longer perhaps speak of these events as miracles but they can provide badly needed hope and courage. For now the real work begins.

View from the Streets
Different Folks, Different Strokes

TEODORO A. CASIÑO

WHEN SUPREME COURT CHIEF JUSTICE Hilario Davide Jr. banged the gavel that fateful night of January 16 and announced, "the no votes have it," the first question that came to my mind was: "Is this it?"

In the weeks prior to that crucial moment, we in Bayan had been wracking our brains thinking of the trigger that would finally let loose millions onto the nation's streets to oust Joseph Estrada. We were certain that the struggle would begin and end in the parliament of the streets and not in the senate impeachment court that was rapidly debasing itself as a political circus. The gun was cocked, and all we lacked was the finger to make it go off. By that time, the numerous bombshells dropped in Estrada's impeachment trial had, in our view, already galvanized the needed broad popular support for his forced resignation or for an unarmed uprising.

Estrada had been on the defensive since October, when Ilocos Gov. Luis 'Chavit' Singson set *jueteng-gate* in motion with his charges that Estrada had received gambling bribes and tax kickbacks. During those heady early days of *jueteng-gate*, several anti-Estrada formations were, to my mind, the major players in the efforts to persuade Estrada to resign, be impeached, or be forcibly ousted from power. The groups were Bayan, the Estrada Resign Movement (ERM), the Council on Philippine Affairs (Copa), the United Opposition (particularly Lakas-NUCD), the Kangkong Brigade and the Kongreso ng Mamamayang Pilipino (Kompil II). There were other organizations like the People's Consultative Assembly, Couples for Christ, Bigkis Pinoy, the Makati Business Club, Barangay RJ and the Jesus is Lord Movement.

Apart from these, there were individuals whose influence was crucial too—former Presidents Corazon Aquino and Fidel Ramos, Jaime Cardinal Sin and Vice President Gloria Macapagal-Arroyo. The visible military groups included the Reform the Armed Forces Movement (RAM) and the Federation of Retired Commissioned and Enlisted Officers (Forces). But there were many more in the chain of command, only they chose to keep a low profile.

Of course, there were groups who called for both Estrada's and Ms Macapagal-Arroyo's resignation and a snap election. The most vociferous among them was the Sanlakas-BMP group headed by the late Popoy Lagman. These groups eventually distanced themselves from the others due to their "resign all" stance, which threatened the fragile united front and which, many of us thought, stood to benefit none other than Estrada.

To say that it was not easy for all these groups to come together is an understatement. We had various organizational, political and ideological differences. Many of our groups were wary of each other, and accusations, direct or implied, of one-upmanship and misrepresentation were common. It was interesting how we at Bayan ourselves learned to adjust ourselves just for the sake of maintaining that united front against Estrada.

In a press conference to announce an October 18 Ayala rally, I found myself beside Alex Aguilar of the TUCP (a rival of Bayan-affiliated KMU) and Commodore Domingo Calajate of the RAM. Like myself, they were clueless about the press conference since we were all invited by Pastor 'Boy' Saycon of Copa just for a "small meeting" at former Rep. Jose 'Peping' Cojuangco's home in Dasmarinas Village. I was surprised by the horde of reporters, photographers and TV cameramen. I also remember an instance when Sen. Ramon Magsaysay, Jr. called me and KMU chairperson Crispin Beltran to the stage at an Ayala rally just to shake hands with Gen. Edgardo Abenina and Calajate. Or the preparations for the November 14 people's strike, with the contending political blocs refusing to join and instead choosing either Ayala, Welcome Rotonda, or Liwasang Bonifacio for their separate rallies.

Launching an open and active campaign to remove an elected and admittedly popular president was not an easy decision, not even for the militants at Bayan. We were chided for being quixotic. There were many within our ranks who doubted the political wisdom of sounding what they thought a premature call. Others were afraid of the possible backlash and counter-attacks from the government. Sure, Estrada was progressively becoming exposed and isolated, but the president was still the president.

To my mind, the first to publicly call for Estrada's resignation was the women's group Gabriela. This was as early as the "Manindigan para sa

Demokrasya" rally at Ayala Avenue on August 20, 1999. Despite pleas from rally organizers, including Cory Aquino, not to make the rally an anti-Estrada affair, the Gabriela women came with their banners and placards slamming the president. Moreover, the 20,000-strong Bayan contingent was even prevented from marching close to the stage.

The next sector to call for Estrada's removal was composed of church people under the Church Against Rising Tyranny (Christ) and Promotion for Church People's Response (PCPR), who joined the nationwide "Never Again" protests on September 21, 1999. They were followed by the youth and student groups, the human rights organizations, then the peasant associations under the Kilusang Magbubukid ng Pilipinas (KMP), whose main slogan, "Oust Erap", was featured in the front-page photo of the *Inquirer* on January 23, 2000. These calls for Estrada's ouster, made mainly by the poor in rallies and demonstrations, reflected how, despite his popularity with the masses, the president had managed to antagonize, one by one, every class and sector that had once supported his presidency.

Scandal after scandal broke out involving the president, his families and cronies. These served to agitate the middle and upper sections of society, including the otherwise politically passive business sector, against Estrada. By February 2000, a broad range of classes and sectors, most of them marginalized and oppressed, had had enough. Erap's popularity was in the pits. It was during last year's commemoration of the anniversary of the 1986 EDSA uprising that Bayan came out publicly with the slogan "Oust the US-Estrada regime." For its part, the September 21 Committee cried, "Enough is Enough, Enough of Erap."

Allies in the parliamentary opposition and in big business said they agreed wholeheartedly with us, but chose to stay on the sidelines, saying they were not ready to confront Estrada: "You go ahead, you guys are used to that kind of thing." Any talk of impeachment was dismissed as *"suntok sa buwan"* (a shot at the moon). But in a few weeks, the middle classes had found their voice through the ingenious "exclamation point" stickers of the Silent Protest Movement.

On April 3, Teofisto Guingona, then the senate minority floor leader, called for Estrada's resignation. That night, in a hastily called meeting, we met with several leaders of the "social democratic" bloc, the first in a series of bilateral talks with various political forces meant to forge an anti-Estrada front even broader than the existing September 21 Committee. Things moved quickly, and Estrada's popularity was taking an even worse beating.

But by May, reports on the severe fighting in Mindanao would hog the media. For a while, the regime's "wag the dog" scenario seemed working. Estrada was being projected as a strong, decisive leader who was saving the country from Moro terrorists, bandits, and secessionists. Many did not want to criticize Estrada for fear of being branded as destabilizers or sympathizers of the Moro Islamic Liberation Front.

We at Bayan felt the need to expose these squid tactics. We were particularly concerned that Estrada's popularity was being propped at the expense of the Moro and peasant communities. We refocused our efforts to oppose the government's all-out war policy, and for that purpose, spearheaded the formation of the broad alliance Kalinaw Mindanao. By the middle of 2000, the Estrada regime's genocidal war in Mindanao had drained the national coffers and was taking its toll.

It was at this time that we met with former Budget Secretary Salvador Enriquez, who broached the idea of a broad formation called the People's Consultative Assembly (PCA). The PCA would attempt to bring together all anti-Estrada groups into a coalition that would work for his ouster and replacement by a council of leaders acceptable to all the political blocs. Unfortunately, other groups were unhappy with Enriquez's close ties with Fidel Ramos and Gen. Jose Almonte. The PCA would later be one of the groups focused on bringing in the military to the anti-Estrada movement.

On September 21, 2000, many more cause-oriented groups were again calling for Estrada's ouster through slogans like "Never Again," "Oust Erap," "Erap Out" and "Enough of Erap." At the rally sponsored by the September 21 Committee at Liwasang Bonifacio, members of Lakas, led by Sen. Teofisto Guingona and non-street parliamentarians like Liwayway Vinzons-Chato, Perfecto Yasay and Philconsa Chairperson Camilo Sabio, came out publicly against Estrada. It was around this time that Singson opened the proverbial can of worms, providing the much-needed boost to the ouster movement. Singson's expose, signaled a major break within Estrada's criminal syndicate, inducing the first wave of defections from Estrada's erstwhile supporters.

Singson unleashed *jueteng-gate* on October 9. A week later, Bayan, along with 23 other people's organizations and NGOs, filed the impeachment complaint in Congress. It was endorsed by 77 congressmen. This was followed by sustained protest actions nationwide, among them a KMU-led rally on Mendiola on October 13, a KMP-led rally on October 19, the weekly Ayala rallies (October 18, 25, November 8), the November 4 EDSA

Prayer Rally, the nationwide People's Strike of November 14, the Luzon-wide Lakbayan of November 29-30, the Jericho March of December 7, the Parada ng Bayan on December 18, and the People's Countdown from December 27-31.

The daily airing of the impeachment trial, despite the legal gobbledy-gook and procedural contortions resorted to by defense lawyers, height-ened the people's shock and anger at Estrada's rapacity and rottenness. There were three possible triggers that we felt would be the beginning of the end of Estrada's presidency: one, Estrada's acquittal by February 12 or thereabouts; two, a major rally to be called at EDSA on January 26, where sections of the military and the police were expected to announce their defection; three, as we all know, the least expected, a major development in the impeachment trial that would ignite massive public outrage.

The nationwide protests and demonstrations continued until the night of January 16, the start of the four-day People Power 2 uprising. I was at the senate that evening, watching the proceedings from the gallery with my co-signatories to the original impeachment complaint. We were all set for a walkout, having been informed over the weekend by private prosecu-tors Romeo Capulong and Simeon Marcelo that the defense and pro-Estrada senator-judges were going to push for a vote on the opening of the contro-versial second envelope.

I came out of the gallery shouting *"luto"* (fixed) and texting like mad. In a few minutes, I learned that the Bayan secretariat had already sched-uled an indignation rally for 11 a.m. the next day. The plan was to sur-round the senate and, if possible, conduct a siege to dramatize the people's protest at this abomination. Again, the question that kept ringing in my head was: "Is this it?"

If there was anything that we believed in aside from the need to re-move Joseph Estrada, it was the reality that no one could do it alone. No organization, political bloc or institution could claim to have a monopoly on strategy and tactics, or the necessary influence as well as resources to oust him. It was a case of all or nothing. And so, as early as August 1999, we in Bayan resolved to reach out once again to our longtime ideological and political rivals: the social democrats.

Those in activist circles know of the longstanding struggle between the "socdems" (social democrats) and the "natdems" (national democrats), which stretches as far back as the First Quarter Storm of 1970. The last time that there was any formal coordination or joint actions between the

NDs and SDs was in the mid-90s, before the breakup of the ND bloc into the "reaffirmists" and the "rejectionists," where the SDs chose to ally themselves with those who had bolted from Bayan.

When the SDs formed Kompil II in October last year, we decided to keep out. We felt it was unnecessary to place ourselves under the Kompil II umbrella as this would have led to organizational entanglements and tactical debates, which we all could do without. We also went all-out in forging alliances with the Right, specifically organizations of big business, the conservative shurch hierarchy, traditional political parties and, indirectly, the military and police—all who wanted Estrada out.

It felt strange; it was tricky but definitely a learning experience for those of us who saw up close how the elite in the anti-Estrada alliance thought, plotted, and moved. In time, I became a regular guest in palatial homes in Dasmariñas, Forbes Park, and Ayala Alabang. We were their "new friends", which meant, among other things, being subjects of many a souvenir photo session.

On the broad united front, it was the military and police elements we were most wary of, but it was the business sector we found most difficult to deal with. The businessmen were the most cautious (some would say paranoid) and *"makunat"*, as it were, choosing to provide resources only to the moderate groups of Kompil II and to the politicians of the United Opposition, whom they felt most comfortable with.

The November 29-30 Lakbayan, which included the famous People Power lunch, was supposed to be supported by the Makati business groups. But only a handful of their executives and employees came down to join the marchers.

Indeed, more than the Makati businessmen, it was the households of Forbes Park, Dasmariñas, Urdaneta, Bel-Air, San Lorenzo, and Ayala-Alabang who took up the challenge of feeding 10,000 hungry marchers for two days. People like Ching and Serg Montinola, Josie Bantug, Rosanna Fores, Marichu Soriano, Triccie and Louie Sison, Cora Tanjuatco, and Teddy Javier became allies and good friends.

The Left's wariness of the military and the police was especially true for Bayan, with their harrowing experiences at their hands. In one meeting sponsored by the People's Consultative Assembly, RAM forces, through Gen. Edgardo Abenina and Commodore Domingo Calajate, even offered to "subordinate" themselves to Bayan just to facilitate certain joint actions. But we would always reject hints of military actions to complement our rallies and demonstrations. We stood our ground and said that the military's task was simply to announce the withdrawal of its support for Estrada, and then to disobey orders, if any, to attack the anti-Estrada forces.

Our critics would always needle us about our "opportunism" and the "watering down" of Bayan's sharp political line. They chided us for being "too soft" and accommodating toward those they perceived to be our political and ideological enemies. But we chose to look at the other side of the coin, and appreciated the fact that people who at other times would not touch us with a 10-foot pole were now marching with us, arm-in-arm to, of all places, on Mendiola. They included people like former Solicitor General Frank Chavez, economist Solita Monsod, and civic leader and socialite Margarita 'Tingting' Cojuangco. Even the University of Santo Tomas fathers joined our vigils on Mendiola. Mainstream bands like Color it Red, Moig, Slapshock, Put3Ska, Brown Man Revival, and—would you believe?—the Executive Band performed at our rallies. We were building a broad base of support for militant street actions and preparing for the ultimate showdown with Estrada.

Of the major groups we worked with, the Estrada Resign Movement (ERM) and the Council on Philippine Affairs (Copa) were the most resolute in using the parliament of the streets to oust the president. Copa was particularly instrumental as one of the major organizers of the weekly Wednesday rallies on Ayala Ave. in Makati City. For demonstrators like us who are more at home at Liwasang Bonifacio and Mendiola, Copa provided the network and resources to reestablish the presence of the militant groups in the Makati business district. Copa and PCA leaders gave many hints about their efforts to draw in the military and police forces within the framework of a "civilian-led, military-backed struggle." At least twice they egged us to hold massive rallies to give their military allies a chance to defect or initiate preemptive strikes against pro-Estrada factions in the AFP and PNP. The first military action would have been some time in the second week of December. The second would have been a planned mammoth rally on EDSA on January 26, to be preceded by a four-day hunger strike at the People Power Monument.

The no vote on the second envelope and Sen. Teresa Aquino-Oreta's infamous dance routine came on the night of January 16. No group could have predicted what would happen. We were all surprised at the swiftness of events and were forced to think on our feet as we tried to steer the final showdown with the Estrada regime.

After the walkout at the senate, at around 11:20 p.m., I called the Bayan office to inform them that Jaime Cardinal Sin would be saying Mass at the EDSA shrine. I was informed that Bayan forces led by KMU, Gabriela and AnakBayan were already massing in Cubao to go there. We decided to inform all the mass leaders and mass formations to go straight to EDSA. Upon arriving at the EDSA shrine a few minutes past midnight, I saw members of the Couples for Christ, Migrante, ERM San Juan, Bayan, Sanlakas, and Ateneo students. In a while, our Cubao contingent arrived. It was there, in the midst of all the shouting and hooting and blowing of horns that I told myself, "this is it."

We cancelled the indignation rally scheduled the next morning and at 1:10 a.m. sent out a message saying: "Go out into the streets. This is the final push. People Power 2 has begun."

Bayan joined the Mass celebrated by Cardinal Sin at the shrine. Our office in Quezon City was deluged by calls from here and abroad. In the next few hours, our local chapters spearheaded or participated in protest actions in the urban centers of Davao, General Santos, Cagayan de Oro, Butuan, Iligan, Marawi, Zamboanga, Kidapawan, Pagadian, Ozamiz, Koronadal, Malaybalay, Digos, Cebu, Iloilo, Bacolod, Tagbilaran, Albay and Naga.

Around 4 a.m., January 17, the first among several meetings among the major formations at EDSA was held at the Linden Suites in the Ortigas Center. Among those present were me and Carol Pagaduan-Araullo of Bayan and Estrada Resign Movement; Paul Dominguez, Sen. Alberto Romulo and retired generals Lisandro Abadia and Renato de Villa of the United Opposition; Dan Songco and Francis Pangilinan of Kompil II, Satur Ocampo, Nathaniel Santiago and Vicente Ladlad of Bayan Muna; Joey Lina and Gary Cayton of the Kangkong Brigade; and Triccie and Louie Sison of Couples for Christ.

We identified the requirements for getting as many people as possible to mass on EDSA and mapped out our immediate tasks. Bayan was tasked to bring in the warm bodies, which would come from its organized forces in the youth and student sector, and workers and urban poor communities in Metro Manila.

A real organizational nightmare during the days of People Power 2 was the marshaling of the stage on EDSA. Politicians and VIPs would come with their *alalays* (assistants) and bodyguards in tow, expecting everyone to be accommodated and often leading to shouting matches and a lot of shoving and pushing. Especially annoying to the marshals were the body-guards of Cavite Gov. Ramon 'Bong' Revilla, who perhaps thought they were still in their hometown.

The most pathetic sight on stage were the *balimbings*, like Rep. Jose Mari Gonzales and former Interior Secretary Alfredo Lim, who even tried to steal some of the limelight for a chance to wave to the crowd. Fortunately, among the people they encountered on stage were two feisty ladies, Carol Pagaduan-Araullo and Josie Lichauco, who took it upon themselves to block their way. Others who tried in vain to get undeserved approbation were Sen. Robert Jaworski and former Tourism Secretary Gemma Cruz-Araneta. From an angry and worked-up throng of 30,000 on the night of January 16, the crowd at EDSA had dwindled to around 2,000 by early morning. Most of those who stayed were from the organized groups.

Around 6 a.m., the impromptu sound system provided by the Couples for Christ was replaced with the bigger setup arranged by Bayan. This would be augmented by additional equipment in the succeeding days. The first morning, the speakers included, among others, a *balut* vendor, a grand-mother, and a seaman who had just returned from abroad. A constant irritation among the various groups at EDSA was the handling of the 24-hour program. The first two days saw Barangay RJ handling the morning program, Bayan and the ERM (Estrada Resign Movement) the afternoon program, and the Kangkong Brigade and Kompil II the evening program.

When complaints of favoritism and the dominance of politicians on the stage arose, the coordinating group decided to form a committee composed of Bayan, Kompil II and the Kangkong Brigade to handle the program. The committee tried to strike a healthy balance between sectoral leaders and politicians on the program.

Next to the defection of the police and military, a major highlight was the defection of Estrada's colleagues in show business. The prize catch for the anti-Erap camp was Nora Aunor, who held a press conference in the morning of January 19 at the Bayan office to demand Estrada's resignation. Her bombshell: Estrada used to beat her "black and blue". Nora asked that she be escorted by the Kilusang Mayo Uno's Crispin Beltran and Bayan's Rafael Mariano to avoid being identified with any of the traditional politicians.

By lunchtime each day, students from various schools would start to arrive in numbers. So would members of the various labor unions, urban poor communities and other sectors. On January 18, a nationwide student boycott was declared by the Estrada Resign Youth Movement, the College Editors Guild of the Philippines (CEGP), National Union of Students of the Philippines (NUSP), League of Filipino Students (LFS), Student Christian Movement of the Philippines (SCMP), and the AnakBayan. Among the sizeable contingents were those from the University of the Philippines in Diliman and Manila, Ateneo, University of Santo Tomas, Miriam College, St. Scholastica's College, La Salle schools, St. Joseph's College, Maryhill School of Theology, St. Benedicts College, Fatima College and the Poveda. The UP Los Banos contingent used more than 40 jeepneys and 15 buses to transport their demonstrators.

On January 19, the Workers Against Estrada (Wage), which includes the KMU, declared their own walkouts. On this day, too, contingents from Southern Tagalog, Bicol and Central Luzon started arriving. By the afternoon of January 19, when the AFP and PNP leadership had withdrawn support for Estrada, crowd estimates were as high as 300,000.

By January 20, things had to come to a head—at Mendiola.

Although it was always Bayan's position that Estrada's ouster could only be ensured by massing a million people around Malacañang, it was actually the representatives from Kompil II who brought up the idea that it was time to march to the presidential palace, to which Bayan readily agreed. This was approved by the coordinating group on the afternoon of January 17 and promptly announced to the public by Kangkong Brigade spokesperson Joey Lina. The next day, however, a plea was made by Jaime Cardinal Sin and former President Corazon Aquino to postpone the march indefinitely. We at the ground level were not given clear reasons for this, except that Cardinal Sin was worried about the marchers' safety, and wanted a much bigger crowd before proceeding to Mendiola. A pretext was made that the postponement was requested by the regional contingents who wanted to join the march but could not make it by January 19.

The indefinite postponement of the march created quite a stir among the groups at EDSA. While it was agreed that we still had to muster a bigger force, many objected to the unilateral decision-making process. More importantly, Bayan leaders knew the multitudes spontaneously gathered at the shrine could not be sustained indefinitely, and so the march or the final showdown had to happen by Monday, January 22, at the latest.

We deemed it only natural that a few hours after the defection of the AFP and PNP top brass on January 19, the plan to march to Mendiola was revived and reset for the next day. The United Opposition was surprisingly assertive this time. They said they had already gotten the consent of Cardinal Sin and Cory Aquino. They said they had a negotiating team dealing with Estrada. A deadline for Estrada's resignation was set for 6 a.m. the next day.

Many of us were worried by the fact that the leaders of the United Opposition had arrogated it upon themselves to negotiate with Estrada. The rest of the groups at EDSA were never informed of these negotiations. It was only much later, when we were already at Mendiola, that we learned they had agreed to give Estrada five more days to stay in Malacañang. We prepared at once for the march. The countdown began and the 6 a.m. deadline was hyped up. By late evening, the EDSA crowd was fully pumped up. The most popular chants were "Mendiola, Mendiola" and *"Sigaw ng bayan, arestuhin si Erap."*

And then a curious thing happened. Sometime past midnight, our Kompil II counterparts in the program committee began admonishing us for agitating the crowd. They told us to keep quiet about the Mendiola march because something had come up. We were to discover later that Cardinal Sin, upon discovering the revived plan, had once again opposed it, as did Aquino and Vice President Gloria Macapagal-Arroyo. Was this part of the negotiated "graceful exit" for Estrada?, we wondered.

This appeal by Sin, Aquino and Macapagal-Arroyo created the largest dilemma for Kompil II, whose members were closely identified with the three leaders. At a meeting in yet another condominium unit at the Ortigas Center, Nath Santiago of Bayan Muna and I declared that the march was non-negotiable. It had to push through at 6 a.m. Many Kompil II leaders agreed, but were visibly torn between what they felt was right and their loyalties to Sin, Cory or Macapagal-Arroyo.

Finally, a solomonic solution: Leave it to the individual members to decide. The march to Mendiola would be treated as part of the continuing actions of People Power 2, and those who chose to stay at the shrine would be asked to pray for the marchers. Good enough.

The objective of the march was simple, and this was to bring the uprising to the very gates of Malacañang. We would show the nation and the world that Estrada had ceased to rule as president, and that he was being held hostage by his own people. The march would hopefully be the start of a grander plan to force Estrada's resignation by encircling the Palace with a million people.

At the last minute, Msgr. Socrates Villegas appealed to the crowd not to leave EDSA because Macapagal-Arroyo would be sworn at the shrine at 12 noon. Curiously, a Sanlakas spokesperson appeared on national TV prodding the people to "preserve the gains of EDSA" by not joining the march. Still, a huge number of the people marched to Mendiola.

We were confident that the march would be peaceful because, for one thing, the armed forces and the police had already been neutralized. In fact, the blueprint for the march was finalized by Nath, me and police Generals Edgar Aglipay and Sonny Razon. Imagine that. The only problem we had were the 100 or so pro-Estrada holdouts on Mendiola.

For me, the march from EDSA to Mendiola was the most memorable part of People Power 2. Indeed, it was a shining moment for the Filipino people. I saw and felt our people's determination to fight for what was just and morally upright and true. People came out of their homes and flooded the streets, bringing with them water, food, and lots of smiles and cheers. There was solidarity in the flesh, and it seemed for a moment that we could do anything.

As we were winding down our program on Mendiola, one thought that kept popping up in my head was "what if we didn't go ahead with the march?" Estrada would have stayed on in Malacañang for at least five more days. In that time, who knows what he and his cohorts could have done?

People Power 2
A Business Perspective

GUILLERMO M. LUZ

A WEEK BEFORE Ilocos Sur Governor Luis 'Chavit' Singson came out with his expose on President Joseph Estrada, I bumped into columnist Teddy Benigno at a hotel lobby as I was leaving a cocktail reception. Benigno called out to me excitedly and told me to watch out for something about to break out. He had recently seen documents that might be the equivalent of the Valachi Papers, he said, referring to the insider whose testimony on a celebrated Mafia godfather and his family in the United States led to his trial and conviction.

"Watch this closely," Benigno reminded me, "because you may be forced to comment on it. It may change the course of history."

One week later, on October 9, 2000, Governor Singson called a press conference at Club Filipino and did a Valachi, accusing Estrada of taking a share from *jueteng* (an illegal numbers game) proceeds and a kickback from the share of Ilocos Sur in the tobacco tax. It was a shocking tale but something none of us in the business community could verify at the time. It was, as it stood, merely one man's word against another. At any rate, our researchers were promptly put on it.

But when, a few days later, Sen. Teofisto Guingona delivered his "I Accuse" privilege speech in the senate, prompting a call for senate Blue Ribbon committee hearings, Singson's word began to acquire a ring of truth. As Singson, meanwhile, revealed, more key items began to be validated. When Singson disclosed a ledger of listing payoffs on the eve of hearings, Senators John Osmeña and Tessie Oreta came forward to admit that they indeed had received P1 million each the year before and were now returning it with interest, which they did, making a show of it, on the first day of the hearings. Former Presidential Spokesman (and later newspaper columnist) Jerry Barican then wrote that he and Director Lenny de

Jesus of the Presidential Management Staff had also received money, though in much smaller sums.

It was this time that former President Corazon Aquino asked us for a briefing on the repercussions the scandal might have on the economy. Our research staff quickly began to assemble data, while I sat down to map out scenarios, resignation among them. We submitted our report to Aquino in the afternoon of October 16. The next day she and Cardinal Sin came to the EDSA shrine for a Mass and to give their first statements on the issue.

I caught Aquino's speech on the radio. She spoke about the crisis of confidence that the whole affair brought and proposed that the president take a leave of absence to allow an impartial investigation. It was one step short of a call for resignation, but nonetheless a challenge to the president and an open announcement of a crisis of leadership.

Blue Ribbon Committee Hearings

OUR CONGRESSWATCH TEAM continued to monitor the senate hearings, while our economic researchers watched the economic indicators more closely than ever. By this time, the business media had begun to call more often. I myself ran into ambush interviews when I attend public events. The question of the day was whether we thought President Estrada should resign. Resignation was only one of the scenarios laid out for our research—a mere part of the analytical model. We felt there was not enough evidence at the time to justify a call for resignation. Since I had been in touch almost daily with Makati Business Club (MBC) Chairperson Ricardo Romulo to exchange notes and seek advice on how to respond to media questions, I somehow knew what to say: "the charges looked serious and we should follow them to their logical conclusions". But the president should come "with specific denials against the specific charges", I added.

In fact, more testimony came up to corroborate Singson's story. If there was one item that seemed to make believers out of people, it was the charge about the tobacco-tax kickback. While grabbing a share in *jueteng* money was a private matter (although illegal just the same), getting the kickback was a public matter. At the senate hearings, branch managers from Landbank recounted how the tobacco tax money was released to the provincial government of Ilocos Sur, then transferred the very next day to three accounts in Manila, all belonging to young individuals who opened each account with a minimum balance of P1000. The tale of P30-40 million transfers, their withdrawals, and disappearance echoed Singson's story down to the last detail.

On October 17, the MBC held a special board of trustees meeting. It had become increasingly clear that the president was involved in the scandal. His only claim to defense was that his conscience was clear—he would come out with an explanation at the appropriate time, he said. The MBC board was unanimous: The president would eventually have to go. However, it wanted to know what the members and other major business associations thought. I was instructed to organize a joint board meeting among the MBC, Management Association of the Philippines (MAP), Financial Executives Institute of the Philippines (Finex), Bishops-Businessmen's Conference (BBC), and the Bankers Association of the Philippines (BAP).

Survey

BACK IN THE OFFICE, we formulated a simple one-question survey that asked our own Filipino members how they felt the president should act in the face of the allegations—resign, be impeached, or stay on? The survey was set for the following Monday, October 23. We also asked the MAP to do a similar survey. To our surprise, members responded unusually quickly and overwhelmingly to the survey question. By October 25, 230 MBC members had responded: 90% felt the president should resign immediately. Very few felt he should resign even go through the impeachment process; fewer still felt he should stay on. The MAP results were a little different: 80% called for resignation.

On October 26 we held the first of several closed-door joint board meetings we had called among business organizations to build a consensus on the courses of action to take. Earlier that day over lunch, a standing-room-only crowd at the Dusit Hotel listened to Bangko Sentral Gov. Rafael Buenaventura speak at an MBC forum to say there were limits to the economic managers' powers to stabilize the foreign exchange rate in the face of a political crisis of confidence. In the open forum, it became plain that the audience was agitated insisting to know what the president or his economic managers could—and would—do to address the political crisis, which had begun to have grave repercussions on the economy.

After lunch, a number of us transferred to the Manila Peninsula Hotel for the joint board meeting of the MBC, MAP, BBC, BAP, and Finex. We had decided to switch hotels to avoid the prying eyes of media, who stayed behind to interview Governor Buenaventura at the Dusit's ballroom.

At the Peninsula, we sat down with the CEOs, who represented five major business associations. Although our groups have had a long history of working together, we had not needed to get together this way since the coup attempt against President Aquino in December 1989. The meeting was unusual for another reason. In order to get the discussion rolling, we invited three outside individuals—none of them connected to any of our organizations—so that we could get independent assessments and prognosis. We invited former NEDA Secretary Cayetano Paderanga to present economic scenarios, former Defense Secretary Rene de Villa, for a military and security reading, and Randy David, for socio-political assessment. Afterward, MBC Chairperson Ricardo Romulo presided over an open discussion. Sentiments reflected the surveys. Only the BAP was less vocal. It felt it had to go back to its foreign members, whose number was considerable, before coming out publicly.

At any rate, the other four groups decided to release its first statement on the issue calling for the president's resignation. We immediately agreed to prepare the draft for approval by the four organizations the next day and to book the advertising space for the following week. We also agreed to release the survey findings that evening with advance notice to Finance Secretary Jose Pardo and Trade Secretary Mar Roxas. The Board of Investments press room was advised accordingly. While copies were being printed, I placed calls to Secretary Roxas and Secretary Pardo. Pardo, who was to see the president that evening, asked for a faxed copy to show him. I would later learn that he told the president the results—business support was gone. The story made the late evening news and the front pages story of major newspapers the following morning. The print advertisement of the four business associations came out on Tuesday, October 31, during the week that many thought saw the beginning of the end for the president.

Kompil II is Created

FOR ITS PART, civil society was consolidating its own network of non-government organizations. One such network was the Kongreso ng Mamamayang Pilipino or Kompil. The first Kompil meeting had been organized way back in 1984, in the battle against the dictator Ferdinand Marcos. In preparation for Kompil II, organizers Dinky Soliman and Dan Songco contacted the MBC for support and participation. The MBC and the other three business groups agreed to participate in the Kompil II conference, Sunday, October 29, at the Ateneo high school gym.

The conference brought together a large broad-based group of leaders—professionals, urban poor, academics, peasants, fisherfolk—resoundingly disputing the Estrada camp's stock claim that the president enjoyed the support of the masses and that the opposition was elitist. Former President Cory Aquino was the guest speaker and Vice President Gloria Macapagal-Arroyo was there for a dialogue.

Over the course of the crisis, we constantly coordinated with Kompil. Three of us representing the business community with Vicky Garchitorena and Ramon del Rosario Jr. eventually became the regular contact persons. To save time, we would attend separate meetings, an arrangement that proved effective in mounting street rallies.

Isolation, the Key

TO BRING ABOUT his resignation, it was determined isolating the president would work best—isolating him by cutting him off from his key people. The problem was identifying who among them could be persuaded to leave him. For the business community, the obvious targets were the economic secretaries: Finance Secretary Jose Pardo (whom the president trusted deeply), Trade Secretary Mar Roxas (whom the president plucked out from Congress to join his Cabinet), Economic Planning Secretary Philip Medalla, and Budget Secretary Benjamin Diokno. Of the four, Pardo and Roxas appeared the more important prospects. Rafael Buenaventura was never a prospect—Central Bank had to remain insulated from politics.

Pardo, Roxas, Medalla, and Diokno supposedly had come to an agreement that if they at all decided to resign they would do so at the same time. The University of the Philippines's academic community worked on Medalla and Diokno, while individual members of the business community worked on Pardo and Roxas.

Another group identified as an important target was the Council of Senior Economic Advisers, composed of Washington Sycip, Cesar Virata, Gabriel Singson, Vicente Paterno, and Jaime Augusto Zobel de Ayala. They had been designated by the president as economic advisers and had on occasion been called to Malacañang palace to join the economic secretaries at the meetings of the Economic Coordinating Council, the highest economic policy making body. The president was beginning to drop the names of these advisers to prop up his credibility.

For impact, resignation en masse was thought ideal. A meeting was thus set for two representatives each from the MBC, MAP, BAP, BBC, and Finex with the advisers for the late afternoon of October 31, the same day that the business organizations released their first joint statement asking the president to resign.

The meeting lasted about two hours. While the conventional thinking of offering the president a graceful way out was advanced, I argued that it was also important for the business community to be seen as standing on some sound principles, rather than being perceived as a mere pragmatic approach. The question was also raised whether the president was yet capable of reforming, and the consensus was that he was not. The meeting ended with the business groups leaving the Council of Senior Economic Advisers alone to make up their minds.

Senior Economic Advisers Resign

WE WERE TO FIND OUT LATER that four of the senior economic advisors had decided to submit a joint resignation letter right after the meeting; the fifth member, former Central Bank Gov. Gabriel Singson, submitted his own resignation letter three days later. In the meantime, over the All Saint's Day holidays (November 1 and 2), the press kept calling to confirm the reports that indeed the senior advisers had resigned. None of the advisers could be reached at the time so, the story would not break out until two days later.

On that day, as it happened, Kompil held a dialogue with Vice President Gloria Macapagal-Arroyo at the UP chapel, and news began to filter out that Trade Secretary Mar Roxas was meeting with the president and making his exit. By 6 p.m., the news was out: indeed Mar Roxas had exited. With the announcement following that Speaker Manuel Villar and 44 other congressmen were leaving the majority party and signing the impeachment complaint, more resignations followed. At the senate, Senators Franklin Drilon, Nikki Coseteng, and Rodolfo Biazon were also resigning from the party.

All this set the stage for the November 4 Mass and rally at the EDSA shrine that attracted a number of businessmen. The occasion drew the largest crowd to date to openly call for the resignation of the president. The rally was so successful it inspired the sentiment that victory was near.

The following Monday, November 6, both the stock market and the foreign exchange market reacted positively, with the Phisix posting a single-day gain of 16.5% and the peso sharply appreciating to P48.05/US$ from P51.00/US$ the previous Tuesday, October 31 (there was no trading on November 1 and 3). The markets themselves seemed to anticipate an early favorable ending. Malacañang either misinterpreted the indicators or tried to put its own spin to them and announced an expression of confidence in the administration.

Now, Secretary Pardo who by now, like the others on the Cabinet, appeared to have missed their chance for a graceful exit, was being asked to stay on and try to talk the president into resigning. Word was out that another week or so would be needed to formulate the exit strategy. Within that week, however, Malacañang's crisis PR team mounted one desperate strategy yet—"elite-against-Estrada" line. By the following weekend, around November 11, the president was on a PR offensive, using the El Shaddai's annual prayer rally as his platform. Another week later, a documentary run on television showing Estrada with his masses behind him. The end wasn't near after all. Impeachment had to go on, and so had the street rallies.

Regular Street Rallies Begin

ONE OF THE MORE interesting aspects of People Power 2 was the balancing act its organizers had to perform to arrive at some compromise among groups so numerous and varied in philosophies and ideologies and, necessarily, also in ways of doing things. Kompil and the business groups seemed natural allies, but they require a great effort to adapt to the others—groups like the Kangkong Brigade, Bigkis Pinoy, the United Opposition, Council for the Philippine Affairs, the labor unions, Bayan, and Sanlakas.

It was the relationship with Bayan and Sanlakas that proved the most unusual for the business community. Even before the crisis, I had already met with Teddy Casiño, Carol Araullo, and Nathaniel Santiago of Bayan, although only in a getting-to-know sort of way. We exchanged ideas at breakfast. Even such meetings are important in a multisectoral democratic setting such as we have. While we may never agree on everything, the interaction is healthy if only for understanding where each side is coming from and how each side arrives at decisions.

Certainly, Bayan broadened my perspective. Joining its rallies in Makati and Mendiola gave me a first hand appreciation of the extent of its network and its mobilization tactics, of the passion with which it pursued its vision, and its high sense discipline when massed in large numbers. On the other hand, I saw that it had certain expectations and preconceptions about business community. I had the feeling that some of its leaders were under the impression that the business community could simply order its employees to join rallies. In fact, the business community is hardly a monolithic group, and this showed at the rallies. Participation for companies and employees was voluntary. We had to take a two-fold approach: first, we tried to convince individual companies to allow their employees to go to rallies; second, to persuade the employees themselves by explaining to them how important the cause was for them—more important indeed than their work for the time being.

The business community was itself still a sharply divided community with a group for resignation (MBC, MAP, BBC, and Finex), another group for impeachment, and still another for Estrada to serve out his term. We in business decided to build up the network of those for resignation or at least impeachment. Eventually we were able to bring in the Investment Houses Association of the Philippines, Philippine Marketing Association, Bankers Association of the Philippines, Federation of Philippine Industries, Philippine Computer Society, Information Technology Foundation of the Philippines, and Chamber of Real Estate and Builders Association. By December, when rallies had already become regular, they had begun to send representations. A number of provincial business groups also joined the network—Iloilo Business Club, Cebu Business Club, Cebu Chamber of Commerce, Mandaue Chamber of Commerce, Mandaue Business Club, Cagayan de Oro Chamber of Commerce, Muslim Business Forum, and the Mindanao Business Council.

Bayan and Sanlakas particularly, seemed to have got the impression we could easily fund the logistical requirements of rallies. To be sure, one massive street rally alone requires intricate efforts and of planning, organization, and implementation, of course, huge resources. Both fixed costs (i.e. stage, sound system, etc.) and variable costs (i.e. transportation, some food, etc.) vary according to the number of people and the distances they are willing to travel. What many in civil society may not understand is that it is not easy even for professional managers like us to raise money for even the most noble of causes, especially when no budgets or reports on the undertaking are given us. Business demands accountability even if the undertaking does not have a discernible bottom line.

In the early rally stages, in November, a mutual lack of understanding of work styles probably caused some frustration. On November 14, three simultaneous rallies were planned in Metro Manila—Kompil and the Labor Solidarity Movement (LSM) at Welcome Rotunda, proceeding to Mendiola, Bayan at Liwasang Bonifacio, also proceeding to Mendiola, and Sanlakas at Ayala Ave., Makati. I am not sure how the rally site selections were made. In any case, we decided we would support the rallies by inviting workers to attend the rallies most convenient to their place of work. With respect to Makati rally, we were in a quandary because the union assigned to Makati was Sanlakas, by far the most radical among the three rallying groups and the only espousing the "resign all" call idea—that is, everyone in government should resign to give way to a snap election. Planning the three rallies was also a challenge because of the animosity between Bayan and Sanlakas and the difficulty of getting them to sit around the same negotiating table.

Sticky Points

WITH PERSISTENCE and a little luck, we were able to organize a meeting among the TUCP, APL, LSM, Bayan, Sanlakas, Kompil, United Opposition, Copa, Kangkong Brigade, and business groups one Saturday in November. Working out between Bayan and Kompil/LSM such details as the timing of their marches into and out of Mendiola and their respective programs did not prove that difficult. What did was reconciling the positions of Sanlakas and the business group. The first sticky point was, naturally, the "resign all" call. We explained that this was a position we in business would not be associated with under any circumstances. We were for the resignation or impeachment of the president and his succession by the vice-president. We explained that we were not supporting "resign all" rally.

The second point was that, since the idea was to demonstrate solidarity between labor and business, it was important to have all labor groups present at the Makati rally. We stressed that business would not want to appear endorsing one union at the expense of others. But Sanlakas refused to fly its flag alongside those of the other unions, in particular KMU. We were told only the local or company unions could appear alongside competitor unions. As discussions bogged down, we all decided for the sake of unity to drop the idea of "salubungan", which called for all the unions and the business group converging in Makati.

The third point was the thematic color for the rally. There was concern that a sea of red flags on Ayala Ave. would scare off potential rallyists and send the wrong message about the country's financial district. In the end, it was decided that a neutral mix of colors would be used to show a multisectoral rally.

The fourth point was who would speak and what could be said on the stage. Certain ground rules were agreed upon; most importantly, no "Resign All" calls and no foul language. Copa was to handle the program and provide the emcees.

Finally, the fifth point was whether the business community could fund the undertaking. We explained that with such short notice—the rally was only days away—we could not; we did not have the money on hand, and neither did we feel it appropriate to raise false hopes that we could produce the money. We wrapped up the meeting with a press conference, where I was seated between Bayan's Teddy Casino and Sanlakas's Popoy Lagman!

The Ayala Ave. rally pushed through on November 27, though not without yet some hitches. One day before the rally, jeepneys bearing Sanlakas banners around Makati with loudspeakers blaring an invitation to workers to join the "resign all" rally. At the rally itself, one speaker openly called for revolution, stunning the largely conservative crowd.

Another rally, the People Power lunch on November 29 with Bayan and Kompil proved to be more successful, although not without hitches, too. The basic concept behind the People Power lunch was that we would ask office workers to share a lunch with rallyists who would come from out of town on their way to Mendiola. The rally was successful, but the source of success came from somewhere else. While office workers in Makati were either skeptical or indifferent (or just not in the habit of packing lunch), it was the residents of the villages who really came through, providing packed *adobo* lunches.

Adobo and rice multiplied to the point where some rallyists were able to bring leftovers to Mendiola. Incidentally, I went to Mendiola the next day to observe the rally and saw first-hand the discipline and order enforced such a large number of people packed in a small space.

Jericho March

AS THE IMPEACHMENT TRIAL date approached, public opinion seemed to swing toward giving the trial a chance, leading to a temporary silence about resignation. While we understood that most people, including many in the business community, were more comfortable with the trial process, the core group of business associations still felt strongly for resignation. Political machinations would thwart justice.

The stage meanwhile was set for one of the most ambitious rally thus far—the Jericho March. The biblically inspired concept was to march to the senate and around it seven times in silence in rows of seven. At prescribed moments, the crowd would stop and pray while rams' horns would be blown to bring down the walls of the senate—our own Jericho. Preceding the march would be a Mass outside the Malate Church Plaza, about three kilometers away, and after that by a torch relay—the "flame of truth".

Once again, it was important to gather a large multisectoral crowd. The organizing group included the usual groups—Kompil, Kangkong Brigade, Bigkis Pinoy, the United Opposition—and Isang Tugon, a group of young professionals who had been working the backroom, organizing rallies, all this time. I was invited to represent the business group so I could provide inputs and, more importantly, relay the information to the business community, I notified all the business groups of the details and identified the designated assembly points.

On the day of the rally itself, our role was to accept the "flame of truth" from former President Corazon Aquino and Vice President Gloria Macapagal-Arroyo and pass the torch to the Kompil group, represented by Dinky Soliman and Dan Songco. The Jericho March proceeded smoothly until the group attempted to enter the senate grounds. It was there that the march was stopped by police blockades for a few hours. The marchers did not quite get to march seven times around the senate but the Jericho March was large and dramatic enough to attract national attention to the historic events about to unfold. While we were marching outside, we learned that Congressman-Prosecutor Joker Arroyo in his opening argument identified the "Jose Velarde" check and its uncanny similarity of the signature on it to that of President Estrada. It was the first of many bombshells that the prosecution panel would drop in the course of the trial.

The Impeachment Trials

WITH THE IMPEACHMENT TRIAL now under way, we settled into our daily routine of watching it on television. We also tried to get passes to the senate so that some of us could watch it in person. Because of the great demand for passes, however, we were unable to get in as often as we would have wanted. The passes we got were distributed by the Management Association of the Philippines (MAP) to the directors of the various associations by turns. In any case, television provided the vicarious experience.

I asked the MBC's Congresswatch researchers to prepare a report on the daily highlights and to team up with another research team from the Transparent Accountable Governance (TAG) project. The reports were posted to the TAG project's website (www.tag.org.ph). Since there was no way to determine how long the trial would run, I felt it important to prepare the daily summaries so that we could refresh our memories as we felt necessary.

As the trial wore on, it became increasingly evident that President Estrada was guilty. But the trial being a political, rather than a legal process, the senator-judges could vote on the basis of political interest, rather than that of evidence. On the other hand, we felt (or hoped) that some common sense and patriotism would prevail. By the time Clarissa Ocampo testified on December 22, I think that people were more or less convinced of President's Estrada's direct involvement in wrongdoing.

Battling Against the Post-Acquittal Thinking

COMING BACK from the Christmas break in January, we were surprised to hear post-acquittal scenarios. We felt we had to do something.

Both Kompil and Nassa (the church's social action network) themselves were planning conferences on the matter, and we became concerned about it being so openly considered.

For the first two weeks of January, I spent some time trying to persuade the people behind these conferences to amend their agendas. In the case of Kompil, Dinky Soliman eventually told me that the same concern as mine had been voiced out by others and that the agenda had been changed. I attended the Kompil meeting at Mimosa on January 12 and

13. Although impeachment was not on the agenda, it was nonetheless on everyone's mind. It was refreshing to note that the talk was not about post-acquittal but rather about post-trial scenarios.

Sister Roseanne Mallilin, the Nassa national coordinator who was so helpful in assisting us distribute information to all 80 or so dioceses nationwide, called to inform me that Nassa would be holding its own conference in Tagaytay on January 16, two weeks ahead of the semestral meeting of the Catholic Bishops' Conference of the Philippines. She faxed me an advance copy of the agenda, and I was shocked to see listed a discussion of post-acquittal scenarios. I immediately called her to suggest that it might be better to focus on the highlights of the trial because the evidence pointed toward guilt. I felt that that had to be promoted more than the political nature of impeachment. So as to avoid the trap laid by the crisis PR team at Malacañang, I also suggested that among the speakers should be the Kompil lawyers group posting a detailed daily report on the trial on the web. She also invited me to speak about the impact of the trial especially on the Philippine economy.

My basic message to the Nassa social action directors (as well as to various Rotary Clubs I was invited to speak to) was that the economy was slowing and could slow further if the trial ended in an acquittal or were delayed beyond February 12, the last day for filing of certificates of candidacy for senatorial hopefuls for the May elections. Such delay, I said, would make the trial evaporate in the election fever. By that time, the MBC economic research team had been forecasting a GDP growth of only 2.7% for 2001. All the key indicators for the year 2000 had been more or less known by then, and it didn't take a rocket scientist to know that the economy was yet turning for the worse.

Aside from giving the economic briefing, I also walked the social action directors through the trial highlights and argued how they pointed clearly toward guilt. I also mentioned that the implications of an acquittal were a condonation and promotion of wrongdoing.

I came away somewhat relieved, having had the opportunity to speak before a group who not only could reach deep into the grassroots and has the respect and authority of their constituents. Riding back from Tagaytay to my office in Makati, I listened to the radio only to find out that the debate was still going on over the now infamous Envelope No. 2.

The 11-10 Vote

WHEN FINALLY the senator-judges voted on January 16 against opening it, I sat stunned. After all Envelope No. 1 had already been opened and there had seemed no reason why No. 2 should not be. Within minutes of that decision, text messages began pouring onto my cell phone. Within hours, hundreds of people were massing at EDSA.

Coincidentally, members of the boards of business associations had called for a meeting the following morning. Since late October 2000, we had been holding these periodic breakfast meetings to analyze the situation and plan our next steps. Clearly now, a turning point had been reached. By the time we wrapped up the meeting, we had all decided that companies would be encouraged to let their people go out on the streets, to EDSA. There was no need to plan or organize; events were taking a life of their own.

For instance, the "human chain rally" of January 18, almost seemed to have formed itself. The night before, a small group of professionals sat down to think of ways to communicate messages to larger groups to get them to link up with the crowds at EDSA. While the crowd had swelled to respectable numbers from the night of the 16th into the early hours of the 17th, the numbers tended to thin out during the day as people needed to rest or get back to whatever it was they had to do. By late afternoon to evening, the crowds would grow again. The challenge was to get more people out to connect with each other.

The "human chain" achieved this in a manner unlike most other rallies. The basic idea was to form a chain of people stretching from the Ninoy Aquino statue on Ayala Ave. to EDSA shrine. I myself was a bit skeptical that this could be done. Text messaging did it—overnight! Before I got home, I had received the message twice, from people not even at the meeting. The message had gone full circle. By late afternoon of the 18th, the human chain blocked off major stretches of Ayala and was well on its way to connecting all the way to EDSA shrine.

On January 19, the MBC board had one of its regular meetings, over lunch. Before we could begin, a couple of us had been contacted by cell phone and told that Gen. Angelo Reyes was withdrawing his support from the president. We exchanged notes and placed a few more calls to confirm the report. Aware that General Reyes was close to retirement, we tried to analyze what his move, if true, meant. After a few more calls, we determined that the information was correct. We cut the meeting short, headed back to our office, then out to EDSA. We were about to mount People Power 2.

Postscript: In Search of Transparency and Accountability

THE LESSON of People Power 1 was that throwing out a bad government is not good enough; we also need to remain engaged to ensure that the government for the public interest.

One of the key problems of the Estrada administration was its lack of transparency and accountability. Estrada advisers had always held on to the notion that just because he won the 1998 elections overwhelmingly, he could rule as he pleased. People Power 2 threw out a government that was not prepared to be accountable for its actions.

Thus, on the first working day of Gloria Macapagal-Arroyo's administration, January 22, representatives of the same 11 business associations that fought in the crisis sat down again to discuss how it wanted the new government to proceed. The result was a statement calling for transparency, accountability, integrity, competence, and honesty in governance. We all wanted a government that would consult with the people and be open and honest with them for everything, especially in major policy decisions and key appointments. We wanted to avoid going back to "business as usual" or "politics as usual", in which the politics of patronage was the rule of the game. We wanted a government that was going to serve the people because it was the people, after all, who brought this administration to office. We wanted change.

Estrada's Overthrow
in a Regional Context

MICHAEL VATIKIOTIS

PRESIDENT JOSEPH ESTRADA'S IGNOMINIOUS EXIT from power on January 20 solved a thorny problem of bad leadership in the Philippines, but underscored the frail foundations of democracy in the region. Estrada maintains that his removal from office was illegitimate. In fact, despite a Supreme Court ruling to the contrary, the use of popular and military leverage to turf him out of office reflects the weak state of democratic institutions. The fact that democracy in the Philippines has been practiced for longer than many of its other Asean neighbors makes this failing a regional problem.

In the months leading up to Estrada's removal, Filipinos agonized over their poor choice of president. What could they do? Estrada was duly elected—with a large plurality. Constitutional propriety needed to be observed. The good name of democracy in the Philippines was at stake. Governor Luis Singson's revelations helped make impeachment a possibility. But then this legal process of executive sanction ran afoul of an entrenched tradition of patronage. It looked like the constitutional path to resolving the political problem was in jeopardy. Both sides threatened the use of the mob to press their case. There was also the threat of a divided army and resulting violence, so in the end the armed forces commander opted for betrayal and a transfer of loyalty with all its dubious legal trappings. Pressed to justify this train of events, former President Fidel Ramos said: "The people are higher than the courts." Estrada said: "I'm still, legally and constitutionally the president of the Republic."

How did all this play out in the region? In late January, an editorial in a Thai newspaper argued that events in the Philippines "present a prime case of how the leaders of Thailand and Indonesia should retune their thinking. Yes, they may have won the people's mandate, but trust is something that cannot be bought and must be earned. The Estrada downfall is a lesson to all of us." Is it? It may be a lesson in how not to develop a democracy.

What's clear is that the military played a direct, albeit disguised role in bringing Estrada down. The old political elite drew on its ties to retired officers, who in turn leaned on the active military leadership. There is something disturbing about a Constitution, claiming to rest on democratic principles, that permits the military to withdraw loyalty from the chief executive so easily. Some people are troubled by the fact that the voice of the mob influenced the Supreme Court's decision to vacate the presidency on shallow legal grounds.

But whatever they say, Gloria Macapagal-Arroyo has been widely accepted as Estrada's successor, an aim long sought after by the political elite before the corruption charges emerged. The world accepts this fact because realpolitik and pragmatism dictate foreign policy more than many Western nations like to think. After all, the recent change of leadership in Yugoslavia was hailed as the end of a dictatorship even though there was no legal transfer of power. The worry is that, for all the new president's promises, the Philippines remains in the grip of a landed oligarchy that the Catholic church helped cement in place under Spanish rule some four centuries ago. And this bodes ill for bridging the economic divide.

But the real failure in the Philippines was institutional, and the events in Manila leading up to the removal of Estrada from office reflect badly on the roots of democratic governance in Southeast Asia. The broader point here is that democracy has not turned out to be either as easy or as bountiful as the theorists predicted. Reactionary forces remain firmly entrenched and are throwing reforms into reverse in some places; social angst and inequality plague the region. The strong-arm militaristic threat to democracy has been replaced to some degree by the tyranny of the mob.

Basically, everyone was too optimistic about the speed and scope of institutional reform. When Suharto fell in May 1998, there were those who imagined a virtual overnight transformation of Indonesia into a working model of democracy simply by holding relatively free elections. When Thailand implemented a new Constitution in 1997, it was assumed that money and politics would miraculously part ways. So too, in the Philippines, a lot of trust was placed in the democratic process. There had been a peaceful transfer of power from Ramos to Estrada. With this show of maturity, the hope was that impeachment and a senate trial would be sufficient to remove an inept president widely condemned for corruption.

We should have been more realistic. The signs are that around Southeast Asia, democracy has shallow roots and vigilance is required to keep the process alive.

Indonesia's "first democratically elected president" was not actually freely elected. He was a compromise choice of a group of politicians, not all of them elected, who feared their interests would not be served if they chose the person the majority of Indonesians voted for. "His whole election was an exception," one senior Golkar politician told me recently, and he quipped: "Now they're taking exception to the exception."

Thailand's "democratic" Constitution laid the foundations for cleaner government, but before anything can be built, Thai politicians need to kick the patronage habit, and to do that people must start expecting more from government than a few hundred baht at election time. The process of socializing reform will take time and involve conflict-avoiding compromises along the way. So expect reform to take longer than expected.

Malaysia has pulled through the economic crisis and a rancorous political struggle, but its leadership is battered and scarred and the country's precarious plural society is unsettled. Malaysia is set to become a nervous place as it prepares for succession.

By splitting the Malay community over the treatment of his former deputy, Anwar Ibrahim, Mahathir has helped incubate extremist Islamic politics and upset the country's delicate ethnic balance. Desperate to revive support, loyalists are resorting to crude nationalism that will unnerve minorities and neighbors. Mahathir has demonstrated that he may have outlived his welcome as prime minister. Calls are mounting from within for him to make way. Mahathir's exit should be used as an excuse to inject more liberalism into the ruling UMNO party. This won't be easy because the succession will be messy. But failing to do so could give Pas the momentum it needs to mount a serious challenge for power.

And in the Philippines, we should have foreseen that a group of senators who for the most part built their political careers in the Marcos period were not necessarily the best judge of character. In the end, Estrada was removed from office by the military through a back door coup hatched on the golf course and in coffee shops, and disguised by a newspaper advertisement. As former President Fidel Ramos put it recently: "Certain key players had to take a stand."

More worryingly, in all these countries the dull but crucial task of writing new laws and cleaning up the courts and bureaucracy, although initially given a boost by the crisis, has slowed to a virtual halt, hamstrung for the most part by selfish elite politics. Nobody, it seems, wants laws that will put them in jail. The rule of the mob, rather than the rule of law, is driving politics. "The people are the court of last resort," says Ramos. But he also warns: "the rule of the people doesn't always mean good government."

With hindsight, of course, it's easy to be cynical. The region has got a lot of mileage out of early hopes for reform and renewal. The first tentative steps, no matter how ineffective, have been tremendous confidence-building measures as the region emerges from economic crisis. So if we now accept that the actual task at hand is harder than initially anticipated, what needs to be done to cement in place the prerequisites of better government?

One problem, amply illustrated by events in the Philippines, is that Asia's presidential systems are very powerful because they are not supported by mature systems of legal and legislative oversight. In South Korea, Kim Dae Jung is not accountable to parliament, although his party is. Former President Fidel Ramos of the Philippines ruminated recently that what the Philippines lacked was a proper parliament with powers to check bad leadership using the mechanism of a simple no-confidence vote. In the Philippines, it took popular protest and the threat of military intervention to remove a bad president. Similarly in Indonesia, Abdurrahman Wahid could remain in power, however bad his government, until 2004, unless he is removed by military or popular force. Neither should be discounted. The threat to Indonesia's frail democracy posed by politicians using the military to shore up their power, or themselves deploying military force—in the shape of paramilitary militias—is real and scary.

Beyond the elite power struggle, the real challenge for countries like Indonesia and the Philippines is to grapple with concrete reform. Many younger Indonesian politicians are in broad agreement on the need for a special assembly to amend the Constitution, along the lines that Thailand followed, and bring Indonesia's political system kicking and screaming into the modern world. At the very least, if Wahid is toppled or forced to resign, the people should more directly elect a new leader, which would mean fresh elections. Sadly, the political elite will continue to insist that Indonesians are not ready for a system in which political leaders are elected more directly. This can only mean that democracy will be diluted as the civilians turn to the military for support, or themselves become militarized through the use of civil militia.

In Thailand, political flux is the norm because political parties are small and political loyalties fickle. But this time, things are different. Thaksin Shinawatra has secured an unprecedented majority in parliament and built a formidable party on the back of his US$ 6 billion telecom fortune. Using foreign public relations firms to find out what Thai voters actually want and then crafting a relevant, if dreamy, populist platform, he has built an imposing political edifice that worries senior establishment figures used to ephemeral governments and weak leaders. No prime minister has been potentially as powerful since the era of Field Marshall Sarit in the 1950s. The question is what will Thaksin do with all this power?

What everyone hopes is that Thailand is able to consolidate the gains made under the 1997 Constitution. Votes were widely bought in the January 6, 2001 election and there is evidence that powerful political interests lent heavily on the election commission to forestall disqualification or commit voter fraud at the local level. But there were signs that more voters now examine policies and are no longer tied to provincial mafia bosses. Politicians should resist the temptation of amending the Charter to weaken its regulatory powers, even if this means that Thaksin by the end of the year is no longer eligible to hold office. For in the end, Thailand's peaceful reform process is an example to the region of how democracy can be cemented in place without conflict and rancor.

There's another general point here. As much as successful reform is all about measuring progress in concrete terms—laws, convictions, whatever— it is important to grasp that reform in the Asian context is also about compromise and accommodation. And necessarily so. The example of Thailand teaches us that in order to achieve what reformers have achieved so far, which is considerable, great care has had to be taken to ensure that reactionary forces are not pushed up against the wall—that aspects of face and dignity are preserved. This has minimized the effectiveness of the conservative backlash and ensured the survival of the reform process.

A Burmese general surveying the region right now could be forgiven for thinking: What's the hurry? We can still live without democracy. Why? From Thailand, the pressure is about to ease up, as the new government prefers profitable engagement to confrontation over ideals. The military is making a political comeback in the Philippines and in Indonesia, and in Washington you have a government that frowns on sanctions. Similarly, Cambodia, painted as the bad boy of the region for so many years, has seen a consolidation of strong, semi-democratic government without so much as a peep out of the donors that keep the economy propped up.

But there are lessons to be learned here. Political change is, like natural evolution, a slow process. Constitutional and legal change is crucial. Thailand has led the way, by formally shaping a democratic government that fits the context and has the approval of the public. Almost undetected, the core principle at work here is one of the most important ingredients of any democracy—public participation.

Overall, Asian countries should perhaps look towards developing systems of government that rely less on models that provide too much executive power. For the experience so far in Southeast Asia suggests that democracy suffers from an inherent imbalance arising from the social setting. Paternalism encourages the abuse of power when too much of it is in the hands of a single leader. Wahid clearly believes that, as president, he isn't beholden to parliament—in fact, the way the constitution is currently configured, he isn't. Patronage, still too ingrained in these societies, tends to dilute the legislative clout of elected representatives. Estrada could afford to buy off 22 senators because most of them were willing to be bought. Because legal checks and balances on the abuse of power don't function properly, people resort to mob violence and the use of military force.

A more effective blend of democracy would ensure that leaders are more directly elected by popular vote, and can be more easily be removed by their peers. Democracy in Southeast Asia needs firmer legal safeguards. The lessons in the Philippines and Indonesia suggest that in the absence of legal certainty as well as responsible leadership, democracy in its infancy is at the mercy of authoritarian and militaristic tendencies. It is also beholden to mob rule. These lessons should not be wasted.

Hong Kong,
March 2001

The Contributors

Jose V. Abueva, Ph.D., is Professor Emeritus of Political Science and Public Administration at the University of the Philippines. He was president of the university from 1987 to 1983 and has undertaken commissions for the United Nations, in particular the United Nations University.

Fermin D. Adriano, Ph.D., is a political economist. He is a government consultant on regional development and is now at work with his wife, Prof. Lourdes S. Adriano, on a study called "Peace and Reconstruction Imperatives for Mindanao's Enhanced Development", intended as the blueprint for the administration's peace and development efforts for the island.

Arsenio M. Balisacan is Professor of Economics at the University of the Philippines and a consultant at the Asian Development Bank. He has served as Undersecretary at the Department of Agriculture and as Poverty Expert for the World Bank and several United Nations agencies.

Maria Cynthia Rose Banzon Bautista is Professor of Sociology and former Executive Director of the Center for Integrative and Development Studies at the University of the Philippines. She was a professorial fellow of the Institute of International Asian Studies, University of Amsterdam, and visiting researcher at the University of British Columbia in Canada and Sophia University in Tokyo. She has published on the issues of development, class, poverty, and agrarian reform, among other subjects.

John J. Carroll, S.J., is Dean of Social Science at the Ateneo de Manila, Professor of Sociology at the Gregorian University in Rome, and a visiting professor of Southeast Asian Studies at Cornell University, where he received his Ph.D. He has been Associate Director of the Institute of Social Order, Director of Research at the National Secretariat for Social Action, Director of the Institute of Philippine Culture, and Founding Director of the Institute on Church and Social Issues.

Teodoro Casiño has been at the forefront of the social and labor movements. He is Secretary General of the Bagong Alyansang Makabayan (Bayan). He was formerly Public Information Director of the Kilusang Mayo Uno (KMU). He writes a weekly column for *BusinessWorld* and contributes regularly to The Correspondents, a public-affairs program on the television network ABS-CBN.

Karina Constantino-David is Chairperson of the Civil Service Commission. From 1998-1999 she was Secretary of Housing and Chairperson of the Housing and Urban Development Coordinating Council. She resigned from the Estrada Cabinet in October 1999. From 1986-87 she served the Aquino government as Undersecretary of the Department of Social Welfare and Development. She got her Master of Economic and Social Studies from the Victoria University of Manchester and has been Professor of Sociology and Community Development at the University of the Philippines. She has been active in NGOs (nongovernmental organizations).

Randolf S. David is Professor of Sociology at the University of the Philippines. He was the founding Director of the Third World Studies Center and served as a member of the University of the Philippines Board of Regents, representing the faculty, in 1999. He was among those who organized the Coalition for the Urgent Resignation of Estrada (UP Cure), one of the first academic groups to call for the resignation of President Estrada. He is a former chairperson of the socialist group Bisig. He also writes a weekly column for the *Philippine Daily Inquirer* and hosts a public-affairs show on television.

Emmanuel S. de Dios is Professor of Economics at the University of the Philippines, where he received his Ph.D. and has taught since 1981. His work includes several edited, authored, or co-authored books and articles on poverty and human development, economic policy, political economy, technology, as well as topics in economic theory.

Carolina G. Hernandez, Ph. D. (State University of New York at Buffalo), is Professor of Political Science and Carlos P. Romulo Professor of International Relations at the University of the Philippines. She is also President of the Institute for Strategic and Development Studies, Inc., and Asean Co-Chairperson of the Council for Security Cooperation in the Asia Pacific (CSCAP). She has been a visiting professor at the University of Toronto, Cornell University, Virginia Military Institute, and the Institute for International Studies and Training in Japan. She will take up a similar appointment for a semester,